CLOUGH
A Biography

CLOUGH
A Biography

Tony Francis

Stanley Paul
London Melbourne Auckland Johannesburg

Stanley Paul & Co. Ltd

An imprint of the Random Century Group

Random Century House,
20 Vauxhall Bridge Road, London SW1V 2SA

Random Century Australia (Pty) Ltd
20 Alfred Street, Milsons Point, Sydney, NSW 2061

Random Century New Zealand Ltd
191 Archers Road, PO Box 40–086, Auckland 10

Century Hutchinson South Africa (Pty) Ltd
PO Box 337, Bergvlei 2012, South Africa

First published 1987
Revised edition 1989
Reprinted 1990, 1991

Set in Plantin by Avocet Marketing Services,
Bicester, Oxon.

Printed and bound in Great Britain
by Mackays of Chatham PLC, Chatham, Kent

British Library Cataloguing in Publication Data

Francis, Tony
Clough: a biography
1. Clough, Brian 2. Soccer—Great Britain
—Managers—Biography
I. Title
338.7′6179633463′0924 GV942.7.C6

ISBN 0 09 174062 2

Contents

Introduction

It's a funny business – writing the biography of a living person without their involvement. Brian Clough's reaction was: 'Best of luck and thanks for telling me. The last bugger who wrote a book with my name on the cover didn't even let me know!' His own version of events would no doubt differ considerably from what you will read here but then no one sees himself as others see him. As for which is the more reliable picture – that is the great unanswerable question.

Since first bumping into Clough in October 1973, I, like many others, have been intrigued by him. He had just walked out on Derby County, abandoned a town and a football club which worshipped the water he walked on. Indeed if you stepped into any hostelry the length and breadth of Derbyshire in those days, Clough was certain to be a major topic of conversation. The place had come alive through one man and his football team. He even made his resignation seem like a triumph. The players would have laid down their lives and very nearly sacrificed their careers for him. His impact was messianic.

I felt compelled to write about him because he has been one of the most influential figures of our time. Love him or hate him, it has been impossible to ignore him. He criticizes people mercilessly in public and they dare not answer back for fear of provoking an even more damaging tirade. His enemies are as mesmerized by him as are his friends. He happened to shine as a football manager because football was the thing he knew best, but given the necessary education who is to say he could not have shone as a reforming politician, a trade union leader, the head of a nationalized industry or perhaps even a missionary?

If that smacks of sycophancy, it is not intended to. There has been more than enough of that where Clough is concerned. Sycophancy and fear. Some of those qualified to assess the man retreated from my invitation because they were uneasy about doing so. It was as if the wrath of God would come crashing down on them . . . or something worse. It would have been naïve of me not to expect a natural reticence in some quarters but I *was* surprised when a former football administrator of international standing joined the 'My solicitor has advised me to say nothing' brigade. Fortunately he was in a minority. I found a gratifying degree of cooperation from most of those I approached. In all they numbered more than two hundred in the course of my travels from Hartlepool to Jersey, from Middlesbrough to Majorca.

In case you were wondering, Brian Clough did not stand in my way, nor did he prevent me from speaking to anyone. He gave me his blessing to contact his elder brother, Joe, who in turn put me in touch with another brother, Bill. Neither could have been more helpful. Brian himself had already confided to me his thoughts and memories of Derby County days and his explanation of the split with Peter Taylor. Some of that material was published in an earlier book, the remainder is included in this one, and very revealing it is. Equally revealing are the words of Sam Longson, the former Derby County chairman, who agreed to make available his unpublished memoirs of their stormy time together; and the 'testimony' of Peter Taylor, who unburdens himself for the first time over what really happened between them.

Whatever we may think of Clough's more outrageous attitudes, they are consistent with many who have climbed to the top of their respective professions. What set Clough apart perhaps is that he makes no attempt to conceal his gut feelings. For that I guess we should be grateful. The world would be a duller, albeit calmer, place without him. It is too much to hope that he will endorse everything included in the following pages but I trust he will realize that no biographer could possibly undertake the task without a sneaking affection for his subject.

Tony Francis

1
Hey, Young Man

Profound anxiety spread across Europe the day Brian Howard Clough was born. Yet it would be forty-four years before he took the continent by storm. The more immediate concern was Adolf Hitler who sent shivers from Berlin to Birmingham with his plan to rearm the German forces. That Thursday, 21st March 1935, Sally and Joe Clough might just have cast their eyes over this ominous editorial in the *North Eastern Daily Gazette*:

> It is now more than ever essential that we should know whether there is any possibility of German cooperation in the establishment of peace . . . or whether she is determined to rearm as a prelude to another war.

Chances are the Cloughs had other things on their mind. Brian was the sixth of nine children, although the first born, Elizabeth, died of septicaemia aged four. The eldest was Doreen, then came Joe junior, Des, Bill, Brian, Gerald, Deanna and Barry. Only sixteen years separated the eldest and youngest. With the possible exception of his sister Doreen, none was remotely similar to Brian in personality. They grew up at 11 Valley Road on Middlesbrough's Grove Hill council estate – a neat, modern house kept like a palace: whitewashed front doorstep, sparkling windows and so spotless inside, despite the congestion, that you could eat off the floor. Valley Road today is no different from a hundred fading prewar estates but in 1935 roses bloomed in the little front gardens and most of the houses had a fresh lick of paint. Brother Joe describes it this way: 'Ours was no back-alley upbringing. We had a lovely house and a park next door. We didn't have to kick tin cans down the street.'

Grove Hill was a garden city development. Homes fit for

heroes after the trench war. Heroes like Joe senior, who suffered a permanent limp after he had been shot in the ankle during active service. Though in theory the estate had been built to house the working classes, the first tenants included managing directors, insurance agents and school teachers along with railwaymen and steelworkers. It was a novelty for people to live so close to the countryside after years in the smoky streets of town. Visitors to Grove Hill were startled by owls hooting in the trees at night!

1935 was a good year for Middlesbrough: too early for most folk to anticipate further hostilities but late enough for the interwar recession to be over. Young men in this relatively new town looked forward to a prosperous industrial future. If they didn't fancy the shipyard or the steelworks, there was ICI with its giant plants at Billingham and Wilton. At one time or another, Joe worked for ICI, so did Joe junior, Bill, Des, Gerald and Barry. So for a short time would Brian. ICI liked to encourage a family atmosphere.

1935 was also the year Arsenal won the league, Sheffield Wednesday beat West Brom at Wembley and Wally Hammond topped the batting averages. Stanley Baldwin warned Edward VIII about his relationship with Mrs Wallis Simpson; the word 'swing' was coined and a thirty-mile-per-hour speed limit was introduced. A packet of twenty Churchman's cigarettes cost one shilling and twopence; an eight-bedroom mansion in the Surrey stockbroker belt would set you back £3000, and you could sail around the world for £109.

Few of life's luxuries came knocking at the door of 11 Valley Road, although the Cloughs wanted for nothing when it came to love and affection. As Brian's elder brother Bill puts it, 'We weren't a rich family but my God we were happy. Always well fed and well dressed.' The six brothers slept three-in-a-bed in the same room. 'That wasn't so bad,' says Joe, 'but it was a squeeze when the cousins came to stay. We were nose to toe then. No need for duvets or hot-water bottles. You never saw ice on the inside of *our* windows!'

That physical closeness might be a recipe for disaster these days, but in the Clough family it engendered a spiritual togetherness which has endured. As well as brothers and sisters, they were friends, supporting and protecting each other through thick and thin. That is still the case, although Brian and Barry, the youngest member of the family, no longer speak to each other. The reason behind their feud will be explained in a later chapter. Bill, two years older than Brian and the academic of the family, was probably closest to him: 'We were chalk and cheese. I was the quiet, studious one whereas Brian was always centre stage, organizing young and old alike. We got on so well because opposites attract. As a young lad he had strong opinions. It was his nature not to be downtrodden and to demand his rights. He took after mum. She had to be strong to rear nine of us. I think Brian inherited her doggedness. She wouldn't pack in even when she was ill. Day after day you'd see her in the back yard at the poss tub and the mangle, wrestling with mountains of laundry. The washing line was always full. Then she had to bake and prepare meals. How she coped with us all I'll never know. Mum and Brian had a special kind of rapport. He made a terrific fuss of her.'

Sally (her real name was Sarah) was the essence of the working-class British mother of the thirties. If she wasn't bearing children, she was bringing them up. Through the relentless slog of housework she rarely lost her good humour. Barry's wife, Judy, remembers her in later times as the doting mother-in-law and grandmother: 'A wonderful person. You could turn to her for anything. If the babies' feeds weren't just right, she'd tell us, "Thicken those bottles up, got to make these bairns big and strong." All the grandchildren were patted and kissed. She squeezed the boys' calf muscles and said, "Footballers' legs, hen, that's what I like."'

Football was the family passion. Everyone played. Middlesbrough was a football-daft town. At ICI they changed the Saturday shifts when Boro were at home. Sally did not actually join in the kickabouts, but she was possibly more fanatical about the game than any of them. The back bedroom overlooked Acklam steelworks sports ground. Whenever there was a match, mum was up at the window shouting encouragement, even though the pitch was a hundred yards away and partly obscured by trees. 'Goodness knows what the neighbours thought,' says Bill. 'She'd shout herself hoarse then come out in a rash. She was just the same when Brian played at Middlesbrough and Sunderland.'

Father Joe was an unassuming man who enjoyed simple pleasures. He liked a cigar in later life and was quite content to allow his wife to run around after him, as most husbands did before the days of women's lib. Bill says, 'Dad was just another child to mum. She waited on us hand and foot.' He did, however, take an avid interest in Brian's playing career, rarely missing a game or an opportunity to sing his son's praises. Middlesbrough FC got to know him well when he became foreman at Garnett's sweet factory close to Ayresome Park. He was a keen Boro supporter and looked after the team during rationing. On Fridays he made up cartons of reject sweets for the players and sold them at four shillings each. He looked forward to having the lads in. When Harold Shepherdson called he collected a lecture about Brian Clough for good measure!

As a boy, Brian watched the factory workers playing 'bob-a-man' football on the common. You paid a shilling to play. The winning team took the spoils. As often as not, brother Joe would take him along: 'Blokes played in working boots with their trousers tucked into their socks. They were hard matches. You'd get four hundred people watching. Brian dreamed of joining them one day.'

For Christmas every year, without fail, the boys had a new pair of boots each and a ball between them. 'It didn't vary for twenty years,' says Joe, 'and we didn't want it to.' On Sundays, though, football had to stop for a day. The youngsters trooped off to St Barnabas Church Sunday school whether they liked it or not. After Sunday lunch, all those of walking age were taken on the weekly pilgrimage to the countryside and back. 'Sometimes we'd be gone for two hours or more,' Bill recalls. 'The little ones were glad to see the Italian ice-cream van on the way home. A cone each helped them over the last few hundred yards.'

Sally and Joe kept a tight rein on the family. Bill says he did not know what girls were until he was twenty-one! He and Brian got up to the usual mischief of young boys: 'We played pranks on the old chap next door. Nothing harmful, just a bit of fun. I remember he had a crooked finger with a twisted nail. When he waved it at us, we would run back into the house petrified.' Joe, who was eight years older then Brian, sometimes had to take him in hand: 'He had some lip, just like now, but you could clip his ear in those days. He never got into serious trouble because he had a nice way with him and could get away with it. Most times we kids didn't dare open our mouths. It was a case of "speak when you're spoken to".'

The Cloughs were more enlightened than some. Joe says it was not uncommon to see wives banished from the house if they didn't come up to scratch: 'They'd scurry off to their mothers with an armful of screaming kids. Their husbands would be chasing after with a boot up their backsides. There were some tough families about.' Big ones too. Fourteen or fifteen kids was quite normal.

There was no shortage of levity in the Clough household. Sally had a piano in the front parlour and a knack of playing by ear. According to Bill, 'Any tune she heard on the wireless she could pick up and play straightaway.' There were regular sing-songs, especially at Christmas or New Year. Her favourite was Gracie Fields. She changed the words around and sang, 'Sally, Sally, pride of the Valley . . .' Even after the older ones married, Sunday nights were the get-together nights. Visitors tucked into her famous Sunday fry-ups: cold meat and bubble and squeak from the remains of the Sunday lunch. Now and then, Sally would treat herself to a Mackeson.

Holidays could not have been easy for such a big family but the Cloughs managed to get away, even if it was only to stay with an aunt in Blackpool. Paying for ten return rail tickets must have been a drain on Joe's wages. That fortnight was the highlight of the year, as Bill recalls: 'We thought Blackpool was the greatest place on earth. Mum dressed us boys all the same. We must have looked like a family of clones. Every couple of days, we were treated to a stick of candy floss between three. Brian usually wanted the stick to lick afterwards. They'd take us along the Golden Mile to have our pictures taken by the man under the black cape. Mum and dad were very proud of us.'

People flocked to the cinema in those days and Sally and Joe were no exception. They had regular bookings at the Palladium on Eastbourne Road and rarely missed Tuesdays and Saturdays, when the programme was changed. The Palladium featured luxurious blue carpeting, usherettes resplendent in blue uniforms and could hold four hundred people. On Saturdays there was what was called a 'penny push' when you could get in for a copper. Otherwise adults paid sixpence and children threepence. In between raising a big family, the Cloughs also had the odd chance to enjoy music hall at the Empire theatre. The older members of the family took it in turns to babysit.

As the boys grew up, Sally would tell them, 'You must get a

trade.' It was a status symbol to have a tradesman in the family, especially in a predominantly industrial town like Middlesbrough. Bill was pressured into taking an engineering job; Joe became a plasterer. Brian was a bit of a disappointment – the only member of the family to fail the 11-plus. While his brothers and sisters moved on to higher education, he stayed at Marton Grove secondary school until he was fifteen. 'He was a miserable failure,' says Bill. 'But he only had himself to blame. He wouldn't do any homework – couldn't concentrate on anything for five minutes unless it was football. The school was more interested in sport than the academic side and I suppose Brian thought, with national service coming up, he didn't have to bother too much.'

There is of course a distinction between being bright and being academically clever. The young Clough did not have the commitment to be the latter, but he was certainly bright. Tony Rowell was his third-form master at Marton Grove. He taught Clough English, maths, geography, history and religious instruction, as well as games:

'In forty years as a schoolmaster I must have taught thousands of boys, but Brian Clough sticks out in my memory for several reasons. He was bright and alert and seemed to have an opinion on everything. He would argue with the teachers, which was rare in a thirteen-year-old. By that I mean argue in a pleasant way when subjects were thrown open for discussion. Each term I had to produce a set of marks and put the forty or so boys in form order. Clough was invariably near the top in all subjects. He could easily have been grammar-school material. Unfortunately, having failed the 11-plus, there was not much a boy could do.

'He was outstanding at all games. I ran the gymnastic club after school and he was a very keen member of that – damned good too! The lads had to perform in a gym-cum-hall-cum-dining-room with a hot plate at one end and a stage at the other. Clough had a lot of courage when it came to vaulting and agility work. There was so little room to manoeuvre that you took your life in your hands, hoping to pull up at the hot plate or the raised area. He was a sturdily built boy but nimble with it. Loved his football. I can see him now in the school colours: black and white striped shirt and white shorts. Even when he got into the main school team as a third former, he'd be telling the captain what to do. I refereed a lot of those games. Clough was usually right in what he said, but times I had to tell him to shut up and get on with it.'

Marton Grove secondary was a big, bleak Victorian edifice with open verandahs, which were the fashion in those days. Whenever you opened the door in winter the snow blew into the classroom. Those who knew about these things thought it was healthier to have fresh air circulating through the building! It was a tough school, serving a large council estate, although discipline was very strict. Boys did as they were told, but the atmosphere was not conducive to learning. If you missed the chance to move up to Acklam grammar like most of the Clough tribe, it was more or less assumed that you left at fifteen and got a job. Before we leave Brian Clough's schooldays, Mr Rowell gives a revealing insight into his character. No wonder he remembers the boy after all these years:

'As PE master, I was pretty adept at throwing things. If boys didn't pay attention, I could hit them between the eyes with a piece of chalk. One day after PE we were in the classroom when Clough's mind seemed to be wandering. On the desk was a gym slipper. I threw it at him as hard as I could, but he *was* paying attention and saw the missile heading his way. He ducked and the slipper crashed straight through the window and out into the corridor. It so happened that we had a very severe headmaster, who was walking down the corridor when the slipper landed at his feet accompanied by a shower of glass. He stormed in to find out which boy had done it. I had to confess that it had been "sir" and in front of the whole class he gave me the biggest rollicking I've ever had. When he'd gone, Clough stood up and said, "Sir, it wasn't fair of the head to do that. We want you to know that the whole class is behind you." It takes a remarkable boy to stand up and be counted in a situation like that.

'I always thought he'd make it. He seemed to be successful in everything he did and you couldn't fail to get on with him. He was popular with the other boys too. There was always a laugh and a smile when Clough was around. When I see him on television today I can recollect him as a young boy with exactly the same attitude and responses.'

Brian's mind was set on a career in football, but in the meantime he had to get out and earn a few bob. The clerk's department at Casebourne's cement works, part of the ICI complex, would do for now. Uninspiring, but better than manual labour. Clough and work, however, did not seem ideally suited to each other. He was intrinsically lazy and not at all taken with the idea of getting up at the crack of dawn. Bill was his saviour: 'He'd have lain there all day if I'd let him. I bounced him out of bed at six o'clock, revived him with a hot cup of tea, and practically dragged him onto the seven o'clock bus. He never had time for breakfast. He'd go straight into the canteen for a bacon sandwich when he got to the office. Becoming a professional footballer must have been paradise after that. We teased him about his easy money. "How's the ninety-minutes-a-week job?" we'd ask. He'd say, "I do more work in one day's training than you lot do all week!"'

Sometimes Joe took his brother on the wagon he drove at the plasterer's yard: 'I told him it was no use his wasting away at the office. If he wanted to be a footballer, he had to have balanced proportions. I was a great believer in that. I made him lump sacks of plaster to strengthen his biceps and chest. He didn't like it much, but he did as he was told.'

A year after leaving school, Clough was playing with and against men in the Cleveland league. Not just any men. This was a league devised for farm labourers from the villages. Some of them were big enough to blot out the sun on the few occasions it shone! The team was Great Broughton, named after an unspoiled village nestling at the foot of the Cleveland hills about twelve miles out of town. A curious place for a city lad to start. It came about through Bill, a modest player by his own admission, who had been with Great Broughton for a full season when he recruited Brian: 'He was only sixteen but being a keen competitor he took up the challenge. He played one or two games the first season, then became a star.'

In the 1952–53 season, the team included four Clough brothers, Joe, Des, Bill and Brian, plus Doreen's husband, Sid. In addition there were two more sets of brothers, leaving room for only one player from the village! Apart from Brian, Des was the pick of the Cloughs. He went on to play for Bishop Auckland and captained Whitby Town: a quick, brave centre-half, who was still playing league football in 1986 in his late fifties! Once, while playing against Great Broughton's arch-rivals, Dunsdale, Des took a nasty cut over the eye. They rushed him to Guisborough to have stitches put in, then he came back and finished the match. Made of strong stuff were the Cloughs. They had to be. The wind fairly howled around those parts. The pitch was a simple farm field with goalposts. They had to clear the sheep into the next field before they could play and even then they could hardly make out the pitch markings. As for the ball, according to Joe it was 'a big leather thing that nearly knocked your head off'.

Bill describes the atmosphere of those cold and frequently grey Saturday afternoons: 'The rivalry between the villages had to be seen to be believed. As "townies" we weren't used to it. Home games were the highlight of the week for the farming communities. Spectators even took side bets. They'd be there on the touchline in all weathers. It was a lovely way of life.'

Clough graduated to Middlesbrough Juniors in his second season, but it did not prevent his playing for Great Broughton in the afternoon, having already played a match in the morning. One of the Great Broughton farmers collected the Cloughs from Middlesbrough in his potato truck. The pick-up point was the Linthorpe hotel, where Des, Joe, Bill and Sid, the brother-in-law, would be anxiously waiting for Brian to get over from his morning match. Joe continues: 'We made a point of getting to Great Broughton early so we could have a pie and a pint in the Black Horse. Brian only drank lemonade then. After a game of darts we got changed in the little Temperance Hall. Sometimes it was so cold you couldn't get your laces tied. The trouble was the hall was about a mile from the pitch. Once, eight or nine of us piled into an old Austin Seven but usually the visiting team gave us a lift in their bus. That was alright but we had to watch we didn't hammer them too hard or they'd make us walk back!'

Brian was outstanding for his age. He was by far the youngest in the team, but not afraid to have his say. Derek Chapman, one of his team mates, remembers making the mistake of wearing his shirt: 'I was cycling past the Temperance Hall one Saturday lunchtime and thought I'd pop in and collect a shirt to save myself a journey. I didn't see which shirt it was. I was having quite a good game when Brian shouted at me: "You might have the number-nine shirt on, Derek, but *I'm* the centre-forward around here!" I shouted back, "Why don't you try running for the ball and save our legs?" That shut him up. He never ran much. Liked the ball played to him so all he had to do was score.'

How he scored! The goals came in threes and fours; once – in a cup tie against Skinningrove, a steel town down the coast – they came in double figures. Clough and his colleagues cleared three inches of snow off the pitch, persuaded the referee to play the game, and won 16–0, with Clough scoring 10. He met his match in another cup tie in the unlikely shape of a sixty-year-old centre-half called George Cowan who had once played in Scottish League football. Clough fell about laughing when the old-stager was introduced as a late replacement. Derek Chapman remembers: 'George came on wearing ordinary shoes and trousers rolled up to his knee. We thought it must be some sort of a joke, but the old boy was brilliant. Brian couldn't do a thing against him. Never saw the ball! That's the only time I can remember anyone getting the better of him.'

Another curiosity about Great Broughton was the manager. Her name was Nancy Goldsborough, a roly-poly postmistress who used to straight-talk the men: 'If you don't do your stuff, you'll have me to reckon with!'

Joe thinks she came to be manager because she was one of the few villagers who could write: 'She was a jolly, cuddly lady, always there with a flask of coffee and a spoonful of rum when it was bitter cold.'

Because the manager was a woman, discipline was tight. There was no bad language. Not on the pitch anyway. Nancy stopped short of visiting the changing room. She would wait outside to collect the kit – dark green shirts and an assortment of shorts and socks. It was a rarity then for players not to have to take their kit home. Nancy washed the lot herself, which was good news for Mrs Clough!

Another of the villagers threw open her hearth to the team after the game. They'd sit around a blazing coal fire, sipping mugs of tea, before washing their hands and faces for the long bus ride back to Middlesbrough. A long day for Clough finished when he staggered back to Valley Road at about seven thirty in the evening.

Great Broughton was not the ideal shopwindow for him to display his talents. However word got around that the village had a demon centre-forward of tender years. George Camsell, the former Middlesbrough and England centre-forward, has often been credited with discovering Clough, but that was not the case. Camsell watched him and *rejected* him. He had been sent by Ray Grant, the headmaster at Hugh Bell secondary school, who ran

Middlesbrough Juniors. Grant had been tipped off by a friend and asked Camsell to watch Great Broughton playing in a Jefferson Cup match at nearby Stokesley. 'Won't make it,' was Camsell's verdict on Clough, but Grant persevered.

'I insisted Clough play for Middlesbrough Juniors against Huddersfield,' says Grant. 'I respected my friend's original opinion. I knew there had to be something to this lad. The match was at Heckmondwike. I shan't forget it because there was a stream running nearby and a bucket on the end of a rope for fishing the ball out of the water. Brian had a quiet match, then he produced something which made me take notice. Our outside left, Albert Mendham, decided to bypass him and hit a ball out to the other wing. He struck it with terrific power. As it was passing behind Brian – or so it seemed – the Huddersfield defenders moved over. Brian, who was facing the opposition goal, turned around and flicked the ball at right angles up and over his shoulder. With the defence flat-footed, he burst through the middle and, from the edge of the penalty area, hit a screaming left-foot shot into the top corner. I thought: good heavens, that's either a complete fluke or he's a genius. Later it was obvious that he was blessed with a touch of genius. I sent a message to the club: "Ignore previous report from George Camsell – this boy can play." It gave me untold joy to see him come good but it was a sad day for Middlesbrough when they let him go. He was capable of thinking beyond the level of most players.'

Clough was on his way. Success was to make him rich and famous and take him around the world, but spiritually it failed to uproot him from the soil of Teesside. Peter Taylor says Clough has always been the small-town boy from the north-east who never wanted to leave. Indeed, in fifty-two years he has lived in only two areas of England: the north-east and Derby. Throughout his travels, he remained close to his parents and his brothers and sisters, visiting them at regular intervals, and inviting them to matches at Derby. He took his father to some of his political meetings. Sally, his mother, would curl up with embarrassment at some of Brian's more outrageous interviews. When he was Hartlepool manager, she once told Harold Shepherdson she had to switch off the radio when he was speaking because she could not bear to hear what was coming next. Both parents lived to enjoy Derby's 1972 championship celebrations. They were on holiday with Clough in the Scilly

Isles when news of the championship success came through. However, Sally did not survive to see his walkout from the Baseball Ground the following year, nor his sacking at Leeds, nor, of course, his greatest success, at Nottingham Forest. She was taken ill on that holiday in the Scillies and died less than twelve months later on Clough's thirty-eighth birthday. She was seventy-two.

That same evening, Clough saw Derby through an important European Cup round at the Baseball Ground before breaking the news to Barry, who was at the match with him. Sadly, his father faded fast after the shock of his wife's death and slipped quietly away himself two years later.

2
Hotshot

Wherever Brian Clough went, controversy was sure to follow. It happened at Hartlepool, where he helped to force the chairman's resignation; it happened at Leeds, where they threw him out after six weeks; it happened at Nottingham Forest, where he fell out with directors and eventually split with Peter Taylor; it happened at Derby, where the team mutinied to have him back. But it started years before that when, as a twenty-one-year-old in his demob suit, he tried to take charge of Middlesbrough Football Club. Remarkable that someone so young should wield such influence, but he was no ordinary young man.

Ray Bilcliff, the stalwart Middlesbrough full-back who played five hundred games for his club, first noticed Clough's ambition when the two of them were playing for the juniors. 'In the taxi coming back from a match, this young fellow started analysing everybody's game – telling them what they should and shouldn't have done. It was the first time I'd ever clapped eyes on him. I wondered who the hell he was.'

Clough loved arriving in style at Ayresome Park each morning. He timed his entrance so that the rest of the squad would already be half changed, then he would swagger in as cool as you like, bike clips tucked into the pocket of his gabardine overcoat, hair clipped regimentally short beneath his favourite flat cap, eyes burning bright with purpose. He seemed from another world. In front of a captive audience, he would peel off his cap, toss it towards the changing-room peg and, five times out of six, hit the target.

'You've got to do something about Clough,' trainer Jimmy Gordon used to warn his superior, Harold Shepherdson, but it was like spitting in the wind. Shepherdson was one of the most experienced and respected coaches in the game and worked under successive England managers Walter Winterbottom and Alf Ramsey. But he had seen nothing to compare with this for arrogance. He and the Middlesbrough manager, Bob Dennison, would rack their brains about how to handle the young tearaway. They never fathomed him.

It was not unusual to see Dennison and Shepherdson fidgeting nervously at the railway station before an away game. The object of their anxiety would invariably be Clough, who still had not shown up when the train was due. Moments before it pulled out, he would make his grand entrance, bag in hand, boots strung around his neck. The players swore he did it on purpose, hiding on the platform and emerging in the nick of time, for maximum dramatic effect. As a boy, Clough spent many Saturday afternoons on the terraces of Ayresome Park with his father and brothers admiring players of the calibre of Wilf Mannion and George Hardwick. He eventually joined Boro as an amateur in 1951 and signed professional forms a year later, at the age of seventeen. It cost the club the minimum registration fee of £10. Naturally, the teenage Clough was excited, but in truth it was no big deal to be signed by a league side in those days. Youngsters were rounded up by the busload, usually to prevent their falling into the clutches of a neighbouring club.

Two years' national service interrupted his ambitions. Clough was initially posted to Dumfries, where he caught the eye of the Scottish League side Queen of the South, but then spent most of his service life at Watchet in Somerset. There he played for the station team, but failed to reach the dizzy heights of the full RAF representative eleven. He regarded those as wasted years and resolved upon moving back north to make up for lost time. It was his misfortune to be saddled with a club content to muddle along in the Second Division. Middlesbrough were poor relations to the other north-eastern giants to whom football was a religion. Len Shackleton, the Sunderland and England inside-forward who later reported on soccer for the *Daily Express* and *Sunday People,* describes it this way: 'If Newcastle and Sunderland had achieved half the success of Liverpool and Everton today, the crowds would have been queuing in July for the first match of the season! Middlesbrough didn't count. They were Yorkshire folk. They wanted Bovril and a bullfight at half-time.'

Once established as a first-team regular, Clough grew

increasingly frustrated at Middlesbrough's inability to escape from second-grade football. He could not personally have contributed much more, scoring 38 goals in his first full season, and following up with 40, 43, 39 and 34. As early as April 1956, after a mere nine games in the first team, he slapped in a transfer request. He thought he could better himself elsewhere. Further investigation by Dennison revealed that Clough had sold the story of his transfer request for £50. The manager warned him, 'I don't mind you earning a few bob from the papers, but for goodness sake let me know first.' Clough had already learned how to manipulate the press.

He had by now fallen under the spell of Peter Taylor, a solid if unspectacular goalkeeper who had not fulfilled his immense promise as a sixteen-year-old in Nottingham schools football. Taylor's head was full of the teachings of Harry Storer, under whom he had served at Coventry. He was dazzled by the man's no-nonsense approach and his ability to come straight to the point. If Middlesbrough were in London at the same time as Storer's Derby, Taylor would make a point of checking train times and trying to catch a word with him after the game. At twenty-six Taylor realized that his playing days were numbered. He first spotted Clough in a Possibles versus Probables match and almost battered down Dennison's door until he took notice. That brief encounter changed both of their lives. Clough, cocky and confident of his own ability, became unbearable to his team mates. Taylor made bullets for him to fire, feeding his considerable ego, encouraging his arrogance. Clough was only too willing to listen.

Jimmy Gordon had seen the danger signs ahead of most: 'Brian played hell with Shep and Mickey Fenton when he saw them standing against the radiator after training one day. Wanted to know why they hadn't been out in the cold and wet like everyone else. He never forgave them for that.' A tougher manager than Dennison might have clipped the young player's wings there and then. Instead, Clough was allowed to behave as he wished. What's more, Dennison made him captain, saying he wanted someone to do the managing for him on the pitch. Shepherdson was not in favour: 'Clough was a bad influence on the team. He created jealousy. He and Taylor were loners who chose certain people to communicate with. I wasn't one of them. It was very difficult to know what he was thinking. I tried to work him out but couldn't. He ordered the rest of the team around something terrible. "Get that f------ ball over to me," he'd shout. "I'm here to put it in the net, not you." Poor Edwin Holliday was terrified of him. Holliday used to visit the lavatory several times before a game as nerves got hold of him. Once, after his umpteenth visit, Clough belittled the poor fellow in front of his team mates by saying, "Eddie, I hope you've washed your hands, have you?"

One man who was not terrified was Brian Phillips, the craggy centre-half who kicked like a mule and sometimes appeared not to care who or what was on the end of his boot. During a practice match at the Hutton Road training ground, Phillips grew tired of Clough's persistent niggling. Clough was an expert at tugging shorts and elbowing – anything to put the centre-half off his game: 'You always knew which way Cloughie was going to turn when he had his back to you – round to his left with the ball on his right foot. It was as regular as clockwork. I caught him with such a crunching tackle he went down like a sack of spuds, moaning and groaning in the mud. I did enjoy it. They called off the practice and carted him away for treatment.'

The other players didn't like the way Clough held back during training. Phillips comments, 'When he first came he was a good trainer, but Taylor used to tell him, "Don't leave it on the track, save it for the next match." After that, he was in the back bunch doing as little as possible. That suited Taylor down to the ground, but it got up everyone else's noses.' Neither did they appreciate Clough's habit of staying upfield while all hell was breaking loose in the Middlesbrough goalmouth. Again Taylor had been the guiding light. 'Be selfish,' he told the young centre-forward. 'You've no business dropping back to help the defence.'

'We'd be flogging our guts out for a nil-nil draw,' says Phillips, 'and Cloughie would be strolling around up the other end quite unconcerned. He did bugger all when the pressure was on. Then we'd have to read in the *Gazette* what a great game he'd had.'

Gordon despaired of him too. He told Clough many times, 'Instead of scoring 30 goals a season, why don't you score 25 and help someone else to score 15? That way the team's 10 goals better off.' All he could get out of Clough was: 'My job's scoring goals not making them. Let the others do that.' Gordon was to serve Clough in later years at Derby, Leeds and Nottingham Forest and was involved in all the major triumphs. No one who witnessed their arguments at Middlesbrough would have believed they could ever work together. Sometimes Gordon would abandon team talks because they degenerated into slanging matches between Clough and Phillips, the only one who stood up to his pontificating.

'It was exasperating,' says Gordon. 'The lad was getting goals, so no one could say anything to him. The rest of the team knew Clough was their best hope of a £2 win bonus. He was horrible to them, bossing them around and telling them what *he* expected them to do. He had no time for anyone who didn't give a hundred per cent. There were two ways of doing things: his way and the wrong way!'

Dennison wanted Clough to prosecute his will on the field of play but Clough took it a stage further. His bossiness spilled over into the dressing rooms and the hotels. Shepherdson had the unenviable job of checking that players were in their rooms on Friday nights before a match. More often than not, they had gone AWOL. He'd find half the team at a briefing in Clough's room.

An unsuspecting Alan Peacock was having breakfast at a London hotel on the morning of a match against Charlton. Taylor came over and announced there would be a team meeting at eleven o'clock. Peacock duly reported, to find only five others present: the rest of the forward line plus Taylor. 'I wondered what the hell was going on,' Peacock recalls. 'Billy Day, Edwin Holliday, Derek McLean and myself sat all looking at each other, when Clough stood up to speak. Then I realized we were in his room. He told us Walter Winterbottom would be watching the match so we were to make him look good in front of the England manager. All we had to do was put it on a plate for him. He'd do the rest. He was so self-centred, you couldn't help but smile. In the event he didn't have a very good game.'

Whatever they thought of him, none could dispute his value to Middlesbrough. He had become the fifties equivalent of a sporting superstar, although his worshippers were confined to the north-east and his lifestyle was by no means extravagant. By the age of twenty-two he was earning £24 a week, with winning bonuses on top, but he was still living at home. It would be three years before Jimmy Hill successfully campaigned for the abolition of the maximum wage. The average pay at the time over the four divisions was well below £20. When the back-garden path was re-surfaced at Valley Road one of the brothers traced the word 'moneybags' in the wet cement. It was their nickname for Brian. He was the only one with a car – a maroon Ford Anglia – and adoring female fans would flock to catch a glimpse of him. Despite that he nursed a secret fear. He wrote in a newspaper article:

> I have no trade outside football. If I could start again as a bright-eyed youngster living his every moment for football, I would take an apprenticeship. After all, everyone doesn't make the grade. What happens then? If a man has no trade he has little future. That might have been me.

Sooner than he imagined, that very dilemma would test his strength of character. In the meantime, his goal-scoring prowess – 200 in only 219 league games – drew crowds of 30,000 to Ayresome Park. Unlike today, the grounds would be swollen with families and groups of young girls who came to see the good-looking lad with the golden boots. One girl found her way from the terraces into the Clough living room as an indirect result of one of his goals. Judy Armstrong was hit in the face by her own rattle as the crowd surged forward to hail another Clough thunderbolt. Standing behind her was Brian's younger brother Barry. He helped her deal with her injury and the couple started courting. Barry and Judy married a few years later. It was a union of which Clough approved. If he didn't approve, woe betide the suitor! A case in point was Esmond Million, one of the club goalkeepers, who took a shine to Brian's younger sister, Deanna. Clough thought Million a man of no prospects and took a dim view of his visits to the house. When the team bus dropped them off at Valley Road, he would run ahead of Million and stand at the door, 'Push off, Es, you're not seeing her tonight.'

With an international forward-line of Day, McLean, Clough, Peacock and Holliday, Middlesbrough should have waltzed into the First Division. Why they did not win promotion is a matter for conjecture. Clough made his feelings perfectly clear when he stormed into the *Middlesbrough Evening Gazette* offices to write his weekly 'captain's column'. He told his ghost writer, Cliff Mitchell, 'As fast as I score, they're chucking two in at the back. That's what I want to write about this week.' Mitchell blanched: 'Do you realize what you're saying, Brian?' Clough answered, 'Of course I do, but I've complained till I'm hoarse to Bob

Dennison and he won't do a bloody thing about it. They're letting the club down and making money.'

He was referring to the cancer of fixed-odds betting, which had started to appear in different pockets of the country. In those days, players were allowed to bet against their own teams and Clough suspected that this practice had sabotaged Middlesbrough's promotion aspirations. The *Gazette* editor prevented Clough's column from going into the paper, but Mitchell wrote it up anyway and read it to a group of the players with the warning: 'We know what's going on. If you don't pack it up, we're running this story next week.'

Before Clough had become a first-team regular, there had been the peculiar case of Rolando Ugolini, the Scottish goalkeeper who immediately preceded Taylor. Middlesbrough were drawing 2–2 at Port Vale when Ugolini appeared to allow a soft shot to bobble into his net for the Port Vale winner. Back on the bus, when the results showed that he had correctly picked Aston Villa and Rangers for home wins, Ugolini let out a loud cheer. 'I've done it, I've got the treble,' called the goalkeeper. But which was his third team? When he replied 'Port Vale', they almost lynched him. One of the players took him by the lapels and said, 'My kids could have had a pair of shoes each if it hadn't been for you.' Ugolini never played again for Middlesbrough. It must be stressed that there was nothing illegal in his actions, deplorable though they might have been. The growing custom was to hedge your bets by going for a defeat. If the team won you got your bonus; if it lost, you won the bet.

Thanks to a painstaking series of inquiries by the *Sunday People* in the ensuing years, a widespread bribery racket was discovered in the English game. There was no suggestion that Ugolini was involved with anything on that scale, but two Middlesbrough players of Clough's day, Brian Phillips and Esmond Million, were ultimately gaoled and banned from football. Million admitted throwing two goals into his net when he played for Bristol Rovers after leaving Ayresome Park, and Phillips admitted offering him the bribe. By then Phillips was playing for Mansfield, the home of bribery's Mr Big, Jim Gauld. Another former Middlesbrough player, Ken Tompson, was also ensnared in the police net while he was playing centre-half for Hartlepool. Phillips is adamant that no organized racket was operating at the time of Clough's complaint. 'If there had been,

I'd have known about it,' he says. Bilcliff is less certain: 'There was talk about players betting against the team, but we didn't find out who they were.'

Dennison was reluctant to probe too deeply. When he had taken over as manager, Middlesbrough had been in sufficient turmoil – £60,000 in the red and still reeling from the scandal of missing money from the club safe and unstamped insurance cards. It coincided with the suicide of the club secretary. One of the new manager's first tasks was to travel to Seaburn to identify the body. Dennison had put the club on an even footing but it was heading nowhere. They used to joke that Clough had to score a hat-trick to avoid defeat! Goals leaked in at the back as regularly as they flew into the opposition net. In vain, Clough and Taylor protested that Middlesbrough had to buy if they wanted success.

The pair had the manager's ear on most things but not that. Phillips found out through a liaison with Dennison's secretary that Clough and Taylor were in the manager's office most Fridays helping him to pick the team. 'Fortunately for me,' he says, 'they both appreciated my uncompromising style. They liked a centre-half who could put it about. Taylor was more than grateful to have someone like me protecting him.'

Clough put his disappointments behind him and continued to turn heads with his goal-scoring feats. They at last brought him to the attention of the England selectors, albeit in a modest way at first. He was outstanding in the England 'B' international against Scotland in Birmingham, scoring once and laying on 2 more in England's 4–1 win. Where it really mattered, though, Clough still struggled to make impact. His buring desire was to get into the senior team for the forthcoming World Cup finals in Sweden. Unfortunately, he had few opportunities of impressing the selectors. This was surprising because sad circumstances had seemed to work in his favour. The Munich air crash had robbed England of three important members, including the centre-forward, Tommy Taylor. Would Winterbottom come knocking? He certainly inquired. Dennison told him, 'He's not the most brilliant footballer in the world, but you won't find a better goal scorer.' Shepherdson, the England manager's right-hand man, was in a better position to influence the selectors, but he reported, 'His goal-scoring record speaks for itself.' Hardly a glowing testimonial, but the Middlesbrough coach knew better than most that behind the statistics was a difficult personality. Clough believes that Shepherdson obstructed his international progress. He should also have asked questions about Harry French, one of the England selectors and a Middlesbrough director. In those days, selectors nominated players of their choice and the poor old team manager had to go along with it. No recommendation of Clough was forthcoming from French.

It does seem odd that, with two such influential figures in the club, the most prolific goal-scorer in the country managed only two caps for England.

Clough did not assist his own cause by being openly anti-establishment. He and Taylor, for instance, spurned the chance to enrol in an FA coaching course which aimed to do away with outmoded training systems. The man behind it was Walter Winterbottom, the national director of coaching, who wanted to instil more thought and flexibility into playing practices. Endlessly lapping the field seemed to him a fruitless and tedious pursuit, which indeed it was. Clough and Taylor thought Winterbottom and his men were bogged down in theory. 'Soccer's a simple game,' says Taylor. 'We couldn't be doing with those schoolmaster types who tried to make it complicated. They had no professional experience of the game. Brian and I laughed at their blackboard talk.'

Nevertheless, Winterbottom planned to give the rebellious Clough a run-out for England during the Iron Curtain tour of Russia and Yugoslavia in May 1958, a month before the World Cup. Before doing so, the manager (or, rather, the selection committee) decided to give Derek Kevan one last chance to prove himself. Winterbottom admits the big West Brom centre-forward was 'as slow as a carthorse' and did not have class, but he was impressed with his work rate. So Kevan it was who picked up the number-nine shirt vacated by Tommy Taylor. The England manager rationalizes it this way: 'I knew Clough could score from any distance and any angle, but Kevan had this tremendous energy.'

It was Clough's bad luck that the energetic Mr Kevan scored twice when England beat Scotland 4–0. Even so, Clough was on the trip to Belgrade shortly afterwards and believed he would be playing after Winterbottom had a private talk with him during the flight. It seemed that Winterbottom indeed wanted Clough to play against Yugoslavia, but that he had his mind changed for him by the bewhiskered gentlemen selectors. They preferred Kevan, having been impressed by his partnership with Bobby Charlton. In searing heat, England were beaten 5–0, but Kevan kept his place for the Russia match and scored in a 1–1 draw.

Afterwards, Winterbottom took Clough and Jim Langley aside and broke the bad news. Neither would be in the World Cup squad. Both players were puzzled. Clough took it very badly. It seemed pointless to him to drag a player halfway across Europe, fail to give him a game, then reject him. He made his feelings plain.

When the party returned home, Clough confronted Shepherdson at Kings Cross station before boarding the train to Middlesbrough: 'I scored 42 goals in the league and cup this season. They count in the matches we play for Middlesbrough but apparently it wasn't enough for this lot.'

He was referring to the collection of ageing club directors and FA officials who made up the selection committee. They had the power of veto. Winterbottom submitted a team based largely on the committee's observations, and they agreed or disagreed as they saw fit. It's absurd these days to think of amateurs picking the team.

England acquitted themselves reasonably well in Sweden, drawing three games and losing 1–0 to Russia. Kevan played all four games, scoring twice, but the hoped-for partnership with Charlton never materialized. The young Manchester United winger was suffering from the delayed effects of his terrifying escape at Munich and didn't make the trip. According to Winterbottom, 'You could hear his knife and fork jangling when he ate. I couldn't possibly take him.'

Clough devoted himself to Middlesbrough and his new job as captain. As if to show the selectors what they had been missing, he scored 5 goals in the opening match of the 1958–59 season against Brighton and repeated the dose for the Football League against the League of Ireland in September. The following 21 March, his twenty-fourth birthday, he helped himself to 4 more in a 6–1 win over Swansea. But still he was overlooked for three internationals that summer. Winterbottom argued that Football League representative matches were no guide. Eventually, the selectors bowed to increasing press and public pressure. Clough was awarded his first cap against Wales at Cardiff on 17 October

1959. His Middlesbrough colleague Eddie Holliday also made his debut on the left wing. This was the team: Hopkinson; Howe, Armfield; Clayton, Wright, Flowers; Connelly, Greaves, Clough, Charlton, Holliday.

In the excitement, Clough forgot his boots. Dennison's wife received the distress call and had to travel to Cardiff with them. She needn't have bothered. Clough hardly got a kick. Grahame Moore equalized Jimmy Greaves's goal with the last kick of an awful game.

Winterbottom and the selectors fell out over the next fixture, a midweek game against Sweden at Wembley. Two thirds of the Swedish side, including Gunnar Neilson and Nils Liedholm, had played in the World Cup final against Brazil sixteen months earlier. The England manager said it would be foolish to take on such an experienced team with the same young players. The selectors overruled him. Their idea was to keep the youngsters together and allow them to mature like the Hungarians had.

Sweden won 3–2 but it could have been worse. Jimmy Greaves says, 'They took us apart. We didn't know what day of the week it was. Cloughie was anonymous in that match, but so were we all. Afterwards, he was very outspoken in front of Winterbottom. When someone pointed out that he hadn't had much of the play, Cloughie said, "What do you expect? How can I play centre-forward alongside Charlton and Greaves when we're all going for the same ball?" That upset me a bit. Then I realized he was right. It was daft to put all three up-front together.'

Dennison, who had taken the rest of the Middlesbrough team to Wembley to watch Clough and Holliday, has an even sharper recollection of that conversation: 'He told Winterbottom he would have to drop either Greaves or Charlton. No wonder he didn't get another chance. Those matches seemed to me to prove something that Clough could never accept – he wasn't quite up to it.'

Greaves disagrees with that assessment: 'Playing in the Second Division didn't help him. I believe he'd have scored just as many in the First with a fashionable club. Another time and another place, he could have been an England regular. He was everything you have to be as a striker: fearless, physically and morally tough, and greedy. I get annoyed when modern strikers say they don't care who scores the goals as long as someone does. They're paid a fortune to do it themselves. Cloughie was like me.

We didn't care who scored as long as it wasn't anyone else! We'd do anything to get a toe in first.'

Middlesbrough had a forward called Arthur Fitzsimons who would vouch for that. Arthur had a reputation for dribbling around three defenders and shooting over the bar. Clough soon put a stop to that. He would take the ball off Arthur's toe to score himself. Once he barged his team mate off the ball before going on to score. When challenged about it he answered, 'I'm better at it than he is.' He was right, as he was so infuriatingly often.

Peacock, who followed Clough into the England side, saw plenty of examples of his selfishness: 'Players would be shaping to score when they'd hear, 'Out of the way,' then bang! Clough would have scored himself. Goals were everything to him. He hated it when I scored a hat-trick – sulked if his name wasn't in the headlines.' Peacock settled well into Clough's boots when the number nine left for Sunderland. He was rewarded with three England caps, one more than Clough. On being awarded the third, he was heard cheering, 'I've done it – I've beaten him!'

Why did Clough fail to get more caps? Shepherdson admits that he deserved more but was his own worst enemy: 'As soon as he was among the England lads, the old cockiness and big-headedness came out again. I had a hell of a job getting players to room with him. Bryan Douglas fell unlucky once and complained to me afterwards, "Your bloomin' pal never stops talking football, does he? Drives you barmy."' Clough's opinions were always delivered with that slightly superior air. Even among internationals it appears that he talked down to people. Shepherdson says, 'I've never seen anyone so obsessed with football and his own ability. It put people off him.'

Others might think those are precisely the qualities required in a footballer, especially a striker. If Clough and Taylor had received such a report on a player when they were managers, they would have signed him in a flash. For a more detached view of Clough's playing ability, there could perhaps be no better judge than George Hardwick, the Middlesbrough and England full-back who played thirteen times for his country just after the war and later became Clough's manager at Sunderland. 'Gorgeous George', as they called him, because of his fatal attraction for the fairer sex, was football correspondent on the *Middlesbrough Evening Gazette* when Clough burst upon the scene:

'His potential from the start was tremendous. His was the

Look at the determination on the face. Clough the centre-forward hated goalkeepers

Sunderland days were happy for a while. Then came the injury and the sack

Left: Action man: Clough was set to break records when injury ruined his career at Sunderland

Below: Young man with big ideas. Ray Bilcliff *(left)* and Brian Phillips weren't smiling when Clough started throwing his weight around

Bottom left: A rare picture of Clough, the full England international. He and Jimmy Greaves *(also in shot)* should never have been in the same side together, Clough told Walter Winterbottom

Bottom right: Clough's first manager was the local postmistress Nancy Goldsborough *(centre).* He rarely answered back in those days

Training at Middlesbrough wasn't always this popular. Taylor used to tell his protégé: 'Save it for match days'

Taylor's all-star team to play the Inland Revenue in 1959. It includes David Pleat, Ian Storey-Moore, Tony Hateley and Peter Grummitt as well as Clough

Hartlepool days. Clough puts Eric Phythian through his paces. Later he put the striker through another ordeal altogether

Quite a family. From left to right: Brian, Barry, Doreen, Des, Mum (Sally), Bill, Dad (Joe Senior), Gerald, Deanna and Joe

greatest finishing talent I've seen before or since. Clough wasn't a goal poacher like Jimmy Greaves, but a goal scorer – from anywhere. Even thirty-five yards out there was a good chance he'd hit the net. If not he would certainly hit the target, forcing the goalkeeper to make a save, or striking the woodwork.

'I was the only reporter to criticize him. Everyone else patted him on the back and told him how marvellous he was. I thought he could improve. On Monday mornings he used to charge into my office full of rage about what I'd written. How dare I criticize him? We'd end up having a cup of tea and discussing the game's finer points. From that sprang a close friendship.

'It suited Bob Dennison to have Clough knocking in the goals. It pleased the public and made the manager's job secure, but it was no good for Clough. He wasn't being encouraged to improve his ability. He could lay off a first-time ball to the wing like his son, Nigel, does today, but he wasn't getting away from his marker. I told him I couldn't see him scoring so many goals in Division One because top-class centre-halves weren't likely to be beaten by his quick reflexes. They'd have smothered him before he got into position.

'That's what happened in his two international appearances. Against Sweden I watched with great sadness. The local press put it down to the poor service he got from his wingers and half-backs, but every time they looked for him, he was heavily marked. He didn't escape – never got into space. His coaches at Middlesbrough should have worked on him.'

Needless to say, Clough was depressed at his performance. Goalless games were hard to bear at the best of times. When he got into a barren patch at Middlesbrough he was like a bear with a sore head. Dennison would play youngsters against him in training to make it easier to score. Anything to satisfy his craving for goals.

After the trip to watch Clough at Wembley, Middlesbrough played a league match at Brighton during which Clough was noticeably subdued. The following day the team boarded a train for the long haul to Edinburgh, where they were to play Hibernian in a friendly. The trip had added poignancy for Clough. His opposite number for Hibs was Joe Baker, a Sassenach widely tipped to replace him in the England side.

On the six-hour journey, most of the Middlesbrough lads settled into the card school or played dominoes. Clough wasn't interested in card schools. He and Taylor sat in a compartment alone analysing the England match and talking of little else but football and Clough. Their aloofness did not go unnoticed. It confirmed the growing feeling that Clough was too wrapped up in himself to be captain.

Two players in particular would be glad to see the back of him. One was Brian Phillips, originally a friend, but lately one of Clough's biggest critics. Others were telling him that he would make a better captain. The second dissident was Bill Harris, a Welsh international inside-forward with lovely, silky skills but no ball-winning ability. Clough gave him a terrible time, moaning at him for not winning tackles and once calling him a 'coward' on the field of play.

A third team mate took part in the whispered conversation on that seemingly endless train ride. Willie Fernie had joined Middlesbrough from Celtic and rubbed up against Clough almost at once. The Scots international was another ball-playing inside-forward, but with more fire in his belly than some. Sparks flew many times when Fernie failed to deliver the ball to Clough's feet but chose instead to beat another defender. Clough would turn away in thinly disguised disgust, and eventually helped to turn a section of the Boro faithful against Fernie. 'My ball Fernie' was Clough's nickname for him.

Derek Stonehouse, the Middlesborough full-back, had travelled up separately from the rest after recovering from injury. He got on better with Clough than most and could detect a chilly atmosphere at the team hotel in Edinburgh: 'The minute I walked in I knew something was wrong. Clough and Taylor weren't there and I could hear a group of players talking about them. Phillips seemed to be the spokesman, but it was all done in whispers. Underhand, so to speak.'

A week later, Taylor got wind of what was going on when Phillips interrupted his training: 'We're not happy about your mate being skipper and we're getting up a round robin to give to the directors.' Taylor was too close to Clough to have noticed the resentment. He warned Phillips he was out of order, but the petition went to Dennison and the board. It carried only nine names, but that was sufficient to persuade the chairman, Eric Thomas, to investigate. The letter complained about 'harsh words on the pitch' and accused Clough of 'sulking' after defeat – a clear reference to the train journey.

Thomas called the whole team and the coaching staff into his office for what was supposed to be a confidential meeting. Word had leaked out, however, and the press converged on Ayresome Park. Anything to do with Clough was headline news. Don Mosey, writing for the *Daily Mail*, recalls arriving in Middlesbrough to the accompaniment of loudspeaker vans touring the streets and proclaiming, 'Clough in round-robin protest. Read it exclusively in the *Daily Express* tomorrow.'

When confronted by the chairman, the signatories backed off. It seemed that Bill Harris had instigated the petition, but support from players like Phillips and Bilcliff was easy to secure. It was Phillips who spoke up: 'He's not well liked by the players. In fact some of them hate his guts, Mr Thomas.' Harris countered with: 'Oh, I don't think it's quite as bad as that.' Clough in the meantime sat with his head in his hands, deeply wounded and close to tears. He said nothing but told friends and relations later that it was one of the worst moments of his life: 'When your own team mates gang up on you, it can't get any worse.' His family felt there was more to it than 'harsh words' and 'sulking'. Bill Clough believes it was tied up with Brian's earlier complaints about players throwing matches, though there is no evidence of that. Clough did not deny the allegations contained in the round robin. He agreed that he *was* sometimes harsh on the field and, yes, defeat *did* hurt. He didn't want to play cards interminably after a game – he wanted to analyse, find out why Middlesbrough had lost. What was wrong with that?

The incident was glossed over, but two of the signatories paid for their temerity. Phillips was offered reduced terms for the next season and had no option but to leave and join Mansfield Town. He appealed against his life ban for bribery and now manages Rainworth Miners Welfare near Mansfield. In 1982 he had the honour of leading them out at Wembley for the FA Vase final. Bilcliff was soon on his way out of Middlesbrough too.

Things were never the same again. Clough demanded a transfer, a move regarded by his disaffected colleagues as a ploy to attract cheap publicity. It was common practice for footballers to leak stories for money. Most correspondents had their pet informants. In an age when footballers' earnings were minimal, no one objected too strongly. Even members of the FA selection committee leaked Winterbottom's teams before he could announce them.

Dennison poured oil on the transfer waters, declaring that Clough was staying at Middlesbrough and that the players' protests had been ironed out. Clough promised, 'I shall be in there on Saturday fighting as hard as I can.' He was as good as his word.

Hardwick recalls the home match against Bristol Rovers: 'I shall never forget watching him leading the team out that Saturday. The crowd barracked him, which was a surprise. Clough took it without any obvious reaction. Then, twenty minutes into the game, he received the ball in the inside-left position about ten yards over the halfway line. He ran diagonally for twenty yards with the opposition backing off, thinking there was no immediate danger. Clough suddenly hit the ball from thirty yards out and it screamed into the net. You had to admire him for doing that while under such personal pressure. He resisted the temptation to walk around the ground with two fingers up to the crowd. He just played on. What tremendous strength of character.' He scored two more that day as well – each from twenty-five yards or more.

But Clough's transfer was imminent, however hard Dennison tried to keep him at Middlesbrough. The manager offered him several financial incentives to stay. Clough had told Dennison he would be happy if he could run a small business. First port of call was Albert King, a wealthy ice-cream merchant from Redcar who later joined the Boro board. King realized the market potential of Clough's name and came up with four or five business ideas along the lines Clough was indicating. King agreed to buy a general store or a newsagent's for £2000 and allow Clough to pay him back over a period of time. Clough was not sure how his new wife, Barbara, would take to living over the shop. He hesitated for so long that King lost interest.

Dennison tried one more idea. He was well connected with a boot manufacturer near Northampton. The company had done very nicely out of a range of football boots endorsed by Tom Finney, and Finney himself had made a good little earner. Dennison persuaded them to market a Brian Clough boot, which would require only a minor design change. He drove Clough to the factory to discuss the idea and he seemed keen. On the way back, he amazed Dennison by saying, 'Two and a half per cent isn't much, is it, boss?' Dennison explained that two and a half per cent of a lot was a lot. Tom Finney had had the same deal.

'It's not as though you have to do anything for it,' his manager explained. 'Just make a couple of personal appearances and sign autographs.' The pair made another journey the following week to collect the freshly drawn-up contract. Clough sat on it for two weeks. The company could not get an answer out of him despite repeated phone calls, and finally offered the deal to Jimmy Greaves instead.

That summer of 1961, there was talk of Arsenal coming in with a bid for Clough, who had been placed on the transfer list at £55,000, but Alan Brown of Sunderland made the decisive approach. He wanted a quick answer before Clough and his wife left on a Mediterranean cruise. Clough wasn't sure about joining another Second Division club, albeit a big one like Sunderland with crowds of 45,000 filling Roker Park each home game. He turned to his mentor Taylor, who was holidaying at Scarborough, one of his favourite bolt-holes. Clough found him in his deckchair on the beach and outlined his predicament. Sunderland were keen but he preferred Wolves. They'd won the league title in 1957–58 and 1958–59, following up with the FA Cup in 1960. More to the point, they played Clough's style of football: long ball out of defence and two fast wingers to provide the crosses.

The snag was that Wolves manager Stan Cullis had shown no interest. Not for the first time, Taylor played middleman. He had tried to 'sell' Clough to Harry Storer at Derby in the early days. Utterly in contravention of league regulations, he went to the nearest kiosk, still in his beach shorts, and phoned Molyneux. It came to nothing because Cullis was away. Clough went on his cruise without giving Sunderland an answer. He didn't know that Brown was as determined as he was.

During *his* family holiday at Bude, Brown discovered that the Cloughs were due back at Southampton at five o'clock one Saturday morning in July. He drove 180 miles through the night to meet Clough off the boat and spotted him in the baggage-reclaim area. The first meeting between these two northern firebrands took place over a five-foot partition. Brown leaned over and introduced himself. 'I've agreed terms with Middlesbrough for your signature. I'm offering you the top wages of the day [about £40 a week] and I'd like you to come up to Sunderland or Middlesbrough tomorrow to sign.' Clough looked at him for a few seconds, then stuck out his hand over the partition. 'Alright, I'll come,' he said, and the deal was done. Brown says now, 'It was the shortest, sweetest deal you ever saw – and this was supposedly the most awkward bloke in the game.'

There were several relieved players on Middlesbrough's books – those who had drawn up the petition to remove him from the captaincy. Even Peacock had to admit that the atmosphere was more relaxed and pleasant once 'Big 'ed' had gone. Shepherdson, Mickey Fenton and Jimmy Gordon were pleased to see him go. Dennison was relieved but sorry; the board thought they had done rather well to offload a troublemaker on their neighbours and make £40,000 in the process.

Brown was equally delighted to have signed Clough: 'I didn't worry about his reputation. I had the same reputation myself. We both called a spade a spade. If people didn't like the truth it was their problem.' The transfer brought Sunderland's spending to over £100,000. In the preceding few months, they had paid £40,000 for George Herd from Clyde and £17,000 for Harry Hooper from Birmingham. The headlines read: 'Bank of England Days Return on Wearside'. Brown and his board, led by the chairman, Sid Collings, had their hearts set on one goal – promotion to Division One the next season. Clough was the key.

The relationship between Brown and Clough was always uneasy. The Sunderland manager was a frightening figure to faint-hearted footballers and he decided to let Clough know who was boss. At an early training session he caught Clough talking on the sidelines to an acquaintance and gave him a fierce lecture in front of the rest of the players. 'The punishment was out of proportion to the crime,' says Brown today. 'Clough recognized authority, but I shouldn't have flown off the handle like I did.'

Sunderland missed promotion by a point after losing to lowly Swansea. They'd suffered a run of six defeats at one stage of the season and Clough decided the manager needed some moral support. To Brown's surprise, he knocked on the office door after training and walked in with sweat pouring off his brow. He looked his manager in the eye and said, 'I've just come to tell you, boss, that we're sorry for what's happened, and to assure you that everything possible is being done in the dressing room.'

'What a gesture that was,' says Brown. 'No other bugger would have had the nerve. Clough wasn't captain, but he was a tremendous influence in the dressing room as well as on the pitch. I could see even then what an asset he'd be on the managerial side one day. My only regret is that I didn't take him under my wing.'

The winter of 1962–63 was the worst since the big freeze of 1946. The snow began on Boxing Day and wiped out football and racing for the next two and a half months. Odd matches were played on rolled snow here and there, but most were played in the minds of the newly created Pools Panel, who met each weekend at a secret London rendezvous and guessed what the results might have been. There was such a fixture pile-up that the Cup Final between Leicester City and Manchester United had to be put back for three weeks.

The north-east, unusually, seemed to have missed the worst of the snow that Boxing Day. Middlesbrough had called off their match with Norwich, but referee Kevin Howley inspected Roker Park at 1.30 p.m. and decided the thin covering of snow was no hazard. The large yellow-grey cloud coming in from the west worried him, but the crowds were queuing outside, waiting for the turnstiles to open, so he declared the game on. Clough was one of the first to approve. He told Howley, 'Well done, ref. That bloody lot down the road have called theirs off. They'd call off anything.'

As the referee had feared, the heavens opened half an hour before kick-off. He stood in the tunnel watching a ten-minute deluge of hailstones turn the pitch into a cold, slimy mudbath.

Several wiseacres have suggested since that the game should never have started. No one complained at the time. The trainer was on the field only once in the ninety minutes and what Johnny Watters, the Sunderland physio, saw as he bent over the crumpled body of Brian Clough made his heart sink. He knew instantly, as did Alan Brown following on close behind, that the player was finished.

The twenty-seven-year-old centre-forward had gone after a misdirected pass with only one thought on his mind. He didn't see Chris Harker, the big, burly Bury goalkeeper, come off his line to challenge. The pair collided in the slush, Harker's shoulder hitting Clough's right knee with a sickening thud. Clough recalls, 'I hit my head hard on the ground and was nearly unconscious. I tried to crawl after the ball which had spun loose. I couldn't move.' His face was as grey as the sky.

While Howley tended to him, Bob Stokoe, the Bury centre-half, complained in his Geordie accent, 'Come on, ref, he's only codding.'

'Not this lad,' replied the referee, 'I've known him a long time. He doesn't cod.'

Clough was stretchered off with a torn cruciate ligament. The injury is treatable today with the insertion of a plastic replacement. In those days, no one recovered. Clough had scored 28 goals already by Christmas and looked set for 50. Sunderland won promotion to Division One but Clough had all but missed his dream. He managed three games in the top flight and scored his one and only First Division goal in September 1964, twenty-one months after the injury and nine months after he was warned he would never play again. He forced his way back into the reckoning with a hat-trick for the reserves the previous week. He was limping now, though, and the sharpness had gone. Clough had one kick in the 3–3 draw with Leeds – and scored.

In the meantime, Alan Brown had left to become manager of Sheffield Wednesday. To his everlasting regret, he and Clough parted on bad terms without so much as a handshake.

'I was too hard on him after the injury. I made him report for training seven days a week at nine o'clock, and run up and down the spion kop until he felt sick. After a couple of months, he came to my office nervously asking for a day off. I let him. It was the first bit of kindness he'd had. When a footballer's getting over a bad injury he's mentally ill as well. It showed in Clough's behaviour. He was under dreadful strain – frightened to death about what would become of him after football. I wasn't as understanding as I might have been.

'My intention was to get him onto the coaching staff but I didn't tell anyone. Least of all Cloughie. I realize now I should have done. It would have eased his anxiety. He was going through hell and giving the trainers hell too. "Get up those bloody steps yourself," he would shout at them. He got upset with me – couldn't work out why I was being so brutal with him. When we celebrated promotion he said, "I'm going to wish you well, but I shan't shake hands." He must have thought I was a beast.'

To this day, Clough has been unable to stand the sight of an injured player. It brings back too many bad memories. When Paul Hart broke his leg playing for Birmingham during the

1986–87 season, the Nottingham Forest team called to see him at East Birmingham Hospital on their way home from a match at Villa Park. Clough arranged the detour but stayed in the coach. During a particularly bad spell of injuries at Forest he ordered everyone out of the treatment room and sent them home along with the physio, saying it upset him to see them lined up on the couch and that it was bad for morale.

Taylor says the injury had a profound psychological effect on Clough. 'For a player who prided himself on his resistance to injury and illness, it was a miserable end. All washed up and only twenty-nine! Management was a poor substitute. All he ever wanted to do was play. It hurt him even more that he never achieved the recognition he deserved outside the north-east. I'm sure that mental pain has been his driving force.'

Clough was in limbo at Roker Park, unwanted by directors who did not take to having a cripple on the payroll, and increasingly unpopular with the players. George Hardwick was appointed manager when Brown moved to Sheffield Wednesday: 'Brian was a very sick and sad young man. He hated every member of the club from the first team down to the "A" team because they could do something he couldn't – go out on a Saturday and play football. Boy was he bitter! He'd meet his team mates in the tunnel at half-time and give them the biggest rollickings. Even told the trainer and coach they hadn't a clue.'

Charley Hurley remembers feeling the lash of his tongue: 'We had a lot of rows but I felt sorry for him. He was broken-hearted. The only release was to take it out on the lads.'

Sunderland slithered to the bottom of the First Division with only 9 points to their name by December. They were heading straight back to the Second when Hardwick arrived. 'Brian was disgusted,' he says. 'He told the directors they should resign. In the end it cost him his job and me mine. I called him into the office and told him he would no longer be getting his money for nothing. He was going to work for his living. I wanted him back every afternoon to work with the youngsters. From now on he'd be with me.

'"Are you serious boss?" he said.

'"Deadly serious. I'm not having you creating hell any more."

'"Hey, you'll do for me. When do I start?"

'"This afternoon."'

Hardwick continues, 'Brian was a revelation. His mind was

occupied and he was achieving something. He *has* to achieve. Eventually I made him youth team manager. He loved working with the kids and they loved working with him. Instead of condemning he was encouraging.'

Clough qualified as an FA coach and could have been excused for thinking that fortune was smiling on him at last. Among the youngsters he guided to the semi-final of the FA Youth Cup was John O'Hare, a player Clough would take with him to Derby, Leeds and Forest in future years. O'Hare says, 'He completely transformed the training routine. We used to dread the business of lapping the field. Under Cloughie we did much more ball work, or rather *he* did. We did the crossing and he did the shooting! It was good for me because he turned me into a striker when I thought I was a wing-half. I went on to play for Scotland, so he must have been right. I found him a real inspiration. He was a nice friendly chap then, before the ambition set in.'

It was not to last. Clough had created too many enemies in the boardroom. Hardwick was called to task by Laurie Evans, the Sunderland vice-chairman:

'What do you mean by making Clough the manager of the youth team?'

'He got us to the semi-final, didn't he?'

'You don't understand, George. We want Clough away from this club. We don't want him involved with Sunderland again. As soon as we get the insurance money he's out of the door.'

'You're talking crazy. This man is valuable. He has a natural flair for getting players to play. He's loving every minute of it and Sunderland are reaping the benefits.'

'I don't care. Get him out!'

'No way. He's doing a hell of a job. In two years he'll be my right-hand man.'

The manager had not told Clough about his long-term scheme. 'He'd have assumed more authority than I had. It was one step at a time with Brian. I had to play it carefully because he was so unpopular with the senior players.'

Hardwick did not get a chance to pursue it. Although Sunderland easily avoided relegation, finishing one place below halfway, Hardwick was sacked. When he pressed Sid Collings for an explanation, the board went into a huddle and came up with two reasons: he had been too friendly with the press, and too hard on the players. Ten days later, Clough received his marching orders as well. Hardwick explains, 'I was fired because I stood by Brian and refused to climb down. Any fool could see that. That's how much they despised him. I don't regret what I did. I had faith in him. Together we could have formed a partnership as successful as the one he had with Peter Taylor.'

How many times Collings and his board reproached themselves after the event can only be guessed at. Sunderland collected £40,000 compensation while Clough had to settle for £1500. With a little help from Hardwick, he made £5000 from a testimonial match at Roker Park before disappearing – almost off the face of the earth.

3
The Odd Couple

If there was one man who could out-talk Brian Clough it was Peter Taylor. Middlesbrough thought they had bought a goal-keeper when they paid Coventry £3500 for him in 1955. But inside that goalkeeper was a manager screaming to get out. For a few years he had made a point of travelling around the country watching football at all levels, even lecturing people better qualified than himself about who could and could not play. Without realizing it, Taylor had already turned talent scout, subconsciously preparing himself for his true métier. He simply could not wait to hang up his boots and get on with the interesting side of the business. Considering he was only twenty-six when he went to Middlesbrough it was fairly precocious. 'Stop preaching,' they told him at Ayresome Park. 'You're here to keep goal not to tell us our jobs.'

His greatest obsession – for that is what Clough was – had flashed across his line of sight during a pre-season practice. Taylor had been at Middlesbrough barely five minutes when he was 'hit for six' by the twenty-year-old with the powerful thighs whose balance and ability to strike a ball cleanly at whatever height it came to him were, in Taylor's humble view, quite exceptional. 'Before you could move, the ball was in the net,' he says. 'No backlift at all. Bobby Charlton used to wind up for his thunderbolts. You could see them coming a mile off. You had no warning with Brian. It was phenomenal. There's been nothing like it since.'

Taylor took the unusual decision to lay aside his own career in order to champion the cause of a swollen-headed, fifth-choice centre-forward rated by no one. His overtures fell on deaf ears, which was not entirely surprising. The opinions of a reserve-team goalkeeper do not normally carry much clout. Dennison might have been excused for thinking that Taylor had a financial stake in Clough's future. Why else would he go to such extraordinary lengths to extol the young man's virtues?

Within a month of joining the club Taylor dragged Clough with him to Hartlepool, where Derby had a match. He wanted his old guru, Harry Storer, to *buy* the so-called wonder boy. Goodness knows what Dennison would have thought about it, let alone the Football League! From talent scout Taylor had made the graduation to soccer agent – all unofficial, of course, and all quite against the rules. Cynics have suggested that Taylor saw Clough even at that embryonic stage as the passport to his own ambitions. It would have taken a man of rare foresight to anticipate what lay ahead. Clough was a willing tourist on their excursions around the north-east. At every available opportunity they would take a bus ride to Gateshead or Darlington, South Shields or Newcastle, to watch the Wednesday midweek leagues. What were they looking for? Taylor: 'I don't know exactly. I just wanted to be involved in football every moment of the day. I loved the atmosphere, loved assessing players. Brian stood beside me on the touchline, so it must have been in his blood too.'

No matter where he looked, Taylor saw nothing to compare with the jewel on his doorstep. On and on he went about 'the best young centre-forward I've ever seen'. Clough must have thought he was imagining it. Most young pros were too busy trying to make a crust to worry about anyone else. Naturally he liked what he heard. It saved him from blowing his own trumpet too often – a habit which persuaded most of his colleagues to give him a wide berth. 'He heard me singing his praises to all and sundry and he was at my side lapping it up,' says Taylor. 'I didn't particularly want to know him as a person. I didn't like him that much and, in any case, I was six years older with a family of my own. I was more like a father to him. Before long I couldn't get rid of the lad!'

Clough had a perfectly good home to go to but, for five nights a week, his mum and dad hardly saw him. When he had finished his game of snooker, he would head across Albert Park to Saltwells Crescent, where Taylor had moved into a rented semi with his wife, Lill, and young daughter, Wendy.

Clough was the faithful labrador following his master home. Each night, Saturdays and Sundays excepted, he would knock on

Taylor's door at around seven o'clock. He did not want anything in particular – just to talk. The subject rarely varied. Football. Especially football as it affected Brian Clough. While other eligible young men were cavorting at the Palais de Danse or snuggling in the back row of the Plaza with their hearts' desires, Clough sat and listened for hours, drinking tea and smoking heavily while Taylor told him how marvellous he was. Is it any wonder he had an inflated ego? While they burned the midnight oil, Lill would rustle up a plate of fish and chips followed by pancakes and Clough's favourite – a 'doorstep' of bread smeared with golden syrup.

Not much of a social life, but Clough was unwittingly sowing the seeds of a brilliant career. Taylor sometimes worried about him. 'You shouldn't be stuck in with me every night,' he would say. 'Haven't you got any girlfriends? Why aren't you out courting or mixing with your mates?' 'Haven't really got any,' was the reply. Clough was not interested in girls – tiresome creatures who got in the way of football. If he miscalculated, he would be leaving Taylor's when the girls were coming off the night shift at Price's clothes factory across the street. According to Lill, 'He hated that. They used to stare at him because he was the local hero. He hid behind the curtains till they'd gone and wouldn't come out until the last double-decker bus had taken the girls away.'

Clough had a couple of flings, one with a girl he met at the swimming baths where the players called in for massage and a Turkish bath. She was only sixteen. The liaison fizzled out after one date. 'He was very nice,' says the mystery brunette, a good club swimmer who now teaches in Middlesbrough. 'One thing you couldn't fault him for was confidence. He thought he was the bees' knees.' But, until he met Barbara Glasgow, girls did not come into it. 'He was in love with football,' says Taylor.

What did Taylor himself get out of the relationship? 'I was glad to make a contact in a new town,' he says. Middlesbrough was a boom town with almost full employment, dominated by dockers and steelworkers. He had little in common with them. Although surrounded by the spectacular open spaces of the Cheviots and the North York moors, the town itself was quite ordinary. A heavy preponderance of manual labour meant that the favourite pastime was drinking. It was a man's world.

Through football, a close friendship developed between the

goalkeeper and the centre-forward. The father–son relationship became less pronounced. Taylor: 'We were like an incompatible couple fatally attracted to each other by a single passion. Football was the love affair we shared, though we had nothing else in common. We couldn't have resisted each other if we'd tried. We turned each other on when we talked about the game. We could have been high on drugs – instead, it was football. We became closer friends than anyone will understand. We slept in the same room on away trips; we had more secrets than a married couple. Brian had five brothers, but I was closer to him than any of them. I loved him like a brother. That's why it hurt so much when it all turned sour.'

Taylor was a popular visitor to the Clough household around the corner: 'I sat down with his parents Sally and Joe many times and talked about Brian. He was battling for survival like we all were. They loved it when I was praising him, telling them he'd play for England one day. I knew all of his brothers and sisters personally. They were a warm, close family.' One of the brothers, Barry, lent Taylor his new bike at the birth of his son Phillip. He pedalled down Valley Road as fast as his legs would take him to fetch the gas and air box from the midwife. Clough and his younger sister Deanna were Phillip's godparents, although, if it had been left to Taylor, there would not have been a christening: 'Brian organized it all. I wasn't going to bother but he said I must. He thought all children should be christened. The family were keen churchgoers. After the service, his mother put on a big spread for us.'

Sally Clough would not have grown rich on the pittance Brian was able to give her out of his salary. He confided to Taylor that he was only earning £7.10s. a week and was struggling to make ends meet. Taylor was appalled: 'I practically dragged him in to see Dennison about a rise. He got an extra £2.10s. a week, which was no more than he was worth.'

Everything Taylor had forecast was beginning to come true. Clough banged in the goals for the reserves and was just as lethal when given an extended run in the first team. One of his goals, against Stoke City, would have gone almost unnoticed by the scorer if Taylor had not gone overboard about it. He had been in the stand observing his protégé:

'Stoke were invincible in those days. They had a great defence, with Basil Hayward in the centre of it. They'd whack you hard, would that lot – do anything to stop you scoring. Brian got the ball on the halfway line as Stoke's offside trap broke down. What he did next was out of this world. He had to go it alone with defenders breathing down his neck. The keeper came out but Brian kept his head and slipped the ball past him. I told him it was the greatest goal he'd scored.

'"It can't be," he said. "What about the rocket shots?"

'"They're not goals. I want to know what went through your mind when you were going clear like that."

'"Nothing. I just put it away."

'"Exactly," I said. "That's why you'll play for England."'

Taylor explained to the incredulous Clough that 'banging them in from forty yards' might get the crowd on their feet but keeping your nerve with time on your hands was a centre-forward's biggest problem. Clough eventually saw the light and was soon passing on the benefit of his experience to Cliff Mitchell, the *Evening Gazette* soccer writer who had dared to suggest in one of his reports that Clough had scored a 'gift goal' after pouncing on an underhit backpass and rounding the goalkeeper. 'They're not gift goals,' Clough admonished him, echoing Taylor's words. 'They're the hardest of the lot because you have to think about them.'

Clough was unimpressed when Taylor revealed his master plan for the forthcoming visit to Derby's Baseball Ground. Playing centre-half for the Rams was a man who frightened Taylor. His name was Les Moore, one of the most uncompromising defenders in the Second Division. Taylor reasoned (and he was only the goalkeeper, mark you) that Clough should stay wide and entice Moore out of position so that Peacock could make hay. The plan worked beautifully, Middlesbrough winning 5–0 and Peacock helping himself to 4 of them. Clough's reaction? 'He knew I was right but he hated it. If he didn't score, he thought he'd had a bad game.'

If Dennison and the fans had known the secret behind Clough's hat-trick against Bristol City in February 1960, they would have been amazed. Clough and Taylor had got into the bridge-playing habit with a couple of Customs and Excise lads from the docks and they played until the sun came up on the morning of the match, which Middlesbrough won 6–3. 'If one of *our* players had done that,' says Taylor, 'we'd have suspended him.'

They were a lonely couple, as footballers often can be. Taylor had no other friend in town and Clough, although living in the bosom of his family, drew little inspiration from the people and things around him: 'Young lads have nowhere to go in football. I had a nice home so it wasn't too bad for me, but you've still got to have some mates. The mates I had in Middlesbrough worked from 8.00 a.m. to 6.00 p.m. No mates were there at half past twelve when I finished work. I knocked about a bit with Billy Day and Eddie Holliday, but Taylor was the one.'

Clough developed an almost fatherly rapport with his godson, Phillip Taylor. 'Any excuse to roll around on the floor with him, and Brian was there,' says Peter Taylor. Equally, Taylor developed a closeness with Brian's son, Nigel Clough, as we shall see in chapter 12.

During the summers of those early years together, Clough virtually moved in with the Taylors at the family home in the Meadows area of Nottingham, only a stone's throw from the club they were destined to turn into champions of Europe. Lill Taylor comments, 'I can see his maroon club blazer on the peg in the hall now. Pete hated that club blazer but he admired Brian's slippers and smart new dressing gown. We couldn't afford such things. Pete was green with envy.' Taylor's brother, Don, managed the local Co-op fruit and veg shop, where both would help out on Fridays, the busiest day of the week. 'It was good exercise and it taught us a lot about how to handle people,' says Taylor.

Clough was put in charge of the dried peas - traditionally a favourite dish in Robin Hood country - but he was confused when customers varied their demands: some wanted peas by the pound, others by the half-pint. Taylor remembers, 'He stood there with a couple of sackfuls of peas surrounded by impatient shoppers, not knowing whether he was coming or going. Out of despair he shouted to our Don, "How do you sell these peas?" Back came the answer: "As fast as you bloody can!" We fell about laughing.' For years after the war, food prices were controlled and money was tight. Residents of the Meadows, one of the poorer parts of town, would haggle if they thought they had been charged a halfpenny more than they should have been. Don knew the troublesome ones. He warned his new shop assistant that, if he heard the words 'put the kettle on', it meant 'difficult customer, watch out'. Don: 'I was working in the back when I heard Brian shouting, "Don, put ten kettles on!" He'd got into a row with an old dear who used to terrorize the shop. She didn't agree with the co-operative system and specialized in causing trouble when the place was full. Poor old Brian. I hadn't seen her coming.'

Clough was a stickler for fair treatment himself, though. He could not stand to see someone get a raw deal out of authority, for which he had about as much respect as Bonnie and Clyde. Taylor says, 'If the bus conductor rang "bus full" when their were spare seats on top, he used to shout down the stairs, "It's not full. Do your job and let those people on!" They were terrified of him.'

Summertime meant cricket to Taylor, a useful medium-pace bowler in the local league. Clough, for all his protestations to the contrary, was not a good player. A sharp fielder with lightning reflexes yes, but thoroughly average when wielding the willow. In a typical performance in a celebrity match organized by Taylor against the Inland Revenue, Clough was caught for nought by the local tax inspector. He came off the field vowing that the taxman would never catch him again! Clough has said he would have loved to open the batting for England – a clear case, Taylor says, of ambition outstripping ability. A former Middlesbrough team mate, Derek Stonehouse, helps to explode the myth: 'We persuaded Brian to play in a game at Redcar once and, because there was a bit of an audience he wanted to impress, we arranged with the fielding side that he would get some runs. Brian knew nothing of the deal. It was pathetic – they were dropping catches, diving over balls on the boundary, everything. Brian was deadly serious but we were laughing our heads off. He made 40-odd so he was happy but he was no cricketer – not in a million years.'

Gambling would get Taylor into financial trouble more than once, but Clough and his money were not easily parted. Despite his pal's best efforts, betting on the horses never appealed. 'I took him to Redcar races one August Bank Holiday,' Taylor recalls. 'Packed, it was – getting on for a hundred thousand spectators. After a lot of hard work, I got Brian to put ten bob on a horse called Cornplaster. It won at 7–2 and I was game for more. Brian wouldn't hear of it. He was very tight with his money. What he earned he stored away.'

In the days when social life revolved around coffee bars and dance halls, Rea's ice-cream shop in Ayresome Street was the focal point for the young folk of Middlesbrough. Being close to the football ground, it attracted not only the players but local girls who came star-spotting. It was here that Clough used to see Barbara Glasgow, a pretty brunette who lived in a nearby row of terraced houses. The Glasgows were regarded by some of their neighbours as 'a bit posh' because they spoke nicely and behaved in a more civilized way than others. Posh they were not, however. Barbara and Brian played tennis in the park (he was a useful player), and he had the occasional game of bowls at Middlesbrough Bowls Club, where members recall Clough and his future father-in-law Harry dropping in on a Saturday night. Clough might have a half of lager in the clubhouse, but did not seem interested in drinking. The courtship with Barbara was a fairly brief one, and the couple married at St Barnabas Church with Bill Clough as best man and Barry as usher. It was a quiet enough ceremony, but the reception at the Linthorpe hotel went off in a blaze of publicity. Fans perched in the surrounding trees to see their hero. Clough was already big box-office. They soon bought their first house in Newham Avenue, Tollesby. It would have been natural if marriage and the adventure of setting up home had taken Clough away from Taylor, but that was not the case. The pair remained as devoted as ever. According to Taylor, 'The bond between us was so strong that nothing could have weakened it in those days. We still saw a lot of each other and went out in a foursome once or twice. I remember we all went to see *Saturday Night, Sunday Morning* when that was the rage. Mostly though, we didn't mix as couples.'

Though both Clough and Taylor play it down, the bond between them inevitably put a strain on their marriages. They spent more time in each other's company than in that of their wives and children. In 1961, however, the odd couple were temporarily forced to part when Clough moved to Sunderland.

4
Edge of the World

'People said you could drop off the edge of the world if you went to Hartlepool. When we trained on the beach it was so bleak and cold I thought they must be right.'

So spoke Clough about his first managerial assignment. He was fortunate that the opportunity came only three months after his sacking. 'If it had been any longer, he'd have gone to pot,' says Taylor. 'He was a no-hoper: jobless, boozing heavily and on his way out.' Taylor had almost lost contact with his mate in the intervening four years. It was a shock to see how the bright-eyed adventurer had lost his spark: 'He'd been having a really rough time. One minute the world was at his feet, the next his career was at a dead end. It was an overweight and careworn Brian Clough I was looking at. He had a young family to support and Hartlepool was the only hope.'

Taylor had tried to push some work Clough's way in the preceding year, commissioning him to check on a few players for Burton Albion, the Southern League club Taylor was now managing. On Clough's say-so, he signed his namesake, Carl Taylor, from Darlington, but the winger never came up to scratch. Now fate had brought Clough and Taylor back together at the Chase hotel in York, where they agreed to go into partnership. It was a bold decision by Taylor. Burton were top of the league and Taylor had just been offered a new three-year contract. He made the trip to York on the strength of Clough's unexpected phone call: 'I've been offered the manager's job at Hartlepool. I don't fancy it or the man who made the offer but, if you'll come, I'll take it.'

Hartlepool were a joke, forever at the foot of the league and seeking re-election. Taylor would have to sacrifice half his wages to move back to the north-east, but the lure of a league club, however run-down, was irresistible.

If he had known the truth behind the offer, Taylor might well have turned tail. Clough had acted without the knowledge of the board. Ernest Ord, Hartlepool's Napoleonic chairman, did not much like the idea of paying two salaries, but was presented with a *fait accompli*: 'Clough didn't consult me at all – just recruited Taylor off his own bat. It was bad enough giving *him* £40 a week, without having to pay someone else as well. I didn't want Taylor. I had no time for him, but I had to go along with it because I wanted Clough.' By the time Ord left the club, the music had changed more than somewhat, but we will come to that in due course.

The joint managership was signed and sealed, and Ord had become a reluctant pioneer. No one had two managers. Not Manchester United, nor Wolves, nor Spurs, let alone a half-baked outfit like Hartlepool. Indeed, no one since has worked in the way that Clough and Taylor did then. The idea belonged to Len Shackleton, who first recommended Clough to Hartlepool: 'As soon as Ord offered him the job, I told Cloughie to fetch his mate. I knew they'd be better working together. He saw it straightaway. Couldn't understand why he hadn't thought of it in the first place.'

Shackleton realized even before Clough and Taylor did that they needed each other. He had seen the unofficial partnership in operation at Ayresome Park – noticed how the pair fed off and protected one another. Clough, in particular, worked better with familiar faces around him. There have been countless examples since of his need for constant reassurance from people he knows he can trust. He approached another former colleague – Jimmy Gordon, who was now coaching Blackburn Rovers. Clough turned up on Gordon's doorstep holding his son Simon in the carry-cot and came straight to the point. Gordon remembers his response: 'I told him I couldn't possibly give up Division One for Division Four. You can't get any lower than Hartlepool. Peter though he could persuade me but I never considered it.'

One look at the Victoria stadium would have convinced Gordon that he had made the right decision. Years of neglect showed in every nook and cranny. The roof of the club offices let in water by the bucketful; one sheltered corner of the terracing was ankle-deep in poultry feathers because a previous manager had kept bantam chickens there; and the old wooden stand erected during the First World War would have disintegrated with a gentle nudge. Hartlepool often wished it would! Frank Perryman, the genial old secretary, used to tell of the day it had caught fire and was saved from destruction by an enthusiastic young fire officer. The fire chief apologized: 'Sorry he saved the stand, Frank. Young fool got the wrong idea. I did everything I could, bar pushing petrol up the hose!'

Given half a chance, the new management team would have pushed something rather more painful in another direction! They came into immediate conflict with Ord, a millionaire tailor who made his fortune during the war years. Unfortunately, the size of his bank balance did nothing to compensate for his lack of inches. The chairman stood five feet nothing in his drip-dry nylon socks and seemed to have a complex about it. A word of criticism of any sort and he was on the attack. He once banned the local newspaper for daring to slate the team and reporters had to sneak into the spion kop and pass notes to a dispatch rider through the iron railings behind the goal. You simply could not please Mr Ord. His favourite trick was checking up on people. Most days at 4.55 p.m. the phone would ring in Clough's and Taylor's office. 'There was never anyone on the other end,' says Taylor. 'As soon as we answered, it went dead. We knew who it was.' A quick look around the place had convinced Taylor to import his Burton Albion team to Hartlepool virtually lock, stock and barrel. Soon afterwards, he received a letter written in green ink complaining about the move. It was signed 'Percy Vere'. 'We knew who that was too,' Taylor says.

It has been asked a thousand times: 'how did the partnership work?' The answer has remained elusive, like the key to any worthwhile mystery. Certainly there were no clear demarcation lines, no list of duties, no written code of conduct. Clough and Taylor would live or die in the cut-throat world of soccer management by their instincts alone. Another two men thrust into the same poky office might have struggled to avoid duplicating each other's efforts, but not so Clough and Taylor. The telepathy they had developed during those years at Middlesbrough had made job definition unnecessary. They each knew what they had to do. Clough gravitated towards press and public relations; Taylor, relieved of that worry, dug into his little black contacts book and busied himself with finding a new team.

He was the streetwise one, although it would not take Clough too long to catch him up.

Taylor explains: 'Brian loved playing the front man; I loved telling him I'd found a new player. When I did, he'd ask, "Who? Where? When? How much?" and it was done. No messing about. Mentally we were inseparable. We knew exactly what the other was thinking and had complete respect for each other. I sensed in the early days that we were heading for the top. Without any planning it worked that the things he was good at I wasn't, and vice versa. Two can discuss systems, tactics and players and sort out problems with directors, which we always had. One man on his own would have been up against it.'

To the outsider, Clough was the dominant partner: the charismatic public speaker, the comedian, the man-motivator – in short, the face of Hartlepool United. Without Taylor in those early years, he would have been nothing. Behind the scenes, the older man was the driving force, Clough the avid listener. 'I passed on the indoctrination I'd received from Harry Storer,' says Taylor. 'Clean sheets, building a team from the back, the importance of winning away from home. Brian took it all in. If I'd told him it was snowing during a heatwave he'd have believed me!'

The difficulty – small enough really – was finding a job title for Taylor. Assistant manager? Joint manager? They settled for 'trainer'. It was an insult to Taylor's intelligence but it kept Ord sweet.

Taylor had to content himself with a trainer's salary, £24 a week, and be prepared to run out with the sponge on match days to keep up the pretence: 'Sometimes Brian took pity on me and did it himself. I hated doing it but it was a small price to pay.' The chairman put them into a couple of his own semis at the seaside resort of Seaton Carew and charged only a modest rent. For that at least they were grateful, although both took school coaching jobs to supplement their incomes.

Picking the team each Friday went like clockwork, as Taylor describes: 'From day one at Hartlepool to the last match together at Forest we simply sat down and did it. Sometimes we disagreed about a certain player but one of us would always back off if the other had a stronger view. We arrived at our decisions quickly and without ever exchanging a cross word.' Clough and Taylor were so much in unison that it never occurred to them until years later, at Nottingham, to request separate offices. It is a rare partnership that can flourish for so long at such close quarters.

The only sticking point was money. Neither had yet come to worship the god mammon, but Clough was tight and Taylor always on the lookout for more. His elder brother, Don, was an unwilling witness to one of their interminable debates on the subject when invited to join them at the George Hotel in Taunton before Hartlepool's match against Exeter. That Friday evening, Don Taylor drove seventy-two miles from his home in Plymouth, had a few drinks with them and retired to bed early. He takes up the story:

'I was fast asleep when they burst into my room. Pete wanted an extra £2 a week and came looking for moral support from me. I didn't want to get involved. Brian kept saying the time wasn't right for an increase. He knew the only way was to take £2 out of his own pocket and he wasn't prepared to do that. They argued the toss from eleven o'clock at night until three o'clock the next morning. In the end I shouted, "Give him the two quid and bugger off, the pair of you." But Brian was adamant. "No," he said to Pete. "You'll have to wait."'

This was perhaps an understandable reaction from a man who spent his days trying to make a silk purse out of a sow's ear and his nights touring the colliery clubs with his begging bowl. Taylor was spared most of that. Clough occasionally took a group of players with him on the rounds, and sometimes John Curry, one of the club directors, who says, 'The hours Brian put in were nobody's business. We trailed around from club to club, supping half-pints outside draughty committee rooms, waiting for them to give us the go-ahead. As soon as they did, Brian would be up on stage regaling the members in that magical way of his. I marvelled at his energy. He loved every minute, but my goodness he'd be on his knees by the time he went home.'

Clough has a vivid recollection of those times: 'It warmed the cockles of your heart to see how people were prepared to put money into the club. They were so loyal; even the old-age pensioners offered half their weekly incomes. The football club was a little oasis to them. I think the word unemployment was invented up there. We battled on with their help, put a new roof on the stand, had floodlights installed and built a team that went on to win promotion the year after I left.'

A by-product of his evangelism was the building of the Brian

Clough image. He had long since learned to use the power of the press; now he was a master at it. Saatchi and Saatchi were not required. Clough was the first of the modern breed of 'cult' managers who would generate more publicity than the players themselves. And he would be in the vanguard of that movement for the next twenty years. Considering Hartlepool's league status, the amount of column inches devoted to them was faintly absurd. As now, Clough had only to click his fingers for the press to come running. He was a brilliantly inventive self-publicist – taking a public service vehicle licence in order to drive the team coach; volunteering to go without wages for a month before Christmas so that players could be paid. For the first and only time in its history, Hartlepool was on the map and Clough, at thirty-one, was a legend.

Incidentally, Clough did not go without wages but he *did* loan the club £1000 of his testimonial money on the strict understanding that the gesture was not made public. 'Don't breathe a word of it,' he instructed Curry. 'Just tell the board it came from an anonymous wellwisher.' The money paid the first-team wage bill for a month, although it nearly crippled Hartlepool to repay Clough when he left.

The scrimping and saving went on. Training kit was so threadbare that Clough had to borrow a hand-me-down set from his old manager, Alan Brown, at Sheffield Wednesday. It was nothing to see players in their ordinary street socks. They were the ones in late for training. Taylor went round the dressing room collecting tie-ups, which were recycled for another week, and the chip shop just off the A1 at Wetherby made a cheap and nourishing canteen after away matches. The smartest trick of all was dodging the Football League ruling that every match had to kick-off with a new ball. It was a good double act: Clough kept the referee talking while Taylor whipped the new ball off the centre spot once it had been inspected and substituted the re-polished ball from two weeks ago.

It would, however, be wrong to assume that Hartlepool always had to slum it. Accommodation was one area in which Clough refused to stint. 'We always stayed at decent hotels because Brian thought it was important to look after his men,' says Curry. 'He didn't want them getting a complex about belonging to an impoverished club. He was angry when the papers made a fuss about us eating fish and chips in the street. He made sure the team was always well turned out, and short haircuts were the order of the day.'

Interestingly, Clough and Taylor were sticklers for discouraging cliques within the ranks. The rule was two to a room and, to ensure that it was not the same pair each week, Taylor would put the names into a hat and draw lots to see who was sharing. He knew from personal experience that factions were damaging for morale. He also knew that players had a habit of gathering in one room after lights-out. Clough and Taylor had been the instigators of this custom at Middlesbrough. Now the team would play cards until eleven o'clock. Clough would look at Taylor and say, 'It's time, gentlemen.' Off they would troop to bed, followed fifteen minutes later by Taylor on the prowl for miscreants. There were none.

Anyone who looked down their noses at Hartlepool's ragbag of soccer desperadoes did so at their considerable peril. Once, in a smart hotel down south, Clough was warned by the head waiter, 'None of your players are permitted into the lounge. They smell [of embrocation].' Clough's reply almost scorched the paper off the walls: 'I can assure you, young man, that my players have one or more baths every day of the week. Either you assure me that your other guests are the same or we're leaving right now!'

He was learning fast. Hartlepool taught him a lot about football economics – a subject into which few managers delved in those days – and it taught him very quickly that the only way to survive in the game was as a dictator. That lesson was central to his future success. It was no good consulting players or treating them like equals; a manager had to be in complete control. While underpinning his extraordinary career, that philosophy was to turn some people against Clough. For the moment, it was the only approach to take. From Taylor's description, Hartlepool was more like one of Her Majesty's institutions than a football club: 'We inherited a real collection of renegades. Hartlepool was the clearing house for every cast-off in the Football League – drinkers, gamblers, womanizers and fighters. Once I had to break up a wrestling match between Les Green, whom I'd brought up from Burton, and one of the established ruffians. Les was fighting our cause and they'd gone under the stand to sort it out. I didn't mind naughty boys. Underneath, many of them had hearts of gold. Gamblers and womanizers I could handle by feeding their vices if necessary. Booze was the biggest problem.

That and drugs. You've no chance with those. Brian was different from me. He preferred the good lads.'

Hartlepool finished eighth from bottom in that first season, 1965–66. Satisfactory enough, but a large black shadow was hanging over the new management team. It was thrown by the smallest thing at the club: Ernest Ord. Clough's first impression of him had proved correct. The chairman was a tyrant. According to Taylor, he had 'toyed' with various managers in the past before sacking them. Most of the directors had been powerless to intervene. Ord pulled the purse strings. John Curry alone was aware of what was going on. He cringed at some of the chairman's antics: 'We went to his firm's dinner dance and were making polite conversation when one of his employees wandered in. He was a big chap, about six foot two and fourteen stone. Just the sort Mr Ord loved. Ord called across the hall, "How much do I pay you a week? These people would like to know." Poor fellow was forced to reveal his salary in front of everyone.'

Ord had a knack of cutting his players down to size too. He regarded it as essential to gather intelligence on the staff: past misdemeanours, domestic problems, anything which might provide useful ammunition. He extracted it by bugging his office and subjecting the players to searching interviews. Ord's cover was eventually blown by the Irish international Ambrose Foggarty, who spotted a tape recorder concealed under the chairman's desk and refused to answer questions. Clough and Taylor were already in his tape library.

One of Ord's edicts was that travelling directors would pay for their own dinners. During a stopover at Thirsk, Curry and a fellow director, Ben Crosby, had barely finished their meal when an embarrassed Clough walked over to their table: 'I'm sorry to have to do this, but the chairman's ordered me to collect thirty bob each from you. It's pathetic but what can I do?' It is difficult to imagine Clough toeing the line in that fashion and it was the last time he demeaned himself in front of a football chairman. The writing was on the wall for Ord. For once in his life, he had bitten off more than he could chew.

The showdown was precipitated by Ord's sudden attempt to split the Clough–Taylor partnership. Taylor was distraught: 'It could have been the end for me. Ord said he couldn't afford two men any more. Brian would work alone and I'd have to find another job. That floored both of us. Brian stood up for me something rotten. It was a good job he did. He'd brought me off a three-year contract at Burton and promised to fight the chairman all the way.'

They found the perfect ally in John Curry. Between them the trio rallied enough support from a downtrodden board to banish Ord and install Curry in his place. It was not quite as easy as it sounds because the club still owed the chairman £7000 – a long-standing loan. 'He tried to reclaim it and break the club,' says Curry. 'We agreed to pay him back in instalments, beginning with £500 from the proceeds of a night match. He turned up after the game with a big canvas bag and demanded the takings. Frank Perryman, the secretary, chased him out of the office!'

Clough had scored his first success over meddlesome boardrooms. It sowed the seed of his lifelong mistrust of directors and chairmen. 'He thought they were all good-for-nothing,' says Curry. 'I told him he was young and had to learn tolerance. Everything wasn't black and white.' When they left the Victoria Ground, Clough and Taylor presented Curry with a table lighter bearing the inscription: 'If we're in the game for a hundred years we will never meet a better chairman.'

Taylor always considered the battle with Ord a major turning point: 'If ever we were destined for greatness, that was the moment. Beating Ord was equal to winning the European Cup. If we'd lost we'd have gone our separate ways, but once we'd survived it I knew we could take any job, face any challenge.'

Ernest Ord had one surprise left in his locker. He turned up unannounced at Taylor's front door, saying, 'I've come to give you a warning. Your mate has finished me and one day he'll do the same to you.' With that he drove away in his Rolls, head barely visible over the steering wheel. It was the last time they ever saw him.

At the time of writing, Ord is back as president of Hartlepool United. He told the author during an interview, 'Despite all the horrible things that have been said about me, I was not a monster. I liked Brian Clough. He was a decent fellow. He had principles. It's just that we didn't see eye to eye. Looking back I suppose I was in the wrong many times.' With that he suddenly broke off, announcing that everything he had said had been recorded and was not on any account to be used in this book.

Clough's and Taylor's brief but eventful incumbency at Hartlepool laid the foundation for promotion. It also unearthed a nugget for the future. Tommy Johnson, the trainer, was told to organize a trial match for the youngsters one Sunday morning soon after the new managers' arrival: 'They strolled around the pitch looking unconcerned. After half an hour Brian said to me, "There's not much here, Tommy, but that young man will do." It was John McGovern, a frail lad of sixteen who had a funny waddle but could kick with both feet and put the ball where he wanted.'

That autumn morning, McGovern had unwittingly taken the first step along the road which would lead to two European Cupwinners' medals, two League Championship medals, two League Cupwinners' medals and a sideboard full of assorted hardware. The 'frail sixteen-year-old with the funny waddle' would become one of the most decorated men in the game's history. Clough signed him four times in ten years. On three occasions the negotiations lasted thirty seconds or so, but Clough had a devil of a job getting started. McGovern's widowed mother, Joyce, wanted her son to stay on at Henry Smith Grammar school and pursue his ambition to be a sports teacher. But he had neglected his studies in favour of football and managed to pass only two 'O' levels. That, despite attending a strictly rugby-only school whose headmaster despised the round-ball game. Throughout the summer holidays, Clough was a regular caller at the McGoverns' terraced back-to-back, turning on his megawatt charm as he tried again and again to persuade the family that football offered a good career.

'He was very determined, but so was I,' says Joyce. 'I wanted John to get a good education. Brian kept telling me football was a great life and that the money John would earn would help me with the pension. He was quite charming, but I wasn't convinced he was right.'

Two things clinched it: first, the headmaster resented having one of his boys involved with soccer and commanded McGovern to stop playing Sunday league if he wanted to stay on for his 'A' levels ('We couldn't believe our ears,' says Joyce); and, second, McGovern's grandmother fell for Clough. 'She thought he was such a lovely, kind man. Couldn't get over such a famous personality drinking tea with us in our humble little abode as if he belonged there.' Granny's vote swayed the verdict and McGovern signed. It did not actually help Mrs McGovern with her pension. Quite the opposite. Her money was cut from £4.10s.

a week to £2.10s. Clough said he would make sure the club made up the shortfall but it never materialized. The board vetoed it.

Clough compromised over McGovern's schooling, allowing him to study two mornings and two evenings a week at West Hartlepool Further Education College.

There began a seventeen-year association as warm at the start as it was ultimately cool and disillusioned. McGovern and Clough had a distant father–son relationship. The youngster's ex-paratrooper father had been killed in a road accident while working on the Volta dam in Ghana. McGovern was eleven years old when the tragedy happened. Although there were only fourteen years between manager and player, he says that Clough was a father-substitute: 'The first time I met him I was petrified. He shook my hand and said, "Get your hair cut, stand up straight and push your shoulders back." It was unnerving for a sixteen-year-old but, when the fear subsided, I worshipped everything he did and said. As a young lad without a father, I was glad of someone to look up to and take orders from. I was only too happy to do as he commanded. He made me feel like a giant on the football field. When he walked into the room he exuded so much latent energy you had to sit up and take notice.'

Clough has never allowed himelf to get too close to his players but there is no doubt he felt for and admired the young McGovern. Mrs McGovern saw what was going on and approved: 'John was like his own son. Brian used to say he wanted his boys to turn out the same way – clean-cut, polite and hard-working. Apart from enjoying the occasional Guinness, John had no vices.'

McGovern's rise was meteoric. Still aged only sixteen he became the first apprentice ever to play for Hartlepool first team, and the youngest player in the Football League. Shortly before Clough moved to Derby, the pair were sitting on the bench for the Bradford Park Avenue match. Clough turned to his substitute and said, 'Watch Bradford's number ten because when we leave we're going to take you with us and two others from this division who can play. He's one of them.' McGovern checked the name in the match programme. It was Kevin Hector. In fact Clough did not have to sign Hector. When he got to Derby, the player was already there.

A parting of the ways with Hartlepool was inevitable. Clough was happy to soldier on but Taylor wanted to better himself.

Every Thursday when Len Shackleton did his rounds, Taylor would bend his ear: 'Come on, Shack, can't you find us another club? We've had enough of this lot.' Shackleton was *persona non grata* at Hartlepool as far as Curry was concerned. Curry thought the Clown Prince of Soccer a bit of a smart Alec and did not trust him. Like any good newspaperman, Shack had got to know which players gambled and offered them money for tip-offs. Clough set a trap to catch the 'mole'. Before a home against Brentford, he called Curry into the dressing room to witness it. Eric Phythian was the chief suspect and Clough had a quiet word with the big centre-forward: 'Pull out the stops today, Eric. Portsmouth and Southampton have sent their scouts to watch you. There's a good chance you'll be away.' Hartlepool won 1–0 that Friday night, with Phythian playing a 'blinder'. The following Sunday, Shackleton's story carried the headline: 'Portsmouth, Southampton chase Phythian'. Clough had the player into his office. Phythian tried to deny the leak but the manager had caught him red-handed. The transfer rumour had been Clough's invention.

Curry was less than delighted then when Shackleton played go-between for Clough and Derby. Shack had earlier arranged for Taylor to be interviewed by Wrexham. Clough had known nothing of it until he opened his morning paper. He stormed around to Taylor's house, where his wife, Lill, was on her own: 'He threw the paper down in front of me and said, "Barbara wants to know what this is all about." He was bitterly upset at the thought of someone abandoning him. I explained that Pete wasn't interested and he calmed down.'

Bigger things than Wrexham were in store.

5
Breakthrough

Triumph and turmoil were running on slowly converging lines when the Clough–Taylor express pulled out of Derby. At an uncertain point beyond the horizon a derailment was inevitable. To the people of Derby who adored Clough, his walkout was inexplicable. There are still those who do not understand how a brilliantly successful club could have torn itself apart. Even in Clough's mind, resignation had been no more than a threat to dangle over the board whenever he felt fractious. He had always believed he was in a position of indomitable strength and did not genuinely want to leave the club. His resignation was a bluff; it backfired because he underestimated the resentment built up against him over six years.

You could argue that Brian Clough was made for Derby in a way he was never made for Nottingham. He has lived there since 1967, his children have all attended local schools and, in the early days at least, he was always to be seen around the place. In most things Nottingham outpaces Derby, but not when it comes to football. However many trophies accumulate in the Forest cabinet, Derby County will always be a more passionate cauldron of soccer. No matter how much Clough may protest to the contrary, be sure that there is a part of him which hurts each time he thinks back to the dark days of October 1973. There are those who believe that he has lived with the quiet dread that Derby would one day re-emerge as a power without him. He knows that he would have achieved European success so much faster at the Baseball Ground if he had not provoked his own departure. Clough himself says, 'Derby were poised to take on everything in football – every single thing.'

This chapter charts the catalogue of anguish which erupted

into the most remarkable scenes ever witnessed in British football. The saga was recorded in the diaries of the Derby County chairman, Sam Longson. Though written up in 1978, they have been confined to his attic until now. They reveal that, only a year into his contract, Derby's directors had had enough of their uppity manager:

> We finished sixth from bottom of the Second Division... and the directors were unremitting in their criticism of me [Longson] and the managerial twosome. Clough described me as the only chairman he could work with and 'the saviour of Derby County'... More than one member of the board didn't like this approach.

Clough had already broken his first promise: 'I had told the Rotary Club that Derby wouldn't finish as low as they had the previous season. With my usual beautiful timing I said it in front of my predecessor, Tim Ward, who was a member of Rotary! I took some stick when we finished one place lower than he had.'

Though he disguised it well, Clough was certain he had made a mistake in joining Derby. Hartlepools' promotion to Division Three in 1968 rubbed salt in the wound. Taylor, the born optimist, had to lift his flagging spirits: 'Brian always needed boosting, but I remember one occasion in particular. We were at my house talking among family and friends when I predicted that Derby would be onto great things next season. I knew we'd get promotion and wasn't afraid of saying so. Brian suddenly perked up and said, "If that's what you think, Pete, I throw my lot in with you." I was staggered at that remark.'

However, Longson notes in his diary:

> Whatever had happened during that season, Brian was able to convince everyone of his unswerving belief in the future. He never stopped talking about his plans, or pinpointing the successes to come.

Who was fooling whom?

Longson had been besotted with Clough from the moment Len Shackleton had nominated him for the job:

> Brian hadn't applied, and no one had even mentioned him in discussion, but I knew instinctively that this was the name I'd been searching for. I was so excited I couldn't sleep that night.

Longson's mind went back to a game at the Baseball Ground a couple of seasons earlier. Sunderland were the visitors and the chairman recalled a confident young centre-forward who seemed to be ordering everyone around:

He was pointing here, pointing there, telling everyone what to do. There was something about him. Others called it arrogance – I called it leadership.

A meeting was arranged at Scotch Corner, a well-known soccer rendezvous, but Longson found his fellow directors in truculent mood:

They thought I was out of my mind. Not only weren't they very impressed by the young man whose success as a manager had been confined to Division Four but I was telling them *they* were to travel to meet *him*. One of them said, 'The only man I'd travel to see would be Matt Busby himself!'

Longson was worried when Shackleton told him West Brom were interested in Clough (a little poetic licence from the Clown Prince), and persuaded the board to relax their principles. That Sunday, Longson, Sidney Bradley, Harry Paine and Bob Kirkland headed up the A1 in the chairman's Rolls. According to Shackleton he was the first to meet the Derby delegation when they pulled on to the car park at Scotch Corner. He says Longson told him, 'If he's suitable we'll employ him without a contract.'

Shackleton replied, 'In that case, as soon as the lad arrives, I'll stop him getting out of his car and you can go home. You're wasting everyone's time.'

The four directors and Clough had lunch and there are no prizes for guessing who did most of the talking. 'He never stopped,' says Longson. 'He was bubbling over with confidence, telling us what he'd achieved at Hartlepool and how he longed for a bigger challenge. You couldn't shut him up. We were all impressed.'

Before they reached the main course, Longson had offered Clough a contract. Shackleton says the chairman wandered over to a nearby table where he and his wife were lunching separately and remarked, 'He's a great bloke, isn't he?' But, to Shackleton's dismay, he apparently did not offer to pay for the lunch, nor to buy him a drink: 'I got a tin of biscuits and a box of chocolates for the wife each Christmas after Derby won promotion. Once Clough left, the biscuits stopped. I'd given a millionaire something money couldn't buy and didn't get so much as a "thank you".' Longson says he assumed Shackleton would have been adequately recompensed by Clough and Taylor for whom he seemed to be acting as agent.

The well-fed Derby contingent motored home pleased with their day's work. Little did they know Clough was ready to turn them down. It took all of Taylor's persuasive powers to get him away from Hartlepool. Both families met at Scarborough's Royal Hotel for a weekend of heart-searching. Taylor recalls, 'He didn't want to go. He was a home bird and insecure about leaving his neck of the woods. He asked me, "How can you say Hartlepool are certainties for promotion and in the next breath say you want to leave after all we've been through?" He had a fair point. I told him Derby had tradition. I'd watched them as a lad and remembered the days of Carter, Doherty and Crooks, when the Baseball Ground was heaving with fans. We could fill it again, I was certain.'

The word 'we' is interesting. At no point during the negotiations had Clough mentioned Taylor to the Derby directors.

Some days later Clough drove the family to Derby to have the appointment confirmed: 'It was a hell of a day with three bairns in the car. I dumped Barbara and the children in Normanton Park near the ground. Elizabeth was in her carrycot on the park bench and the boys were on the swings. I told Barbara I'd be one hour. I'd either come back with the job or that would be it. It was well into the evening when I collected them. I got a right earbashing, I can tell you!'

He had left the board with a sore head too. In the middle of the interview Clough announced that he would only consider the job if he could bring Taylor with him. The directors were speechless. An assistant? Nobody those days worked with an assistant. Either you were a manager or you weren't. They were worried about the money as well as the precedent. Clough had been offered £5000 a year. 'How much is a bloody assistant going to cost?' one of the directors wanted to know. Taylor's initial salary would be half of Clough's. The pair had been fortunate enough to catch Longson in generous mood; the man who first took milk from Chapel-en-le-Frith to Manchester by road had recently sold his haulage business for close on half a million pounds. The new management team was promised £70,000 for new players.

From the moment they first watched the team on a close-season tour of Germany, Clough and Taylor knew what they had to do.

Clough turned to Longson on the touchline: 'What do you expect me to do with them, Mr Chairman?'

'It's completely in your hands.'

'Good. In that case, I'll sack the bloody lot!'

He was only half joking. Eleven household names departed. Sammy Crooks, the chief scout and one of Taylor's boyhood heroes, was shown the door. Next went the groundsman, the secretary, the assistant secretary and a couple of tea ladies who were overheard laughing after a defeat!

The first £21,000 was spent on John O'Hare, whom Clough had coached as a youngster at Sunderland. The man with shoulders as broad as a coathanger went on to play for Scotland, and twelve years later was still good enough to be in Nottingham Forest's European Cupwinning team. O'Hare was happy to drop down a division: 'He signed me on a Sunday, which you weren't supposed to do. He said Derby would pass Sunderland on the way up from Division Two. I knew nothing about Derby but Clough convinced me they were going places. We agreed on £40 a week, which was £15 more than I was getting at Roker Park. They put me up at the Midland hotel next to the railway station and I wondered what on earth I'd come to. Derby was a dreary town. The stadium was dilapidated. Somehow I settled in straightaway. Clough was a much more aggressive person than when I last knew him. He was confident and outspoken. I felt it was only a matter of time.'

That was one of the few Clough signings. From then on, it was Taylor picking the players to rejuvenate this faded football citadel. He began to establish his reputation as a star-spotter with the extraordinary transfer of Roy McFarland from Tranmere Rovers. 'An uncut diamond' was Taylor's initial reaction on seeing the centre-half play against Hartlepool in 1966. Now, with £49,000 still in the kitty, he made a beeline for the lad.

He and Clough watched McFarland play for Tranmere one Friday night, then set about the difficult task of persuading Dave Russell, the manager, to part with him for an acceptable fee. Russell haggled and Clough pulled one of his outrageous strokes. He picked up the telephone and pretended to ask Longson for permission to go up to £24,000, giving the impression that his chairman thought the figure exorbitant. Russell wanted more, but listened resignedly as the bogus conversation continued. In fact Clough and Taylor could have gone up to £49,000 if they had so desired, but the three men shook hands on a £24,000 deal pending the player's agreement. McFarland was not easy to persuade: 'I wasn't even convinced I wanted to be a pro footballer. If I did, my ambition was to play for Liverpool, my home club.'

The determined duo drove through the Mersey tunnel just after midnight looking for the terraced house where McFarland lived with his parents. He was tucked up in bed but they dragged him downstairs in his pyjamas and sat him between them. He might as well have surrendered there and then. The discussion continued until 2.00 a.m., with McFarland asking for more time to think. Clough told him, 'Take as much time as you like but we're not leaving this house without a decision.' The prospect of being bombarded until the sun came up was not a very appealing one. McFarland, his resistance already crumbling, was eventually swayed by his father, a keen admirer of Clough in his playing days. He said, 'If they want you that badly, son, I think you should go.'

Later that Saturday morning, McFarland woke up heavily depressed: 'I couldn't believe I'd been so stupid. Derby County – who were they? In the afternoon I stood on the kop at Anfield watching Liverpool beat Newcastle 5–0. That made it worse. I remember saying to my cousin, who was with me, that I'd just made the biggest mistake of my life. One more day and I'd never have signed for Derby.'

Soon afterwards came Alan Hinton, a former England winger reckoned by his then club, Nottingham Forest, to be over the hill. It took another party piece by Clough to secure that signature: 'They though Alan had shot his bolt. I talked him into signing at midnight as we walked around the Baseball Ground with the perimeter lights switched on. Why we weren't arrested I'll never know. Tony Wood, the Forest chairman, was having a late drink with some of his mates at the Bridgford hotel when I phoned. He said he wanted £30,000 but I didn't fancy paying his price. I told him the deal was being held up because Alan wanted a thousand for himself – could it come off the fee? Wood was absolutely delighted but what he didn't know was that Alan hadn't asked for a penny. It was just me being greedy and wanting to pay less than £30,000. The Forest chairman was boasting that he'd offloaded a passenger. They must have felt sick when Alan dipped his bread with us. We had three magnificent seasons out of him. He was an incredible asset and one of the most talented players I've seen. All for £29,000.'

One of the Derby directors was not convinced by the transfer. 'What colour's his handbag?' he asked Taylor, referring to Hinton's lack of enthusiasm for the physical side of football. Taylor told him to keep quiet: 'Hinton may not have physical courage, but he has more moral courage in his little finger than you have!' When Derby won the league title four years later, Hinton was the leading scorer, with 15 goals. He created many more with his ability to place a cross exactly where he wanted it.

Clough and Taylor found the missing pieces of the jigsaw in Willie Carlin and Dave Mackay. Once they were installed, promotion to Division One was assured, and Derby's Golden Age was underway. Mackay was another remarkable signing. Derby wanted a big-name player whose experience would rub off on the younger ones, but Mackay seemed an unlikely target. He was a household name from the fabulous Spurs side of the sixties, but was older than Clough, a stone overweight and suffering the after-effects of a twice-shattered leg. Clough heard that Mackay was going to Hearts as assistant player–manager. While Mackay was not quite ready to hang up his boots, he was reluctant to make a fool of himself in his native Edinburgh. Clough got wind of his hesitation and drove to London at 6.00 a.m. on the off-chance of signing one of the biggest names in the game: 'I asked to see Bill Nicholson but they told me I couldn't. They treated me like a leper – kept me hanging around in the corridor for ages and had me travelling to and from the training ground. Eventually I got permission to talk to Dave. He asked for £15,000, to be spread over his contract. It was a lot of money. I happened to say, "Yes, you've got it," and he was in Derby before he realized what he was doing.'

Again there was boardroom resistance. One of the directors complained to Clough, 'Do you know we've got the most expensive player in the entire Football League?'

'You might have the best,' Clough replied.

Mackay was astonished when Taylor locked him in the office and broke the news that his days as an attacking half-back were over. He says, 'I thought they were round the twist. They wanted me to play in the middle of the defence. Me? I was fat and tired and a year older than the manager!' Taylor assured him he would not have much running to do: 'We want you to stroll, sweep up behind Roy McFarland. We don't want your legs, just your brains and your mouth. Let the young lads do the running.'

The relationship between Clough and Mackay would take several twists and turns over the years. As a player, Mackay was one of the few Clough never tangled with. He came to team talks if he wanted to and trained as he saw fit. The manager, respecting his wealth of experience, backed off. When Mackay left for Swindon, Clough and Longson negotiated a three-year contract for him with a provision that, if Mackay stopped playing, his contract would continue as a manager. 'Apart from signing him in the first place,' says Clough, 'it was the biggest favour I did him. He did stop playing when he fell among inferior players. He was glad of the deal I'd done for him.'

The two of them would meet up again at the Baseball Ground six years later. In 1973 Mackay would be in the manager's chair and Clough would be an unwelcome visitor.

For the moment, promotion banished most other thoughts. 'Like your first car or the first Christmas you remember,' says Clough, 'it was the greatest joy of my career. I hadn't won anything until then. European Cups couldn't match it.' The club was determined not to stand still. So in 1969 it prepared for its first season in Division One for sixteen years by building the Ley stand along the popular side. The stand cost £230,000 and raised the ground capacity to 41,000. The clamour for season tickets was such that preference was given to supporters willing to pay for two seasons in advance. There was no shortage of takers.

It was typical of Clough to involve himself in every aspect of the club, even the building of the stand: 'I sat down with Indians and Pakistanis negotiating to buy twenty-three feet of factory space. I went into the foundry and the smelting works and came out with a face as black as theirs. I even did plans to buy all the houses on the opposite side of the ground. We had the money. We could have grown into something special but the directors couldn't cope.'

As far as they were concerned, Clough was 'sticking his oar in' rather too much. Longson, who by this time was reduced to the rank of director, writes revealingly:

The dynamic young manager had arrived like a whirlwind. We were all under his spell. Unfortunately for the club, he took more and more control both on and off the field. I had to work overtime to explain to him that a football club is a limited company subject to company law. It is also subject to the rules and regulations of the Football Association and the Football League. Chaos was abounding inside the ground. The young man to whom Brian had given the vital backstage job of secretary and his staff of three part-timers were run off their feet. I could see we were heading for trouble. Brian had a free hand in running most aspects of the club and it was becoming increasingly apparent to me that the time had come to separate the duties of team management and general administration.

Trouble duly arrived after Derby's first season in the top flight. They qualified for Europe by finishing in fourth place. Crowds of 30,000-plus were commonplace. A capacity 41,000 saw them humble mighty Spurs 5–0. John McGovern, who had joined Clough for the second time, was in a dream world: 'Jimmy Greaves shook hands with me as we came off. I didn't wash for the rest of the day!' Europe, however, was dashed from their hopes after a joint Football Association–Football League inquiry found Derby guilty of "gross administrative negligence". Longson's worst fears had come true, although the inquiry happened quite by chance. The league had a policy of conducting routine checks. Out of the blue, two accountants knocked on the door of the Baseball Ground. What a can of worms they opened up.

According to Longson, the annual audit showed a discrepancy of £3000 - money which was not missing but had not been recorded in the books. On top of that, players had not been registered, money had been paid out without official trace, including £2000 to Mackay for articles he had written in the club programme; there was no system for the sale of season tickets and petty cash was paid out without chits. The club was fined £10,000 and banned from playing in Europe. Taylor has his own views: 'I can't pretend we were innocent. Perhaps Brian and I were a bit cavalier at times, but they threw the book at us. They dug up every technicality they could find.'

Clough laid the blame fairly and squarely at the feet of the directors, an accusation that Longson has always resisted: 'He must take his share of the responsibility. He made decisions he considered right and proper but without any account of what the footballing rules said he could or couldn't do. Without a strong secretary behind him, the decisions had stood.'

The upshot was a boardroom coup, led by Longson and assisted by Clough, which ousted three directors, Ken Turner, Harry Paine and Bob Kirkland, and eventually had Longson back in the chair. As was his wont, the manager was gradually tailoring the club to suit his requirements. Requirement number one was a tame chairman. That, he thought, he now had. Requirement number two was a hand-picked secretary, the appointment of whom would not be long delayed. Another prerequisite for success was a trainer he could trust. He went for Jimmy Gordon, which surprised everyone who had worked with them both. Gordon had been one of Clough's greatest critics at Middlesbrough. Despite their long and successful association he remains a critic:

'It was against all my principles to join him. I didn't like him and still don't. Neither was I a fan of Peter Taylor's. It was a hell of a shock when the boss phoned me at Blackburn. I thought he wanted to sign Keith Newton. He said, "It's not Newton I want, it's you."

'"Why me?" I asked. "All we've done is argue."

'He said, "That's why I want you."

'That night he spent five hours at my house trying to convince me. He came for me because I was honest and loyal. I agreed for one reason only - money. Everyone has his price and he knew mine. He gave the groundsman a day off to help me find a house, then got the club to pay £1000 interest-free deposit on it. How could I turn that down? When I got there, the set-up and the players were unbelievable. You could never achieve that blend again. Durban, Mackay, Carlin, McFarland, Hector, Hinton, O'Hare. It was a great side. I noticed early on though that, if you were a nice lad like Ronnie Webster, those two had no time for you.'

Derby were still reeling from their European ban when Clough decided he would have a new assistant secretary. Acting on a tip from Gordon, he invited Preston's assistant secretary, Stuart Webb, for interview. The manager booked Webb and his wife Josie into the Midland Hotel and, next morning, marched the smartly dressed young man into a board meeting he had called to announce that this was Derby's new man. Longson was on holiday. None of the new directors – Bill Rudd, Bob Innes, and Clough's nominee, Mike Keeling – was likely to raise an objection. Webb was ideally suited, but Longson felt *he* had been snubbed: 'I was annoyed – extremely annoyed. As chairman, I wanted to be the one who appointed the secretary.'

If Clough thought Webb was another 'yes-man' he was mistaken. The new assistant had firm ideas of his own which brought him into immediate conflict with the manager. Over the next few months, they had several heated arguments and Clough repeatedly implored Longson to sack Webb. He even went as far as to say that, if the secretary stayed, he would leave. Longson dug in his heels.

Administrative affairs at the Baseball Ground were still in chaos. Webb was astonished at what he saw: 'Success had caught the club cold. The books were in utter disarray. Nothing seemed to be accounted for. There was a cup tie against Wolves early that season, but the ticket office was unable to handle it. In fact there wasn't a ticket office. Clough was running around with wastepaper bins full of cash. So were the apprentice pros. I'd never seen anything like it. One of the bins disappeared. I knew Clough had it and threatened to call the police. He brought it back saying he'd been looking after it. There were hundreds of pounds inside. I'm certain that what he says is absolutely right but, at the time, he was interfering in my side of the business. We were under the microscope after what had happened with the inquiry. I told Clough the money side was my responsibility. He didn't like that. He thought he should be in charge of everything. I pointed out that, as company secretary, I was legally answerable, and that he had no right to be involved. Luckily the board backed me up.'

Clough admits that things were not right: 'I brought Webb into the big world. He was young and we were caught in this whirlwind of success. I'm not sure if we handled it right. I'm certain I didn't. Overnight we had gone from half a bitter to champagne!'

He and Webb, who had graduated to secretary, also clashed over the key to the club safe. Webb went to lunch and left the key with his assistant, seventeen-year-old Michael Dunford. His instructions were not to give it to anyone, including the manager. Clough sent his own secretary to collect the key during the lunch hour. Dunford refused to hand it over: 'Clough then rang me and demanded the key. I said I couldn't release it, even to him. Next thing I know he was in the office shouting, "I'm the manager and I do what I like. Hand over the key and collect your cards – you're fired!'

A tearful Dunford did as he was ordered, but was reinstated by Webb the following morning. Life however continued to be uncomfortable for him: 'I was accused of listening in to his calls once. Brian was paranoid. There was a big rift between him and Stuart and I caught the backlash.'

Having appointed a trainer and a secretary, Clough broke the British transfer record without telling the chairman. Longson had agreed in principle to the Colin Todd deal before jetting off on holiday to the Caribbean. He received a cable after the transfer had gone through: 'Signed you another good player. Todd. Running short of cash. Brian.' Longson had just sat down to dinner at his hotel in Antigua. Derrick Robbins and Arthur Waite, the chairmen, respectively, of Coventry and Crystal Palace, were at the same hotel and bumped into him in the restaurant.

'I see you've been spending again, Sam,' said Robbins.

'I believe so, Derrick.'

'What do you mean, you believe so?'

'Frankly, Derrick, I don't know the price.'

'Well, I do. Finish your meal and I'll tell you.'

Longson could not hide his shock at the figure of £175,000. He pushed his plate away and lit a cigar. He wrote in his diary:

How could any manager go out and spend that sort of money without even a word to the chairman? I was bitterly disappointed that Brian had taken on both Stuart Webb and now Colin Todd without discussing finance. I felt the incidents destroyed something between Brian and myself, a sort of unspoken trust. I don't think the relationship between us, once seemingly untarnishable, was ever quite the same again.

He had every reason to be indignant but the chairman was a proud man, fond of telling people how a farmer's boy made his million. Apart from his haulage business, Longson owned a hire-purchase company, two farms with a dairy herd, and grew raspberries on a commercial scale in the inhospitable High Peak. Judging by this extract from his memoirs, he seemed to *believe* he was the saviour of Derby County. The saviour passing among his disciples:

I had a special relationship with many of the supporters, and used to talk to them regularly on my way to and from a match. Most of them knew me as Sam. It was doubtful whether any of the directors were even recognizable to the fans let alone on such intimate terms with them.

Clough thought he was easy meat. The manager buttered him up with carefully worded eulogies in the press and the club programmes, much as he does at Forest today. Behind his back, he called Longson 'the old twit', but that was pure bravado by Clough. All the indications are that a genuine friendship had sprung up between the two men in those early years. Clough was more than happy to drive around in the chairman's Rolls and liked Longson beside him when he went to sign players. The chairman made the fatal mistake however of allowing sentiment to enter his relationship with Clough. It was something none of Longson's business managers nor his two hundred employees in the haulage company had ever experienced. Indeed to them he was a hard and somewhat intimidating boss, prone to sacking people for the merest indiscretions. He once sat up until 3 a.m. in his lorry park to catch a driver siphoning petrol out of one of the vehicles and dismissed him on the spot.

It was an entirely different Longson where Clough was concerned. He carried a photograph of Clough in his wallet everywhere he went:

'Brian was like a son to me. I knew his mother, Sally, and all the family. In the summer, I used to let them have my bungalow at Red Wharf Bay in Anglesey for their holidays. Often in the early days, Brian would phone me and say, "Come down to the ground, Mr Chairman, I want to talk to you. I can't talk to the other buggers." I was proper daft with him. He used to come to Chapel-en-le-Frith with the kids and I'd give them presents. It got me into trouble with the other directors but I didn't mind. It suited me as long as we were getting success.

'One of the directors complained because we'd spent £1500 on a new car for Brian. I said if the manager carried on the way he was going, I'd buy him a Rolls or he could have mine. That didn't go down very well. They were all for sacking him. He was a great manager with a good business head. We had to put up with a lot from him, but balancing books with transfer deals was one thing we didn't have any problems with.

'One Saturday, we'd lost 2–1 to Huddersfield and I went along to the dressing room. It was the chairman's prerogative. I never heard such cursing and swearing in all my life. It was too much for me and I hurried away out of it. The next Monday at the ground, Brian asked me why I'd walked out of his team talk. I told him, "You'll never get away with speaking to players like that." Do you know what he said? "I'll show you whether I'll get away with it or not!" And he did, didn't he? Even though he used to pull players to pieces and shout at them something terrible, most of them spoke well of him. He made sure they were properly paid and looked after. His technique in the dressing room was to hypnotize people. That's the only way I can think of describing it. He'd break their willpower, then put them under his influence.

'I remember we were travelling to Arsenal for a Cup replay one Tuesday afternoon during the power restrictions. Suddenly on the coach journey, Brian bellowed, "Toddy!"

'"Yes, boss," came the reply.

'"Come here, sit down, look at me and shut up. You're the best half-back in the country, got that?"

'"Yes, boss."

'"Well then, go out there and show the buggers what you can do. And don't take your eyes off me for one moment, do you hear?"

'You see, it was the eyes. That was the power he had over them.'

Clough used to talk about his 'antennae' which could pick up and transmit signals from a distance. He believed he could sit in the manager's dugout and 'make' any of his players look around at him without uttering a word. He told friends he had tried it several times and it had worked. Once on a tour of Spain Clough said, 'I was walking along the beach this morning with Peter and my two bairns and I saw these sixteen blokes running in the distance half a mile away. I thought: what more could I want? I've got 'em insured for two million quid. None of 'em picks pockets and gets up to no good. What a superb bunch of lads – but they can only play when I turn the switch on.'

On the same trip he confessed revealingly, 'Most of the time I feel as if I'm hanging by my fingertips. I like to be right and most of the time I think I am right but I'm not infallible. I constantly doubt my ability to manage. I think it's the bloke who doesn't question himself who goes wrong. If Hitler had sat down and thought for a minute that he was wrong we wouldn't be here today. He'd have sorted himself out and made the right moves.'

Taylor barely merits a mention in the Longson diaries. He was very much on the outside looking in (at least until it suited Longson to befriend him). Longson used to say that the difference between Clough and Taylor was that Clough had wisdom. Not surprisingly, Clough's number two was increasingly resentful as he watched the favours being heaped on his mate. Longson at one point offered to bequeath Clough the rest of his business empire, before thinking better of it. In 1971 he gave him some Derby County shares as a Christmas present, later admitting that it was a foolish thing to have done: 'I knew, as far as football law was concerned, it was wrong but I gave them to him as a friend, not as a manager. That is how highly he figured in my esteem.'

Longson was losing his sense of proportion alright. While others tried to dissuade him, he bought his manager a full-length suede coat, a waste-disposal unit for the house and endless toys for the children at Christmas. His generosity culminated in the £5000 pay rise which did so much to alienate Taylor: 'Longson and Brian were as thick as thieves. They were so close it made you sick. The relationship was false and wrong but they were both enjoying it. Brian was cultivating him at my expense and the old boy got carried away. I felt as though I was doing my job in limbo. There was nothing wrong with gifts but the chairman should have bought two suede coats and two waste-disposal units. By the same token, Brian should have said, "Hey, Mr Chairman, there are two of us, you know. It's not just me running the club." He never did. I was so choked over the perks Brian was getting that I couldn't face the celebrations when we won the title.'

It's little short of astonishing that, amid the recriminations and petty jealousies, Derby remained stable long enough to become English League Champions in 1972. Taylor, for all his grumblings, knew when he was well off. No point rocking the boat with Europe's glittering horizon in view. Whatever he thought about Clough, he did not feel it strongly enough to sling his hook. Perhaps he was more insecure than Clough. His lifelong friend George Pycroft thinks so. Pycroft was a part-time scout for Derby but became the middleman in a curious tug-of-war between Clough and Taylor. Pycroft's friendship switched away from Taylor towards his partner, and Taylor believes that Clough fuelled the growing disaffection between them. While Taylor was recovering from an apparent heart attack in 1970, Clough virtually appointed Pycroft as a replacement. That increased Taylor's sense of vulnerability. He regarded himself as the best scout in the country, and doubtless felt threatened by Pycroft. When neither paid much attention to him as he recuperated at home, Taylor's fears intensified.

Pycroft recalls, 'He was afraid someone might think he was dispensable. He was always looking over his shoulder, worried if people weren't appreciating him. He knew there was only one Brian Clough but dozens of Peter Taylors. It got worse at Forest, where players were more or less instructed to mention his name in television and radio interviews. Taylor had a real complex about it. Once he gave McGovern a roasting for giving credit to Clough and not to him.'

Pycroft and Taylor had fallen out over a scouting mission to Scunthorpe.

'I went to watch a young player at Taylor's request,' says the scout. 'His name was Kevin Keegan. It was nine months before Liverpool signed him and I reported back, "Don't miss this lad." The worst thing you could say to Taylor was that someone could play, because he'd try to prove you wrong.

'He did nothing about Keegan. When the lad joined Liverpool, Taylor said, "I see Shanks has dropped a clanger." I told him that at £35,000 it was a bargain. Later on, he admitted that I'd been spot-on in my assessment and went quiet about it for the rest of the week. Clough telephoned me and arranged a meeting. He said, "I want the full Keegan story." I told him, but got the impression he already knew. Then he confessed that he had watched the player himself, not once, but twice, because he was so impressed the first time. "Why didn't you sign him then?" I asked, but he said it wasn't his department. Taylor was supposed to be in charge of that. To be honest, neither was a great judge of a youngster. Brian used to say to me, "Tell me one youngster Taylor has brought to Derby or Forest." By that he meant schoolboys. There weren't any.'

When Taylor returned to work after his illness, Pycroft's services were dispensed with. The dismissal notice was written by Clough, but, according to the scout, dictated by Taylor: 'He never forgave me for the embarrassment of the Kevin Keegan episode.'

Keegan was in the past. Archie Gemmill was in the future. Derby needed more pace in midfield to mount a championship challenge. Webb told Taylor he knew of just the man. Gemmill was a Scottish Under-23 international who played for the secretary's old club, Preston. Derby paid £64,000 for him, one of the shrewdest investments they made, which is saying a lot. Once again, it needed a little bit of Clough magic to secure Gemmill's signature. His wife was not impressed with the Derby manager. She disliked his abrasive television style. Taylor and Clough turned on their considerable charm but, after a couple of hours of talk, Gemmill said he would decide in the morning. 'That's great,' said Clough. 'I'll sleep on the settee till you do.' He amazed the couple by washing the dinner plates and staying overnight in the spare room. Needless to say, he signed Gemmill over breakfast.

When it came to signing players, Clough had no peers. He started at an advantage because of his reputation. It was that which broke the ice with McFarland's father and indeed, when you consider that most of the new players were not so much discovered as snatched from under the noses of other clubs, you begin to see the importance of Clough's role. Taylor would draw his attention to the player and Clough would do the rest. The strategy came unstuck spectacularly in the infamous Ian Storey-Moore affair.

Moore was a fast, direct left-winger who scored goals, but he had languished at Nottingham Forest until he was twenty-eight. Many had viewed but none had pursued, until Derby and Manchester United were locked in a farcical battle to secure his signature. Most of the farce was introduced by Clough. It cost him the player, Derby £5000 and caused Longson another round of sleepless nights. Manchester United's initial bid of £200,000 was accepted by Matt Gillies, Moore's manager. Gillies and Moore, along with Frank O'Farrell, the Manchester United manager, and Ken Smales, the Forest secretary, met at Nottingham's Edwalton Hall hotel to finalize the deal but talks broke down when Moore failed to agree terms. Clough, ear to the ground as usual, sensed his opportunity and pounced. He made a similar offer to Forest and was invited by Gillies to talk with Moore.

The player takes up the story: 'Clough spoke to me on the phone at the Edwalton Hall and told me to stay where I was, he was coming over. Gillies and Smales drove off and left me alone to negotiate a £200,000 deal. Strange behaviour. It was as though they didn't want to meet Clough. He was a bit overpowering, but Clough and Taylor between them convinced me that Derby were a better bet than United, who were going through a transitional stage. I was impressed by the potential at Derby and signed the forms. As far as I knew, that was it.'

In fact, Moore was so overwhelmed that he signed the forms blank and left Clough and Taylor to fill in the details. Webb countersigned, but Forest did not. In a peculiar display of peevishness, Smales refused to add his signature, thereby invalidating the transfer. Forest had decided that they did not after all want another star player falling into Derby's clutches and tried to resurrect the United deal. Longson was warned by Smales that there would be trouble if Clough insisted.

The chairman, worried out of his wits, phoned Clough: 'Are you sure you're in order?'

'Absolutely certain. Forest can't make him go to a club of their choosing. He wants to come to Derby and I've bought him.'

To make certain, Clough 'kidnapped' the player and took him to meet the rest of the team at Derby's Midland hotel, where they were staying before Saturday's match against Wolves. Moore watched that game ensconsed in the directors' box at the Baseball Ground, having first been paraded around the pitch and introduced to the crowd as 'Derby's new player'. It was an outrageous bluff which did not work. After Derby's 2–1 victory, Moore was hidden away in the Midland for the rest of the weekend. His wife was allowed to join him that Saturday evening. He says: 'I didn't know whether I was coming or going. It was the first transfer I'd been involved in and I suppose you could say I was a bit naive. Walking around the Baseball Ground, I was convinced I was a Derby player. When it fell through it was all very embarrassing.'

Forest stubbornly refused to confirm the transfer. As soon as Moore went home, O'Farrell and Sir Matt Busby arrived on his doorstep at Bingham with a large bouquet for Mrs Moore. The negotiations started again and Moore eventually went to Old Trafford, missing a championship medal with Derby. Against normal custom and practice, Forest had indeed forced a player to join the club of their choosing. Clough was justifiably enraged. He sent a four-page protest telegram to Alan Hardaker and the Football League management committee, pointing out that Gillies had invited him to talk terms with Moore in the first place. Longson was apoplectic. You didn't criticize Alan Hardaker! The chairman sent a second message to the league secretary, dissociating himself and the club from Clough's telegram.

Despite such hiccups, the Clough–Taylor bandwagon was moving forward at full throttle. The pair of them, for all their disagreements, were buzzing in a way they have never buzzed since, not even when Nottingham Forest were winning European trophies. Their management methods were unique and based on the principle 'if you want it, go and get it'. Taylor specialized in delving into players' backgrounds, possibly one of the lessons he learned from Ernest Ord. When they signed for Derby, he'd say, 'Tell us what your vices are – drink, drugs, gambling, women? If you don't tell us, we'll find out anyway.' As an inveterate gambler himself and someone who had been 'skint' more times than he cared to remember, he was in a perfect position to judge. Taylor believed everyone had a skeleton in his cupboard. That is why Colin Todd drove them to distraction. They had nothing 'on' him. Clough teased him mercilessly: 'Toddy, you must lie, steal or cheat in private because you're too good to be bloody true!'

The team was enjoying a celebration dinner in Portugal after knocking Benfica out of the European Cup in 1972 when Clough stood up to speak: 'Hey, Toddy, I don't like you and I don't like your missus either!'

Todd was momentarily struck dumb: 'I said nothing, but it hurt a lot. The next day I went to his office and told him he was completely out of order. There was no excuse for bringing my wife into it. He apologized and said he didn't mean it. By the time I got home, he'd sent a bouquet of flowers to Jenny and apologized to her on the phone. He told her, "I'm doing it for a reason, you know. I'm just trying to provoke a response." He couldn't understand how I could play a blinder then get changed and go home apparently unconcerned. He tried fining me when I wasn't late and swearing at me for not showing any emotion. I never rose to the bait because I wasn't that type of person. In the end he gave up. I can see now exactly what he was doing and he was right. I should have taken his advice and put some more nastiness into my play. I might have got more England caps if I'd had Brian's determination to succeed.'

Clough and Taylor at last found Todd's Achilles heel. Gambling. Not in a big way, but big enough to be a potential problem:

'I got a phone call from Peter Taylor telling me to report to the ground and bring Jenny with me. On the way we tried to figure out what it could be. Jenny thought I must have won an award. We sat in the office confronted by Brian and Peter.

'Peter said, "Any problems, Toddy? Anything we should know about?"

'"No, I don't think so."

'"What about gambling?"

'"What about it?"

'"It's come to our notice that you're in trouble. That you owe Arthur Whittaker £700." (Whittaker's was the betting shop near the ground.)

'"How did you know that?"

'Then Brian chipped in: "If we ever find out you've been gambling again, you'll be out of this club as fast as you came in. We've spoken to Whittaker and one of the directors has paid your debt. This is the last time I want to talk about it.'

'It shook me rigid that they had found out. It taught me there was nothing the two of them didn't know and it cured me of gambling. I've had a few flutters since, but I owe it to Brian and Peter that I'm not ruined.'

The so-called blue-eyed boy John McGovern was also put to the test. Clough could not believe that he was such an upstanding young man and phoned occasionally on Friday evenings to check if he was at home. He invariably was. Fear was an essential part of Clough's management technique. McGovern was afraid to ask for a pay rise. When he plucked up the courage, Clough laughed him out of the office: "A pay rise – the way you're playing? Get out of here!"

McGovern remembers, 'I'd come away thinking I was the worst player in the world but I'd still be in the teamsheet come Saturday. Brian was a master at handling people. Sometimes when he finished his team talks on a Friday and the players were filing out looking self-satisfied, he'd shout after us, "If you think you're that bloody good, you'd better look at the team sheet, because you might not be on it!" The joke was that the team picked itself week after week. It was just Brian's way of trying to guard against complacency. Once, when we had beaten Everton, who were reduced to nine men, Brian decided to punish us. A lot of managers less gifted than him would have been satisfied with a win. That never entered his head. If he didn't think you'd played well, it didn't matter about the result. He had us in for extra training on Sunday morning.'

Few were spared the sword. Alan Hinton endured an on-off relationship with Clough, who was very hard on him, no doubt hoping that it might produce more of a physical edge to his play. Friends would see Hinton prostrate with nervous anxiety after a bad session with the manager, particularly after he missed a penalty against Juventus in the second leg of the European Cup semi-final in March 1973.

Sometimes Taylor would play the despot, adhering to his motto "observe and replace". The moment anyone showed the slightest sign of slipping below the expected standards, he was out. Inevitably it led to Taylor's parting with some players prematurely. Peter Withe would be a case in point. So would Archie Gemmill. Les Green was not. The goalkeeper who followed Taylor from Burton Albion to Hartlepool to Derby was not a favourite of Clough's but he played for two seasons without missing a game. Mackay endorsed Taylor's view that Green was only just short of international class. Nevertheless it was Taylor who gave him his marching orders quite suddenly and without a second thought one Boxing Day.

'On Christmas Eve,' says Taylor, 'Green had asked to borrow £100 for the kids' presents. He was in trouble with gambling debts and being chased by a woman. We helped him all we could but my worries were confirmed when I saw him shaking at half-time during the match against Manchester United.

'I said to Brian, "I'm not happy about Greeny."

'"What do you mean? We're 2–0 up."

'"I still think there's something wrong upstairs. You wait and see."

'I was right. He played a stinker in the second half and we got beaten 3–2. I told Green he was finished. He never played for us again. Brian hadn't seen the problem. He used to say he saw things later than me.'

Where Clough shone was in the half-time talks. Jimmy Gordon saw it over a long period: 'He was at his brilliant best then. The things he could remember from forty-five minutes' play were unbelievable. He could go through the team analysing every contribution and telling them where they had gone wrong. Every incident seemed to be recorded on a photographic memory.'

Simplicity was the essence of Derby's success. There were no blackboards, no dossiers on the opposition to study and commit to memory. Their method was far less formal than that; the psychological approach was very important. It was psychology which turned McGovern into a better player than he had a right to be; psychology which gave Mackay that new lease of life, and brought out hidden depths in players like Hinton and Durban at Derby; Robertson and Woodcock at Forest. Taylor says:

'It's a myth that we didn't believe in coaching. Our coaching went on wherever and whenever we discussed football. They'll tell you that to be a coach you have to put on a tracksuit and spend hours at the training ground. That's rubbish. When we were out with the players every day at training we were only putting into practice what we'd discussed between us. Most of our best work wasn't done on grass. It was done over Lill's treacle pancakes in the old days. We could decide tactics in the dressing room, the tearoom, the boardroom or in the office. We were great believers in group therapy. Often we'd get the lads a pint of beer and sit them around us on the floor. That was psychology at its best. Telling them how to play took no time. To O'Hare it was: "Hold the ball no matter how hard they whack you." To Hector: "Watch O'Hare. You've got to be ready when he slips that ball to you." And to Hinton we didn't say any more than: "Stay wide." The rest was common sense. Players aren't daft. Our opposition used to complicate it – that's why we beat them.

'Brian does it just the same today. He can't change after all these years. We watched teams occasionally but not much. George Best was always worth a look but there weren't many about. It would be impossible to put a percentage on our contributions when it came to tactics. It was equal and spontaneous. Our best moments were after a big win or a bad defeat at the Baseball Ground. We'd sit out the last few moments on the bench and one of us would say, "I think we ought to . . ." The other would finish the sentence: ". . . take them away for a few days." Telepathy. Within half an hour we'd have arranged to take them abroad the following day.

'Yes, we made players play better than they'd ever played in their lives, but we could have done nothing without raw talent. McGovern, no matter what the knockers say, had talent in *that* team. People like John had what the bloke playing next to him wanted. That's how it gelled at Derby.'

But it did not gel so well behind the scenes. Webb says Clough and Taylor were 'always bickering. Some of their stand-up rows were terrible, though we were often uncertain whether it was genuine or another of the many games they played. We knew what Peter was like, but we weren't sure about Clough. He had at least five different personalities. At his worst he had to dominate everyone. If you showed an ounce of resistance, he'd crush it out of you, then rebuild you to his own liking. You could never get a one-to-one situation with him even then. He was constantly surrounded by aides and hangers-on.' The 1972 league championship title was won despite the backstage bickering between Clough and Taylor, Clough and Webb, Clough and Longson, and Longson and Taylor. Derby's challenge also survived an impudent attempt by Coventry City to sign Clough and Taylor.

The bombshell was dropped late in March 1972 when Derrick Robbins asked Longson's permission to approach Clough. Longson was dumbfounded when Clough announced that he was leaving. The chairman resisted: 'I told Coventry they couldn't have him. Not there and then. We were in the running for what looked like being our first-ever league championship and for the manager and his assistant to leave at that stage would have a devastating effect on the players.' The following week, however, Clough handed in his resignation, along with those of Taylor and Gordon. Longson urged them to think about it, but on 11 April all three resignations were accepted.

It was not the end of the story of course. Longson continues, 'Later that evening, Brian and Peter came to my house with Mike Keeling, one of the directors. They indicated that they might be prepared to stay at Derby for more money.'

The board met again and agreed to their demands. It was not

until the next day that Longson discovered the improved offer had been unnecessary. Before his meeting with Clough, Taylor and Keeling, Coventry had called off the deal. Robbins was appalled at Clough's delaying tactics and sent the assistant secretary, Richard Dennison (Bob's son), to Clough's house to deliver the rejection letter personally. Dennison reported the withdrawal of the offer to Webb the same afternoon, but the Derby secretary, knowing nothing of the proposed meeting at Longson's house, had not considered the message so urgent that it could not wait until the following morning. The chairman felt he had been tricked:

I was furious. I'd promised to pay them more money to stay in the firm belief that the Coventry offer was still open to them. They didn't tell me any different. Keeling had gone on about the risk of losing Clough and Taylor for the want of 'a bit more money' and I'd had to make a quick decision. I couldn't go back on my word because they might have resigned again.

A farewell party arranged to mark the move to Coventry turned into a league championship celebration, but there had been sufficient anguish already for all sides to realize that the future was uncertain. Apart from Coventry (twice), Derby had survived approaches from Barcelona, Birmingham City, Sunderland, Everton and the Greek national side for their management duo. Now that Clough and Taylor were in charge of the league champions, anything was possible.

'Even when the parties and the banquets were going on,' Taylor says, 'I sensed it was all coming to an end. We had no relationship left with the directors. They were always criticizing. If it wasn't about my paying more than £100,000 for Terry Hennessey, they were quibbling about a paltry £14,000 for Roger Davies. I ask you, £14,000 for a player we sold for nearly twenty times that amount!'

There were marvellous days in Europe, among them a packed house at the Baseball Ground to see the Eagles of Benfica humiliated 3–0 with a little help from the phantom groundsman. Taylor turned on the sprinklers overnight, believing that Derby would be more at home on a quagmire. Eusebio was confused when he came out of the tunnel. He asked Taylor, 'How come the pitch she is so wet? We get no rain last night.' Taylor shrugged his shoulders and said something about the vagaries of the British climate!

A 36,472 crowd saw two goals by Hector put out Spartak Trnava and give Derby a passport to the semis. There followed a notorious first leg in Turin, in which, according to Clough, 'Juventus bought the referee. Of that there is no shadow of doubt. I was cheated, Taylor was nearly arrested and two players were booked for next to nothing. What surprised me is that Juventus were good enough without that. They were the better side but we could have reached the final if Gemmill and McFarland had played at Derby.'

Gemmill and McFarland were the only two who would miss the return leg if they received another caution. Both were booked for trivial offences within the first quarter of an hour! John Charles, who had played six very successful seasons at centre-forward for Juventus, had travelled with Clough and Taylor to Turin. He warned them just before kick-off that Helmut Haller, the Juventus substitute (and a West German international), had been into the referee's room twice. At half-time, instead of following his team mates to the dressing room, Haller walked away with referee Gerhard Schulenberg, also a West German. Taylor noticed them: 'I hurried after them and asked if they minded my listening to their conversation because I spoke German (I didn't speak a word of it really). Haller jabbed me in the ribs with his elbow and, while I was gasping for air, some heavies grabbed hold of me. I heard John Charles shouting to me to hold onto my passport.' There was no proof of any irregularities between Haller and Schulenberg but, once Gemmill and McFarland were disqualified from the return leg, Derby said goodbye to any realistic hope of pulling back a 1–3 deficit.

At the mandatory press conference after the game, Clough refused to talk to the Italians. He waved them aside with the words 'I don't speak to cheating bastards!' Brian Glanville of the *Sunday Times* had the interesting task of translating Clough's message into Italian.

Back home, Longson could have done with an interpreter. He had lost all semblance of control over his manager and was kept in the dark about two further transfer negotiations. The first had concerned David Nish, bought from Leicester City for £250,000, a huge sum for a full-back with no international caps. Clough was at his cockiest now. He thought he was answerable to no one. Len Shipman recalls how he marched into the Leicester boardroom in the middle of a meeting and announced, 'I've come to buy your full-back.' Shipman, the president of the Football League and chairman of Leicester, had to remind Clough that he couldn't throw his weight around like that. It was a very important meeting and would he kindly get out. 'Very good,' said the Derby manager, 'I'll wait outside.'

Longson recalls:

The deal was done without any consultation between Brian and the board in spite of the fact that such a big fee would have to be very carefully considered. It was another example of how he'd decided to go his own way and expected everyone else to follow. The close consultation that existed in the early years had disappeared completely. We'd always done our best to provide cash for Brian and Peter. In return we expected the right to discuss money. I'm convinced to this day that if the board had been consulted we'd have got Nish for considerably less than £250,000. Nevertheless, such was my respect for Brian that I was prepared to bite my tongue and swallow as best I could the irritations that were cropping up.

If he had known anything about Clough's foray into the transfer market at the start of the 1973–74 season, old Sam might well have bitten his tongue clean off. It emerged several months later in a chance conversation between Stuart Webb and Eddie Chapman, the West Ham secretary, that Clough had made a staggering £400,000 bid for Bobby Moore and Trevor Brooking. Longson and Webb were ignorant of it, but one of the directors, Mike Keeling, certainly was not. By now, Keeling more or less did as Clough commanded.

The manager first went for Moore, telephoning him at home and inviting him to a meeting at the luxury Churchill hotel in London. Taylor had set it up, and was somewhat taken aback when the player recounted the illicit details in his autobiography.[1]

Clough said at once, 'I hear you're interested in winning a league championship medal.'

Moore had been touched on the sensitive spot of his one unfulfilled ambition: 'Who wouldn't be?'

Clough: 'Would you play for Derby County?'

'Why not?'

'That'll do me.'

1 *Bobby Moore*, Everest Books, 1976

The pair headed for lunch in the hotel restaurant and were at first turned back by the maître d'hôtel because Moore was dressed in a casual shirt and sweater.

Clough brushed the protest aside: 'My team will never stay here again if *my* player can't sit in this restaurant.'

Moore protested: 'I don't play for you yet.'

Clough: 'Shut up. You're my player. That's no trouble. I'll ring Ron up now.'

Clough did better than that. He went to see Ron Greenwood in person. That episode is described in Greenwood's autobiography, *Yours Sincerely*:[2]

> He walked into my office with one of his directors. 'I just want a chat with you,' he said. 'Have you got any whisky?' I obliged. 'Any water?' he asked. 'Sure, the kitchen's just around the corner,' I told him. He went out . . . and didn't come back for twenty minutes. 'I've been looking round the place,' he said. 'Isn't it lovely? All nice and spruce.' (I learnt later that Clough had approached our receptionist and persuaded her to open up the directors' box, where he asked her all sorts of questions about the club.)
>
> The conversation in my office got underway. 'I want to sign Bobby Moore and Trevor Brooking,' said Clough.
>
> 'You can't be serious,' I replied.
>
> 'Every man's got his price,' he insisted. I told him there was no point going on because neither was for sale.
>
> 'Well, if I can't have Moore, can I have Brooking? And if I can't have Brooking, can I have Moore?' Clough continued.
>
> 'They're not available, Brian,' I said. 'But I'll pass your offer on to my board.'
>
> Clough carried on talking about money as if he hadn't heard me. The figures were rising by the minute.

So were temperatures in the Derby boardroom.

2 *Yours Sincerely,* Collins Willow, 1984

6
The Tempest

This is the way Clough describes the events leading up to the final confrontation:

'What brought on the bust-up at Derby was a bloke called Longson who wanted success as an old man. He got a partnership which brought him that success, then he wanted a bigger say. When a club mushrooms like Derby did, there's a lot of envy, jealousy and bullshit. Longson suddenly found himself in boardrooms where he'd never been allowed in before, let alone welcomed as chairman. People said to him, "Be careful what that young bugger's doing – he's shouting his mouth off too much." On Sunday mornings at Chapel-en-le-Frith, where he held his unofficial board meetings, he'd get the odd snide remark: "Who's running Derby County, Sam? Is it you or is it that young whippersnapper?" He repeated these conversations to me. I said, "Don't let it worry you, Mr Chairman," but it got to him. They tell me it does when you're in your seventies.

'It wasn't a clash of personalities because half the people we were battling with didn't have personalities. We went to Manchester United early in the new season and we won. Jack Kirkland, who'd just joined the board, wagged his finger at Taylor across the boardroom and said, "I'm coming to see you on Monday because I want to know exactly what you do at the club." Taylor did his nut: "No one wags his finger at me!" Longson then accused me of giving Matt Busby the "V" sign in the directors' box when all I was doing was waving to my wife. It got to a stupid, petty level, which for grown men was incredible. I was very full of myself and there was no way I was going to stand for that. They could stick their club and the new contract up their jacksies!'

Longson's view is somewhat different: 'Brian laboured under the illusion that nothing had ever happened at Derby until he arrived. In fact I'd been a director for 13 years and the club's representative on the Football League for much of that time. He thought we were country bumpkins but he overlooked the fact that I'd been to ten European Cup Finals before he was a manager and knew many of the game's hierarchy personally. If anything, directors in opposite boardrooms gave me a wide berth rather than welcomed me with open arms because of Brian's outrageous behaviour. He thought he was God – thought he could twist me around his little finger like he has everyone else. How wrong he was. When I imposed my will he couldn't take it. He could never accept that there was another authority at the club and it's been his problem everywhere.'

Three days after the Manchester United victory which took Derby to third place in the table, the club was managerless. Players, supporters, everyone in football was flabbergasted. There was no precise beginning to the troubles, as we have seen in the previous chapter, neither was there a definite end to them. It could be argued that the repercussions are being felt a decade and a half later. Clough says there are still people who travel to watch Nottingham Forest rather than their home club, Derby, because of what happened. For certain, Clough had become larger than life – a television superstar mimicked by comedians and in his element when he was laying waste to the game's establishment. Not everybody liked him, but he was in demand. ITV ratings soared (and still do) when that famous index finger started wagging and that strangulated Yorkshire accent clicked into gear. He could name his own price; he could apparently say anything to anyone without trepidation. The nation sat back in awe.

Sam Longson was seventy-three, and unheard of outside his native Derbyshire until he found Clough. He adopted football's angry young man as his own son and encouraged him to appear on television as much as possible. He saw no harm in it to begin with; indeed, it seemed to produce a positive advantage for his beloved Derby County and by association for himself. When the chairman finally decided that Clough's television appearances and newspaper columns were getting out of hand, it was too late. The horse had bolted and was running around the paddock.

At first Longson had enjoyed the reflected glory of Clough's success and fame right across Europe. Now, however, he was having to apologize everywhere he went. Clough was digging at the establishment almost every day of the week. No potential target was safe. Alan Hardaker came in for it; so did Sir Alf Ramsey, Sir Matt Busby and Don Revie. 'He's a bit of a lad, isn't he?' Longson used to joke, but he had long since ceased to see the funny side.

The incidents at Old Trafford were unimportant in themselves but assumed greater proportions because of the rapidly deteriorating situation. At a board meeting on Friday, 11 October 1973, Longson had called for Clough's sacking but failed to get the necessary support. He had been trying for some time to rid the club of its outspoken manager, but could find nothing of sufficient gravity to warrant his dismissal. That changed after Clough accepted a part-time job with LWT's *On the Ball* programme. He had agonized over a £16,000 offer to replace Jimmy Hill as ITV's full-time anchorman, but decided not to leave football.

Derby reluctantly endorsed his decision to go part-time but came to regret it when the manager's television commitments took him to London on Wednesday or Thursday each week for studio recordings. Taylor twice had to deputize for him at important board meetings. The directors took a dim view of this, complaining that the manager's report was more important than television. Now at last they felt that they had something concrete with which to confront him – breach of contract. As Longson puts it:

> His absences did not comply with his undertaking not to allow outside commitments to interfere with club duties . . . it could hardly be argued that for a manager to be away on Wednesday or Thursday was the best way of preparing a team for a Saturday match. In addition, he was travelling to London again on Sundays to contribute comments and analyses. The situation had become well nigh impossible. The final countdown to Brian Clough's resignation had begun.

Clough was appalled at the board's double standards. In the early days, they had been enthusiastic about television: 'When I was invited to sit on the World Cup panel, the directors told me I *must* do it. It would be good for me and good for Derby County. In those days I took Sam on the occasional trip with me. He lapped it up. Then when we got a bit of success and I was in demand just as much, the mood changed. Suddenly it was: "Never mind about all this television – what about doing the job we pay you for?" I told them they were the shits who were *encouraging* me two years before! Taylor stood up for me magnificently. He went into a board meeting and warned them, "If you stop him doing television, you'll take away part and parcel of his job."'

In his own mind, Longson had been a big fish in a small pool until Clough arrived and he seemed to resent the spotlight falling on the manager rather than the chairman. He threw a tantrum in the directors' box one Saturday when someone handed him a back-page newspaper headline reading: 'The man at the helm'. Beneath it was a picture of Clough! Longson admits in his diaries that he could not cope with Clough's increasing stature and notoriety:

> In the early days of our relationship, Brian had leaned on me and sought my advice. During the 1970 World Cup, he not only continued to make a name for himself as a controversial character with the press but also as a television pundit. Now his confidence was growing by leaps and bounds. He had something big to offer football. If you consider that I am stating this because I felt slighted, you are right.

Hell hath no fury like a chairman's wounded pride.

To make it worse, Clough appeared to go out of his way to irritate Longson. In the summer of 1972, for instance, he had refused to go on a pre-season tour to Holland and West Germany after the board objected to his taking the family. Clough battled, but the chairman would not budge. 'This is a working trip, not a holiday,' he told Clough, 'and I'm ordering you in no circumstances to take your family.' Clough pulled out of the tour altogether, leaving Taylor to take charge.

Next came the manager's new newspaper column. Directors beseeched Clough to 'avoid controversy and blunt criticism of the game's leading personalities'. They might as well have asked a baby not to cry. He continued to be as outspoken as ever, complaining once about Alan Hardaker, 'It seems you cannot say he has too much power.' Nervous anxiety drove Longson into hospital for a major operation. He says, 'It was like walking a tightrope. We had been left in no doubt that, if Brian stepped over the mark again, it would be regarded as the responsibility of the club. But it had become clear by now that we had little influence over him.' Longson was super-sensitive in this area. He numbered Hardaker and Shipman among his personal friends and could not bear the thought of upsetting them. Rightly or wrongly he feared that Clough could get Derby expelled from the league. In view of the club's history of serious misdemeanours, relegation, even expulsion, seemed a very real threat to him. He was asked to attend a meeting of the Football League management committee and reminded in no uncertain terms that Derby would face severe disciplinary action if they failed to persuade Clough to modify his criticisms. Longson adds, 'I only regret that no official warning was issued by the league to back up what we were left to say in private to Brian.'

This seems to have been the crux of the matter. As Taylor insists, the television issue was probably a smokescreen for Longson's real motive in wanting Clough out. He was desperately concerned that a fresh Football League inquiry into the club's affairs would bring to light more glaring deficiencies than before.

To confuse matters further, the relationship between Clough and Taylor had reached a new low. Taylor had found out about the £5000 pay rise and other Clough perks. And he was hearing alarm bells from Stuart Webb: 'He told me I must start going to board meetings because Brian was "murdering" me, boosting his own contribution and belittling mine. He said, "I can't listen to it any more. Clough's taking the credit for everything."'

In January 1973, Longson received the following phone message from Clough: 'If Peter Taylor isn't at work by Friday, I shan't be going to Liverpool with the team. I'll walk out!'

'What in heaven's name is wrong?' asked Longson. He didn't get an answer. Clough and Taylor had had a flaming row about the manager's perks and Taylor went home complaining of chestiness. Ten days later he had still not reappeared. Clough sat in the chairman's house begging him to sack Taylor because of his apparently sulky behaviour and the rifts it was causing in the partnership. The two were constantly at loggerheads over money according to Longson. 'Taylor was unable to conceal his envy and jealousy of his more illustrious partner,' says the former chairman. 'Clough became so angry because I wouldn't do as he commanded that he spilled a large scotch all over the kitchen floor. He was shaking with rage and shouting: "I am getting nowhere with you buggers!"'

Taylor returned to work but the fracas started a new train of thought in the chairman's mind. Should he get rid of Clough and offer the job to Taylor? He writes:

The more I considered the idea . . . the better it looked, until I faced the reality that I had to clear my mind of the temptation. The big stumbling block was Peter Taylor's loyalty to Brian.

According to Taylor, however, Longson *did* try to split the partnership – twice:

'He pulled up outside my house in his Mercedes sports car and asked me straight out to take the job.

'"What about Brian?" I asked him.

'"Never mind about Brian. I'll take care of him, he's going."

'I told him to fetch Brian and repeat the conversation in front of him. He said he couldn't. I went to see Brian directly. "What's going on here – Sam's offered me the manager's job? Either make peace or sort something out because we can't carry on like this." From a position where Clough and the chairman had been close, with me on the outside, I'd become the blue-eyed boy overnight. I didn't want that. Not too long before, Sam had the nerve to query my role at the club. "Stick around," I told him. "You'll find out soon enough." Now he was offering me the top job. It didn't make sense.

'He came round again a few weeks later, asking me to write my own contract. Out of loyalty to Brian I didn't even consider it. What kind of chairman couldn't read a situation like that? Did he really think I'd go behind Brian's back?'

How odd, then, that Longson should commit this paragraph to his diaries:

I am delighted that I let my considered judgement get the better of my personal feelings in the matter and I was able to resist the temptation to split them.

He explains: 'Taylor has got it all wrong. It's true I went to his house – to see why he wasn't at work. I was trying to sound him out. I wanted to test the depths of his resentment of Brian. I didn't want him as a manager. He completely misinterpreted the reason behind my visit.'

Two more incidents convinced Longson that the time had come to stand up to Clough. The manager had launched a blistering attack on the Football League and Leeds United.

'I'll sack the bloody lot!' Clough told Sam Longson when he took over at the Baseball Ground in 1967. He was almost as good as his word

Pandemonium as Clough and Taylor resign at Derby County. 16 October 1973

Top: Addressing the Protest Movement at Derby's King's Hall. Don Shaw *(left)* and Bill Holmes were the organizers

Above: Clough makes his charismatic return to the Baseball Ground only a few days after resigning. October '73

Above: Television Superstar. Clough was offered Jimmy Hill's old job but turned it down. Here he is with fellow panellists Sir Alf Ramsey, Malcolm Allison and Pat Crerand

Left: Clough campaigns on behalf of Phillip Whitehead *(seated)* during the '74 General Election

Right: Nigel Clough tries to emulate his father, but walking on water isn't easy in-deep-end-ently!

Below: Quite a handful - Elizabeth, Nigel and Simon

Leeds, under Don Revie, had been found guilty of 'persistent misconduct on the field', but escaped with a suspended £3000 fine. Remembering Derby's £10,000 fine and banishment from Europe a couple of years earlier, Clough declared that Leeds should have been relegated and added, 'The trouble with soccer's disciplinary system is that those who sit in judgement, being officials of other clubs, might well have a vested interest.' He was charged with bringing the game into disrepute – a serious allegation which, if proven, could have resulted in a three-year ban from football. Certain that Derby were now 'for the high jump', Longson snapped. (In fact, Clough was cleared of the charge after he had resigned.)

The attack on Leeds was the last straw for me. I was sick and tired of the whole business. If Clough wanted to quit the game to give himself freedom to speak his mind on any subject under the sun, I told him I wouldn't stand in his way.

In October 1973 England were due to play Poland in a World Cup qualifying round; they had to win to be sure of reaching the Munich finals in 1974. Before that Wembley date, the Poles had a friendly against Holland. Clough, a key figure in ITV's panel for the build-up to the finals, figured that watching England's opponents in Amsterdam would be useful research. He asked Longson if he and Taylor could travel to the game. He would regard it as part of his holiday. Longson approved, on the strict understanding that Derby would not pay for the trip because it was a private matter. Longson reported to the board meeting on 11 October that, despite that conversation, Clough had submitted a bill for the Amsterdam trip. (Derby did not pay it, incidentally.)

Having watched his bid to remove Clough fall on stony ground, Longson tried another course of action designed to provoke a showdown. After the Manchester United game and the acute embarrassment of having had to apologize to Sir Matt Busby and the United chairman, Louis Edwards, for Clough's finger gesture, the chairman instructed Webb to lock the manager's drinks cabinet. For some time, the directors had complained about Clough's drinking habits. They used Webb as the go-between. 'I had to confront Brian over these things all the time. He didn't like it, and he hated me for doing it,' says the secretary. 'They locked his cabinet because they were concerned about the amount of drink Brian and Peter were getting through. Brian was drinking heavily. His office doubled as the boardroom. There was a bar with a constant supply of bottles. He'd have a couple of scotches first thing in the morning and entertain his friends until late at night.'

Taylor confesses, 'We were both drinking to excess. It was a temptation because it was always available. Sometimes I'd take a bottle home. Having said that, Brian's drinking wasn't a problem to me. If I saw him overdoing it, I only had to say, "You've had enough," and he'd stop. In any case, he could hold it well.'

Jimmy Gordon says that Longson could not have chosen a more effective way of provoking the manager: 'Standing between Clough and the bottle was deadly. We knew there'd be hell to pay. The boss couldn't operate unless there was champagne around.' There was an irresistible urgency in Clough's voice when he telephoned Longson the following day. 'Can you come to the training ground at once, Mr Chairman. This is important.' When he got to the Matlock training centre, Clough took him aside and said, 'Can I have permission to sack Stuart Webb? He's locked the bar.'

'I know,' replied Longson, 'Stuart was acting on my instructions. It's nothing to do with you. The secretary is in charge of company affairs. You just get on with managing the team.'

Part two of Longson's attack was a written ultimatum to Clough about his television and newspaper work. He demanded that each article be submitted to the board for approval and the on-screen appearances be curtailed. What's more, Clough would need permission to appear on television. While an enraged Longson was compiling his letter, Clough and Taylor were busy launching a counter-attack to unseat the chairman. Longson received a delegation of three directors who were seeking an end to the troubles. They told him that Clough and Taylor could no longer work with him. The implication was obvious, but Longson parried the thrust by citing all the grievances he had against Clough and explaining his latest campaign. He and the manager exchanged heated words over the phone about clauses in the ultimatum, after which Clough and Taylor offered their resignations. They demanded an emergency board meeting the same evening. Longson refused to drive the forty-three miles to the Baseball Ground, saying he wanted the resignations in writing and would call a board meeting the following morning.

In the meantime, Clough explored the possibilities of an alternative to walking out. He turned first to Phillip Whitehead, his friend and local MP, who begged him, 'Don't give the board the chance to overthrow you, because that's what they want. Only resign if you genuinely don't want to do the job and are satisfied that the sacrifice will be worth it.' That night, Clough also arranged to meet the club president, Sir Robertson King, at a public house in Borrowash. Says Clough, 'He was a lovely man. He asked me if I was sure about what I was doing. I said no, I wasn't sure, but I knew I couldn't possibly carry on working in that atmosphere. He said, "Let's see how it goes at the board meeting."'

He asked Sir Robertson to take over the chair, promising that he would withdraw his letter of resignation if Longson left the board. Keeling was in favour of this solution at the board meeting but the other directors turned it down. That historic meeting was an embittered affair. Six years of niggles, some minor, others more sinister, had come to the surface. Clough, displaying remarkable self-control - or nonchalance, depending on your point of view - went through with his morning's engagements first. They included the opening of a new shop ten miles out of town and a visit to some elderly patients in hospital. Meanwhile, word of his impending resignation had spread. A group of night-shift workers at Rolls-Royce telephoned the ground urging them to avoid bloodshed. Outside the stadium, the first of the protesters had started to gather.

Clough and Taylor were kept waiting in the ante-chamber to the boardroom/manager's office while the directors discussed the plan to unseat Longson. In due course, the chairman opened the door and said, 'Right, you two, let's have you in!' Clough accused him of being narrow-minded and said he would only consider withdrawing his resignation if Longson's ultimatum was thrown out and him with it! He said everything he and Taylor had done was for the good of Derby Country. The club's lawyers pored over Clough and Taylor's contracts while Longson barked, 'Don't even think of a settlement. You're getting nowt!' And he meant it. The resignations were eventually accepted, although Keeling and Sir Roberston King voted against. Longson wrapped it up by demanding, 'Put your car keys on the table and go.'

Clough comments, 'Not one of the directors had the guts to get up and say, "Hold on a minute, Sam, you're wrong." He'd been there a long time and most of them were friends of his.'

Keeling resigned from the board, saying, 'I don't think I can be of any more use to this club.' As it turned out, that would be a grave mistake. Keeling could have done a lot more for Clough by remaining on the board and trying to orchestrate his return from a position of strength. He might just have succeeded. What followed the board meeting can only be described as a pantomime. The arguments spilled over into the executive lounge, where television crews had installed their lights for the news conference. Clough and Longson were holding court at different ends of the room at the same time. That was bound to suit Clough more than Longson. He was used to lights and knew how to handle the media. Longson tried to explain that Clough had broken his contract by getting involved in outside work, but he was so ill at ease in front of the microphones and cameras that Kirkland had to drag him away.

Instead of leaving as they had been commanded, Clough and Taylor strolled along the corridor to the executive lounge to listen to the chairman. Clough told reporters, 'It surprises me a little that people who want to stop me putting two words together can't put them together themselves. I feel embarrassed for the chairman and deeply ashamed for Derby County.' When he left the ground, the board had gone back into session to decide what to do next.

Clough made a move towards the boardroom door, threatening to empty a nearby jug of water over their heads. Taylor put a restraining hand on his shoulder and said, 'Leave it.' As a last act of defiance, Clough hung onto his car keys and drove away in the club Mercedes. Taylor was in the passenger seat. It was the end of their time at Derby, but only the start of a protest movement which was to last for years.

Predictably, Clough gave the board a verbal lashing in the newspapers, to which Longson responded with a long statement, listing a series of allegations against Clough. The statement was opposed by other members of the board. It resulted in a libel action by Clough and an out-of-court settlement in his favour of £25,000 – more than compensating for his lack of pay-off from Derby. Longson was prepared to fight the writs:

I was dead against the settlement agreed by the rest of the board. My statement had been studied by our legal advisors who assured me it was 'unlikely' that I would lose the case. I also believed that the directors and the club had to have their names cleared. Litigation was the best way of achieving that.

Even when George Hardy took over the chair, Longson would not let it rest. At a board meeting, he slammed a cheque for £20,000 on the table and said, 'This is going all the way to court and there's the money for the legal fees!' Hardy tossed the cheque back at him saying, 'If you think that's in the best interests of the club, think again.' Hardy had seen the papers for the libel hearing and feared a slanging match with a stack of dirty linen being washed in public.

Longson in the meantime acted swiftly to find a new manager. His first choice was Bobby Robson, who preferred to stay at Ipswich. That left Dave Mackay. Arrangements for a four-year contract were drawn up by Longson, Bradley, Kirkland and Webb. The two missing directors, Rudd and Innes, were told over the phone. A jubilant Longson thought he detected a certain reticence on their part. It seemed they were not at all sure that the board had done the right thing in accepting Clough's and Taylor's resignations. Longson was in a trough of despair again:

> Bill Rudd was now saying that he would consider taking Brian and Peter back if Brian was prepared to give an undertaking to toe the line. To say that I was shattered is an understatement.

It emerged that Keeling was trying to muster support to have the pair reinstated. How he must have wished that he could have done it from within, taking advantage of the hesitation of at least two of the directors. Clough and Taylor wanted to return to their jobs. Clough said that he would be prepared to relinquish his newspaper column and his ITV work to achieve that end. It confirmed what Longson suspected all along – that Clough had fallen victim to his own bluff and was now regretting it: 'When I first told Brian he'd have to cut down on his television work, he said, "If I have to give up all of this, Mr Chairman, I'll resign." I replied, "Bloody well resign then." He said if he did it would be curtains for me. I spat on my hands, rubbed them together and said, "Right then, we'll see who's right." He had the biggest shock of his life when his resignation was accepted.'

In the face of a potential revolt from within the board,

Longson stood firm, as this extract from the diary underlines:

> I couldn't even contemplate any further dealings with our former manager, or with Mike Keeling, who'd supported him. As far as I was concerned, what was done should not be undone. I'd hoped there might be a reconciliation right up to the last minute. I didn't want to bring Brian down. Why should I? I recognized the massive contribution he made to Derby County but we had to get on with the job in hand, and my plans did not include even considering the reinstatement of Brian Clough and Peter Taylor.

Taylor was soon to be an unwilling accomplice in Clough's emotional campaign to repair the damage. He disagreed with it as much as he disagreed with the original decision to resign: 'We should never have left. I told Brian so. We were doing a good job. There was cash in the bank, about £250,000 if I remember rightly, and we were third in the table after our best-ever start to the season. When we left, Longson said, "This club doesn't need running for three years." It was the biggest indictment he could have made against himself. It was like saying, "Now we've got success we can relax." Astonishing.'

Clough admits that he had second thoughts about resigning: 'I shouldn't have walked out on a four-year contract. I should have told them that, if they wanted me out of the club, they'd have to pay every penny.'

Shortly after the resignations, Derby County reserves had a Central League appointment at Nottingham Forest. Stuart Dryden, one of the Forest committeemen was surprised to see the entire Derby boardroom represented at the game. It was unheard of. Dryden says, 'They paired off with us and I got Jack Kirkland. He was a very outspoken man. He warned me, "Don't ever have Brian Clough at your club – he'll ruin everything." It was an odd thing to say because I'd never met Kirkland or Clough, and Forest had never given any indication that they were considering such a move. When I spoke to the rest of our committee afterwards, each reported that he'd had a similar warning from a Derby director. That's how nervous they were of seeing him set up shop down the road.'

Kirkland had unwittingly given Dryden an idea and, within fourteen months of that meeting, the very thing Derby were dreading came to pass.

7
Mutiny

Dave Mackay had an unpleasant surprise when Clough breezed into his office at the Baseball Ground a few weeks after walking out. With the supreme effrontery which is his trademark, Clough announced that he had come shopping for reserve and 'A' team players to take to Brighton. He had already taken the scouting staff. What a bizarre half-hour it must have been. The Protest Movement, activated and sustained by Clough's brazen desire to get his job back, had made life a misery for Mackay. The team was either listless or downright rebellious and had not won for six matches after he took charge. There was a strong feeling that the players had deliberately performed under par. A man of lesser resolve and character than Mackay might well have buckled under the strain. Until Clough showed up that November day, however, a chink of light had began to break through the gloom.

Roy McFarland had publicly asked the Protest Movement to wind up its activities, and its leader, Don Shaw, a local playwright, had agreed to put McFarland's request to the next meeting. Longson comments:

> It looked like peace at last, but the tinder-dry atmosphere needed only the faintest spark to blow the whole thing up again. It got more than that. It got a flash of lightning in the form of Brian.

At that first confrontation between Clough and his beleaguered successor, the chat skirted around the main issue for a while until Mackay spoke out:

'Why don't you get on with your job at Brighton and let me do mine?'

'What do you mean?' asked Clough.

'You know what I mean. A few words from you could stop all this nonsense once and for all. Call off the protest.'

'Why should I call it off?'

'Because you're being unfair. If I was in your position, I wouldn't dream of interfering with another manager's job.'

According to Mackay, Clough then revealed the real purpose behind his visit and his dealings with the Protest Movement. He was apparently 'out to get' two members of Derby County and wanted to embarrass the club which he believed had treated him so badly. The two in question were Longson and Webb.

Clough scarcely referred to Mackay's quandary, although he must have been aware that any scheme to destroy the club was bound to number the new manager among its casualties. Mackay and his assistant, Des Anderson, had played it cool up to that point. They knew they were inheriting a whirlwind as well as a world-class squad of players.

Anderson says, 'It would have been a tragedy to disrupt the team, however badly they were playing. Many of them weren't giving their best but we were determined to give them time. Each morning when we came into work there would be a mini crisis of some sort. Either Clough had been meeting the players secretly or his pal Mike Keeling had been stoking the protest. We had an offer of £750,000 from Gordon Jago at Queens Park Rangers to take three troublemakers off our hands. He told us to perm any three from Todd, McFarland, Nish and Gemmill. It was a comforting thought, but we wanted to keep those players. There was no way we could replace them. Many times Dave and I thought privately that we'd had enough, but we were both battlers.'

McFarland was the self-styled leader of the players' revolt. He, like the rest, was devastated by Clough's and Taylor's departure. Clough had brought most of them up from very little, given them a good lifestyle, a successful career, international caps in some cases, and medals to treasure for ever. Now he was gone. McFarland advised that nothing should be done on the spur of the moment. He said that wrenching the boardroom door off its hinges would do their cause no good. Along with Nish, Hector and Todd, the centre-half had been training with the England squad when news of Clough's resignation hit the headlines. He walked into the television lounge at the Hendon Hall hotel, where Alan Ball showed him a copy of the *Evening Standard*. The rest of the England party were laughing and joking; the four Derby lads sat grim-faced trying to take it all in. 'No one in their wildest dreams expected them to throw in the towel like that,' says McFarland. 'We had no idea things were so bad behind the scenes.'

After a series of rapid telephone calls to their team mates back in Derby, the players decided to keep a low profile until the England game and the home match against Leicester City the following Saturday had been safely negotiated. Then the board would feel the full blast of their fury. As the four Derby players stepped onto the Wembley turf that evening after the walkout, who should be standing in the centre circle waiting to greet them but Clough himself.

A few confused handshakes were exchanged but little was said. Clough was at the game against Poland as an ITV panellist. It was the game in which he outraged viewers by referring to the Polish goalkeeper Tomacewski as 'a clown'; it was the night Hector made his two-minute debut for England and had a shot cleared off the line in the closing seconds. It was the night Peter Shilton dived over Domaski's shot and England went out of the World Cup.

It was also the night McFarland felt so depressed that he drove home to Derby instead of staying in London with the rest of the team. It seemed to him that, in one short evening, everything had collapsed. Derby's acting manager, Jimmy Gordon, somehow hoisted morale in time for the Leicester game. It was vital to win to strengthen Derby's challenge for a top-of-the-table position. Derby won 2–1 with goals from Hector and McGovern. They did it 'for the sake of Brian and Peter', but the match was overshadowed by the events which preceded it. The protest group, marshalled by Keeling, Shaw and Bill Holmes, the manager of Ind Coope Brewers, was already in full swing. Hundreds of demonstrators boycotted the match and paraded banners outside the Baseball Ground demanding 'Directors out, Clough in'. Police had been warned of possible riots and provided heavy reinforcements while terrified householders barricaded their windows and prayed for Sunday.

There was a feverish buzz of excitement at five to three when a gold Rolls-Royce nosed its way through the back streets towards the ground. It was Clough! Four days after being banished from the club he was back with a borrowed season ticket. The idea had come from Shaw, who had had a job persuading Clough to turn up.

'Are you going to the Leicester game?' the leader of the protesters had asked him the previous day.

'I daren't,' said Clough.

'Why not? If you walk around that running track you'll get an ecstatic reception. Television will be there. Think of the visual impact.'

'I can't do it, Don. They might throw me out.'

'They can't. You created that team. You're the hero.'

Police officers looked on horrified as Clough skipped through the crowds of protesters pursued by a frenzied mob of reporters and cameramen. He bypassed a bewildered steward, nipped through a turnstile and tried to make it to the players' entrance so that he could appear on the running track as planned. The commissionaire blocked his way so Clough went up the stairs into the rows of seats alongside the directors' box. The effect was electrifying. There stood the young manager, immaculate in his pale grey suit, saluting the fans with arms aloft. Players from both teams stopped their warm-ups and stared in amazement.

Just a few feet away, Longson rose to *his* feet to the applause of some of the shareholders sitting behind him. They were outshouted by a 34,000 crowd, most of them rooting for Clough. The pair of them stood momentarily vying for the support of the fans. A case of egos at twenty paces. With the game barely underway, Clough was gone as fast as he'd come . . . out past the same steward, across the street, into the waiting Rolls and away to London to appear in the Michael Parkinson show.

Exactly a week after the resignations, Derby's senior players made their first intervention. McFarland handed in a letter to the board:

> During the events of the last week, we the undersigned players have kept our feelings within the dressing room. However, at this time, we are unanimous in our support and respect for Mr Clough and Mr Taylor and ask that they are re-instated as manager and assistant manager of this club. Nobody can say we have acted on the spur of the moment or are just being emotional.

It was signed by each member of the team except for Henry Newton, who was in Liverpool on business. When told about the petition, Clough said, 'I'm staggered. Whatever happens I will be grateful to them for restoring my faith in human nature.' He arranged to meet the players at his 'local', the Kedleston Hotel just outside Derby. 'Feelings were running very high,' says McGovern. 'We were bitter that the relationship was over. There was genuine love for the man in the club and in the town. I don't think he was wrong to try to get his job back with the help of the players. We were all looking forward to getting back together as fast as possible. As a young player, I didn't understand the legalities of players demanding to see the board.'

Over drinks, the group remembered some of the good times and tried to put a brave face on things. Clough was his usual energetic self but it was the first time he had allowed himself to get emotionally involved with the players. They wanted him back and he wanted to come back. It was agreed that the team should express its feelings personally to the directors.

However, the directors did not want to see them. They had signed Mackay but promised not to announce it until his present club, Nottingham Forest, had played Hull City that night. They shied away from the players, managing only to inflame passions. It led to a sit-in at the Baseball Ground in the afternoon and early evening. The players laid siege to the stadium, believing that a board meeting was in progress. The boardroom lights were burning, apparently confirming their suspicions. In fact, only Kirkland and Webb were there. Hearing the team in the corridor calling for the directors to show their faces, they locked themselves in the boardroom and kept quiet. It was a long wait. Especially for Kirkland. There was a bar in the room, but no toilet. Rather than risk a dash to the outside loo, he was forced to relieve himself in the champagne bucket! Finally, thinking that the players had dispersed, the director and secretary broke out and made for their cars. Colin Boulton and Ronnie Webster had been posted as guards for just such an eventuality. With the players beating on their car roofs, Kirkland and Webb sped off, Kirkland shouting, 'You'll have a new manager in the morning!'

The players knew that it had to be Mackay. McFarland, a close friend of the former Derby player, decided on a direct approach as time ran out. Half an hour before the Hull match kicked off, he telephoned Mackay at the City ground and warned him that it would be unwise to take the job because of the mood of the players. Not being the sort of man you could push around, Mackay swore down the phone and told McFarland he had no intention of turning down the best job in England. 'If ever I needed an incentive to make a go of the job, that phone call was it,' he says. Derby had chosen wisely. Although he had no particular track record as a manager, Mackay was a well-loved figure in the town. He had played alongside most of the players who were in revolt. If anyone could win them round, it was him. Before he did, though, Mackay learned what it was like to walk into a nest of vipers.

Longson writes:

> Never in all my experience have I seen or heard of a case in football where a manager who has been sacked or resigned has rampaged in such a way as Brian Clough did against Dave Mackay. I will never understand why the Managers Association stood by and did nothing. What made it worse was that Dave Mackay, as a player, had done more than anyone in bringing Clough's success at Derby County to a peak.

The reason why neither the Managers Association nor the Football League intervened was probably that Mackay did not utter a word of public complaint.

Clough was in league with the players and the Protest Movement. Don Shaw met him for the first time three days after the resignations. The writer had just beaten a hasty retreat from Israel, where the Yom Kippur War had put paid to the research he was doing for a film. He had nothing to do for four weeks so he threw himself into the campaign to keep Clough at Derby, a club his family had supported since the days of Steve Bloomer:

'I didn't know Brian, so I knocked on his door at Ferrers Way in Darley Abbey. He said, "Come in, sit down, what are you drinking?" We hit it off immediately, though he was a bit of a Philistine when it came to the arts. He readily admitted that he was horrified when the board accepted his resignation. It had been offered in a fit of pique and he would welcome anything I could do to rouse the people of Derby. I felt very sorry for him. He just sat there in a state of numbness not knowing what to do with himself.

'At first he believed that the tide of emotional fervour would sweep over the board and sweep him back to power. Unfortunately at that time the action group had only 750 members. They were taking the mickey out of us to begin with.'

Soon the official Protest Movement was formed after a rally at a bingo hall. It elected a steering committee and collected

£150.53½ in a bucket for the fighting fund. Bill Holmes (a Forest supporter, curiously) told the gathering that five directors could not possibly withstand the wrath of 30,000 protesters. He predicted mass transfer requests by the team. It was that silly. His boasts did not materialize, of course, but the players were in no mood to train, let alone play.

Reason flew out of the window when they met Clough at the Newton Park Hotel near Burton. Clough invited wives and children along and, as the champagne slipped down, someone made an absurd suggestion: the team should fly to Spain to avoid playing for Derby. In the near-hysteria of that autumn evening, most of the players would have agreed to anything. They talked of training on their own in a local park – in short, of boycotting the club. Both notions were eventually rejected, which is just as well. The PFA had reminded Terry Hennessey, Derby's representative on the players' body, that they would be in serious breach of contract. Hennessey turned out to be one of the less militant members of the team. As the protest developed, he was not at all certain they were doing the right thing, a view which made him unpopular with some of his colleagues. The other calming influence was Jimmy Gordon. Though he was ostensibly a 'Clough man', the coach backed Mackay and Anderson to the hilt. While talk of strikes and boycotts filled the air, Gordon called the players around him and told them, 'This is terrible. There are some young kids in this team like Steve Powell – what do you think will happen to them if you go on strike? They'll be suspended at the start of their careers. You can't do that to them.' But it was touch and go, he says.

Clough took this view: 'It was the most natural thing in the world for the players to protest and for me to meet them. We'd been so close it was incredible. We all lived in the same area. I saw them at the shops and passed them on the way to work. I was one of them. In fact, in my own mind, I played centre-forward for Derby every week! How could it be unwise to carry on seeing each other? It was a good, clean, lovable, happy story. I didn't encourage the Protest Movement – it's just that I was friendly with the people running it – and still am. I could have sat around in the area and possibly have taken the Forest job much earlier than I did, but I preferred to go to Brighton and get as far away as I could.'

As far away as he could? Clough never moved from Derby all

the time he was running Brighton. Mackay says Clough spent more time in Derby that *he* did: 'That was the trouble. I'd be heading for London or somewhere to watch players, and he'd be back in Derby meeting my team!' On the day he was to join Brighton, Clough rang Shaw from the Goldstone Ground: 'The whole of the nation's sporting press are here. Should I sign or not?' Shaw replied, 'It's your career, Brian, I can't tell you what to do.' Clough said he would sign, but would be back in Derby that very night for a protest meeting. And he was.

Shaw continues, 'He came to thank everyone who had fought for him. He got as far as saying, "Thanks for everything you're doing, and don't forget to support Roy Mc . . ." when he broke down and cried. He was so overcome he had to hand the microphone to Peter Taylor, who was much more in control. He told the gathering, "We'd better cool it."'

Taylor did not see the protest as a 'lovable, happy story'. Quite the contrary: 'I didn't share Brian's warm feelings towards the protesters. I only went to one meeting. It's not wrong to show your emotions but it depends how far you go. I'm not made that way. Brian's different. He loved getting involved. The players were thunderstruck but they got carried away with the media and the public. They were loyal to us but I wasn't sure how much I wanted their loyalty in a situation like that. I told Brian we weren't going back so we should stop misleading people. He knew it was a loser from the start. All sorts of businessmen were jumping on the bandwagon trying to promote themselves. Brian got involved with meetings after Mackay took over, which was wrong. He had to have his head for a while.'

Clough told Shaw after the meeting at which he broke down, 'This is incredible. If I can get back to Derby I will' – and that on the same day that he had taken the Brighton job! He maintained contact with Keeling, who must have been kicking himself for resigning, especially when Derby went nine games without a win under Mackay and three directors, Bradley, Innes and Rudd, were panicking. (Keeling declined the opportunity to discuss the matter in this book, saying only that leaving the Derby board was 'the best thing I ever did'.)

Clough was often back home in Derby even though he worked on the south coast. Shaw says, 'After a while he started turning up at these strange clandestine meetings I was having in the dead of night with the first-team players. We used to meet them at the

John McGuiness Health Club in London Road. One night we had the entire first team there except for Hector. The door swung open and Brian came clanking in holding a carrier bag with three bottles of brown ale and three glasses. His first words were: "Don, I'll kidnap your children and, John, I'll burn this restaurant to the ground if you damage these players' careers!" Then, one by one, he ordered the players out. He had this Svengali-like power over them. Nish was the last one out and as he dawdled Clough called to him, "David, that would have cost you £10 a few weeks ago." Then he put his bag on the table and said, "I've brought my own beer and one each for you. Now then, gentlemen, what are going to do for me?" I said, "You've just blown it. The players were all ready to come out on strike."'

Shaw and Holmes explained the problem of the PFA warning and the possible implications for the team. The trio then came up with an astonishing scheme, suggested by Clough and taken up by Shaw. Had it gone ahead Clough could have been in serious trouble with the authorities. He told the two protest leaders, 'Go to the Baseball Ground and find Tommy Mason. He's in the second team – nice lad but he'll never make it. Tell him to get the reserves out on strike, then the first team will follow.'

Shaw did the rest: 'I went to see the landlady at Tommy's digs. While we were talking, he came clattering along the street from the training ground. When he saw me he said, "Does Mr Clough want me at Brighton?" I felt rotten letting him down. I told him our plan. He was willing enough. I was being very stupid, but we felt we were so close to getting Brian back that it was worth the risk. The directors were petrified of me and avoided me whenever they could. A strike might just tip them over the edge. Tommy rushed back to the Baseball Ground to rally the reserves, but Stuart Webb got to hear about it. I was told the club was issuing writs against Brian and me. They had a change of heart, thank goodness. I regret trying to start a strike but we were a few weeks into the dispute and looking for another breakthrough. Luckily, we didn't pursue it. Brian didn't seem to realize the dangers of what he'd suggested. He thought he was omnipotent.'

That scheme having been aborted in its infancy, the Protest Movement turned its attention to the first team again. It hatched a plot with the codename 'Snowball'. Shaw and Keeling tried to explain it to Archie Gemmill and Colin Todd at a meeting in Gemmill's house. Shaw told Gemmill, 'When you hear

"Snowball", you and the rest of the team come out on strike.'

'Did the boss tell you to tell me that?' asked the player.

'No. He's the manager of Brighton. This is *me* telling you. Will you do it?'

'Only if the boss tells me to,' Gemmill replied.

At that moment, Clough turned up. Shaw reported to him that Todd and Gemmill were prepared to strike only on his (Clough's) instructions.

'Send the wee lad over,' said Clough, referring to Gemmill, before going into Keeling's flat across the road. Clough asked him: 'Would you go out on strike to get me back?'

'I would, boss.'

'Would you do it without my asking?'

Gemmill paused for a moment: 'No, I'd only strike if you told me to.'

'Brian was giving up by then,' says Shaw. 'He couldn't be seen to be inciting a mutiny.'

On the day of the meeting between Clough and Mackay at the Baseball Ground described at the start of this chapter, the Derby manager had warned the players, 'When you're disappointed in life, the only thing to do is swallow it and get on with living. If any of you don't want to support me, you can leave.' But in the evening most of the squad were at the Cloughs' house with their wives, supposedly for a party to celebrate their imminent move to Brighton. Nine of the wives, along with Barbara Clough, were planning to re-activate the Protest Movement despite the fact that Shaw had all but agreed to call off the dogs. It was at this point that John O'Hare opted out:

'Clough laid on the champagne. It was a real party atmosphere. Then he said he wanted all the wives to march down to the town hall and join in the protest meeting in a couple of days' time. They were supposed to get up on stage to show their support. Barbara was all for it, but to me it was stupid. I wasn't having my wife involved in a thing like that. It had gone too far. I made my excuses and left the house. [Clough shouted after him, 'Goodbye and shut the door when you go out!']

'The next morning, I was just about the only one in training. Dave Mackay asked me if I'd been to the meeting. He seemed pleased when I told him I'd walked out. We waited for a while, but no one else showed up from the first team, so Dave sent me home.'

It is hardly surprising that O'Hare was alone that morning. In his absence, the rest of the team had signed the following letter to Mackay:

> We the undersigned players refuse to report to Derby County Football Club until 1.00 p.m. on Saturday, 24 November, for the following reasons – (a) dissatisfaction with the present management and (b) the refusal to re-instate Brian Clough and Peter Taylor.

The letter was never sent because the gist of its contents had leaked. As discussed at Clough's 'party', however, Barbara marched the wives down to the meeting of the Protest Movement. Far from folding, the movement was given fresh impetus. Mackay, usually so imperturbable, hit the roof. If the team did not turn up until one o'clock, he would play the reserves against the unbeaten league leaders, Leeds. Before that, he called the first team into his office one by one and read the riot act to them.

Anderson says, 'Bringing the wives into it was the last straw. The gloves were off. We weren't prepared to tolerate any more. We told the players that Clough wasn't coming back so they had to decide what they wanted to do. If they wanted to leave, they could go. By their attitude and performance on the field, they were losing valuable win bonuses. It was doing them no good and Derby no good. When we tackled them individually, there wasn't a murmur of protest. We went back to the dressing room and Roy McFarland shook our hands. He said what had happened was water under the bridge. From now on the team was a hundred per cent behind us.'

Derby went on to finish third in the league that season – a tribute to Mackay's and Anderson's resilience in the face of the most profound antagonism. The following season they repeated Clough's feat of winning the championship. Longson suffered only one more major embarrassment, at the annual general meeting in December 1974. Clough's faithful lieutenant, Mike Keeling, managed to drum up more than 7000 signatures on a petition demanding Clough's return. The petition was swamped by a counter-petition bearing 22,000 names. It was a loud and unpleasant meeting, during which Longson, in a state of utter confusion, picked up the microphone and held it to his ear!

Don Shaw abandoned hope of getting Clough back to the Baseball Ground and despaired of the future: 'None of the directors could see that this plain little town in the middle of England was being broadcast worldwide because of Clough alone. He was Mr Derby and the whole town was alive because of him. He made Derby his home, fell in love with the place and people, and they kicked him out. He was a great romantic character with a magical quality given to few. In biblical times he'd have been a prophet. When he said, "Come and follow me," half the town would have been behind him. He was bombastic and cruel sometimes, but I think Archie Gemmill summed it up when he told me, "I hate the bastard, but I'd give him my last half crown!" I have found it difficult to go to the Baseball Ground knowing what the club would have been but for those short-sighted fools.'

The Protest Movement rumbled on along its ragged way for two and a half years, with Keeling refusing to give up. When the knives eventually came out for Mackay, the protesters saw their chance of ultimate victory and found a marvellous ally in George Hardy, a forty-eight-year-old scrap-metal millionaire who had ousted Longson from the chair. In February 1977, Clough and Taylor were invited back to Derby. It was an ill-conceived scheme by an ingenuous if well-meaning new chairman. Hardy admits, 'I was nowhere near ready for the job. Keen to see Derby on the right lines again, but totally inexperienced at running any football club, never mind one in the First Division.'

Hardy's avowed intent was to restore Clough to what he believed was his rightful place. Another fiasco of an AGM had given notice of what was to come. Overnight, Derby acquired more than 300 additional shareholders when Keeling split his shares into single units and sold them to the rest of the pro-Clough lobby so that they could wreak havoc at the meeting. Hordes of supporters descended from the terraces to disrupt the AGM with riotous behaviour and ridiculously impassioned speeches about Clough. It was music to the ears of Hardy. He had a vision which took the form of a newspaper headline: 'Clough returns – New chairman achieves impossible dream'. Mackay was duly sacked and Colin Murphy, the new manager, was far too inexperienced to stay in charge for long. Hardy put his master plan into operation.

On a tour to Sweden the chairman 'worked' on three directors, Innes, Arthur Atkins and Richard Moore. He knew his only hope of attracting Clough was with as near a united board as possible. In the event, he did not manage it but not for want of trying. Longson, who was still on the board, would never agree but Hardy figured that 80 per cent support ought to be enough. All four – Innes, Atkins, Moore and Hardy – agreed that an approach should be made to Clough, who was by now managing Nottingham Forest. On the plane home, Moore sat across the aisle from Hardy rubbing his hands with anticipation and professing that he 'couldn't wait to get back to Derby'. Unaccountably Moore changed his mind the same night. He phoned Hardy the next morning to break the news. The chairman, who was by far the strongest personality on the board, feared that Atkins and Innes might now have cold feet. At best it was three (Hardy, Atkins and Innes) against two (Longson and Moore). With hindsight he would have done better to abandon the whole idea. Naively, Hardy believed he could still force the issue, though he recognized that a split board was his Achilles heel. If Clough got to know (which he was bound to), there was no chance.

Hardy and Webb, Clough and Taylor met at Hardy's house, then at the Riverside hotel near Burton, having first obtained permission from Brian Appleby QC, the Forest chairman. Hardy offered Clough £17,000, the same salary he earned at Nottingham. It was not an impressive start. He added, 'It'll be adjusted in your favour once you're back.' Hardy explained afterwards, 'I couldn't see how the board could object if Clough was coming back on the same money he was already on. I was trying to make it presentable to all sides.'

Clough was not keen. He asked for an extra £5000. Then the conversation got around to cars and bonuses. Hardy's bravado was beginning to wear thin. He was in no position to agree to any of their demands. What he had underestimated was Clough's and Taylor's bargaining skills, especially Taylor's. But as the evening wore on, Clough surprisingly was warming to the idea. Taylor was even keener. At ten o'clock, the foursome shook hands on the deal and opened a bottle of champagne. The prodigal son was coming home at last. That was the very firm impression Hardy had anyway. Webb too: 'When we left it was all smiles. Taylor was clowning, pretending he had a bad leg and hinting that it had to be an automatic car this time.'

Clough, although aware of Hardy's hesitancy over the question of the united board, nevertheless promised that he would clear his desk at Nottingham the next morning and contact the chairman to arrange a pick-up time for the news conference. As they said goodnight, Clough added, 'I want to be sitting alongside you, Mr Chairman, at Anfield next week.'

Hardy, understandably, was looking forward to the news conference but he became worried when Clough failed to telephone at the appointed time. Still, Clough was known to be unpunctual. Television cameras and reporters hovered between the two cities waiting for news. Back in Nottingham, Clough was having serious doubts. His second coming would not be on a white charger with directors tossing garlands around his neck. Longson was still in the background and Webb was still in the foreground. He could not tolerate the thought of working with either again. Taylor was longing to go back. Webb had made the approach through him because of his well-publicized affection for Derby. In Taylor's words, 'I was born in Nottingham, but I've always felt more at home in Derby. I love the place, love the people and love the club. I would have gone back in a flash. If we'd stayed in the first place, Derby would have won the European Cup long before Forest did.'

It also occurred to Clough that, while Derby were a First Division outfit, that status was under threat. Would he rather be with a club which might just squeeze promotion or with one that could well go down? At any rate, after talking it over endlessly with Appleby and Taylor, he turned to his partner and said, 'Come on, Pete, let's go and face the music because we ain't going. At least I'm not going.' Taylor, disappointed but resigned, did not have the stomach for the trip to Derby. 'You'll have to face the music on your own,' he said.

Appleby comments, 'It would have been catastrophic for us to have lost him. I don't think for a minute he'd have gone anyway. He was just settling a few old scores. Brian loves it when people are so much in love with him that they fall over backwards. I don't think he has much respect for them.'

Yet Clough has always believed that Appleby wanted him to go – a belief shared by another director, Stuart Dryden, who was suspicious of the chairman's first words on arriving at the City Ground that morning: 'Has he gone?' asked Appleby.

The chairman had been defending a man on a murder charge at Nottingham Crown Court during the upheaval. The case was adjourned at midday and, as Appleby walked past the dock, the defendant tugged his robes and said, 'Don't let Brian Clough go to Derby, Mr Appleby.' Nottingham folk disliked Derby County intensely.

Fifteen miles away, nerves were jangling in the Derby boardroom and poor Murphy, the caretaker manager, was running up and down the corridors like a headless chicken. Directors gulped their gin and tonics and nervously fingered their wristwatches. Reporters had picked up a strong rumour that Clough had reneged, but still there had been nothing official. Finally, Clough phoned in mid-afternoon to say he was on his way. He brushed past cameras, dodged reporters' frantic questions and headed straight for the boardroom.

'Can I speak to the chairman in private, please?'

The directors were puzzled. Speak to Hardy alone? Why? Hadn't it all been settled? They vacated the boardroom while Hardy and Clough went in alone.

Clough told the chairman, 'I shan't be coming.'

After a brief silence, Hardy replied, 'You bastard. Get out!'

But Clough had one more surprise for him: 'If you put Longson's and Webb's heads on a plate, I'll be your manager.'

'I can't do that and you know it,' said Hardy. Clough was playing games now.

Two minutes later both men emerged white-faced. Clough told the waiting press, 'I've never been so flattered and elated as when I was approached for this job. That's why it's taken so long to say no. I wanted to come back to Derby so badly it was unbelievable but now I'm staying at Nottingham Forest and as far as I'm concerned that's where it's finishing.' On his way out, he patted Murphy on the back and said, 'Glad to see you're in the job, Colin. I wouldn't have taken it anyway.'

Derby were left with enough egg on their faces to make an omelette.

Later that evening, Hardy telephoned Clough at home, resolved to find out what on earth had happened in the missing eighteen hours: 'I felt so angry and so let down that I had to know for my own peace of mind what had gone wrong. Now the heat was off, I thought Clough might tell me.'

So anxious was Hardy to retrieve a lost cause that he offered Clough £50,000 to reconsider. Not the sort of conversation you would expect on the phone. 'Split it between you and Peter any way you wish,' said Hardy. '£30,000 for you and £20,000 for him, whatever you think best.'

Clough said he would think about it – his stock answer to an invitation he does not fancy. If he did give it any thought, he did not tell Taylor, who discovered the facts in a chance encounter with Hardy several months later.

Clough and Derby was effectively a closed chapter, although there would be one further attempt by Taylor to take his partner back to the Baseball Ground, about which more later. The Hardy episode had the hallmarks of sweet revenge. The inescapable conclusion was that Clough had made Derby dance to his tune, set them up for the kill, then slaughtered them. Taylor insists that that was not the plan: 'I know that's what everyone thinks but I for one could never do that to Derby. It wasn't revenge. It just happened that way.'

Hardy will never be persuaded of that: 'I was strung along. If he was worried about facing hostility from some of the directors, why didn't he mention it the day before and save everyone's embarrassment? Even when I called him that night, he still didn't give me a reason. I believe that deep down he wanted to come to Derby. Perhaps he was worried that he couldn't perform a second miracle. It took me a long time to get over it. I couldn't see how he could have had any animosity towards us. We were a completely different board from when he was last there. He accused me of being naive about soccer. I accept that. Brian promised he'd make a football chairman out of me when he took the job. I didn't mind that either. When you've shaken hands on a deal, you're entitled to assume there's an agreement. It was a very sad day for Derby. The club was made into a laughing stock. It taught me a valuable lesson about the game. You wouldn't get me within a hundred miles of a football club again.'

Clough comments, 'If it had been done better, I might have gone. Hardy didn't try hard enough. He had no idea. He thought he could talk down to people who were better at their jobs than he was at his, despite his Rolls-Royce and his million out of scrap. Offering me £17,000 then telling me not to be greedy? Who did he think he was kidding? In the next breath he was telling me he'd bought his eighteen-year-old son a Ferrari. I said, "Who the hell do you think you are, telling me that cock and bull story then offering me less than I was getting at Forest?" He told me it was a delicate situation and it would be hard to get me back. Bullshit! After I met the chairman I wasn't tempted for a second. You might say, why go then? You always do. You have to go to explore. I didn't enjoy the ructions because it was a different set of people. If it had been the same board I might have enjoyed it.'

If it is any consolation to Hardy, Clough has a history of allowing himself to be courted by clubs, then turning them down. The philosophy of 'you have to go to explore' has driven a few chairmen to distraction over the years. That was never more true than during his eight-month rehabilitation by the sea at Brighton, where he openly used the club as a stepping stone back to the big time. Offers came from Sunderland, Aston Villa and Teheran, among others. In each case there was the rigmarole of 'will he, won't he' as Clough basked in the publicity. Each time the answer was negative. Mike Bamber had a devil of a job getting him to Brighton at all, although he was assisted by the fact that Clough still had the threat of suspension hanging over him after his charge of bringing the game into disrepute. 'We could have been paying him for three years but losing his services after five minutes,' says the Brighton chairman.

Bamber reminded Clough of that threat when he telephoned Clough's home within days of his departure from Derby inviting the out-of-work manager to take over at Brighton. He received a dismissive reply: 'Brighton – they're Third Division, aren't they? I might consider it. If I do, I'll be in touch.' To be frank, he was not that interested in job offers. He planned to take two or three months out of the game. In any case, if he *was* starting again, there was always the possibility of Nottingham Forest on his doorstep. No house move needed; the children could stay at school, etc.

The Forest offer came unofficially from Stuart Dryden, who was later to become a good friend of Clough and go into business with him. Dryden was only a committee member at Forest when he arranged a secret night-time rendezvous with Clough and Taylor at a friend's office in the city. Dryden explained that Matt Gillies had left and that he (Dryden) thought it was time that Forest had a shake up. Would they be interested?

'Are you offering?' Clough asked.

'I'd like to but I've only been on the committee for a few weeks.'

'We're interested,' was the reply, 'but we're not applying.'

'You've got to do something to help me get you there,' said Dryden. 'What about phoning the club at 11.00 a.m. tomorrow and making a discreet inquiry about the vacancy? I'll make sure I'm there to take the call.'

It never came. In the meantime Keeling had telephoned Bamber at Hereford, where Brighton were on the verge of a 3–0 defeat. Bamber left the directors' box at half-time to take the message. He was told, 'Brian says why don't you get the team coach to come through London on the way back and he'll meet you at the Waldorf.' Bamber and the team did a twenty-mile detour. The players sat outside in the coach while the chairman had a brief chat with Clough. He was staying at the Waldorf courtesy of LWT. The meeting was inconclusive but Clough telephoned later in the week to say, 'Meet me in Derby.' Bamber and Harry Bloom, the Brighton vice-chairman, travelled up by train but were kept waiting for two hours at the Midland Hotel. Bill Wainwright, the hotel manager, who acted as a go-between/agent/bodyguard and foodtaster for Clough, kept them well supplied with sandwiches, beer and apologies. 'At last he turned up in a scruffy old tracksuit, mumbling some weak excuse,' says Bamber. 'We were furious after travelling all that way. I told him it was out of order.' Nevertheless the deal was practically signed and sealed, with Clough and Taylor offered more than they had been earning at Derby.

Behind the scenes, though, Clough was ready to do another of his disappearing tricks. It led to a flaming row with Taylor. 'We'd done a great deal,' says Taylor, 'I went to bed early that night ready for the flight from East Midlands airport the next morning. I couldn't wait to get there. Brian rang me in the early hours with Keeling by his side. He said he couldn't go through with it. I said if that was the case I was finished with him and slammed the receiver down. There was no point my going if he didn't. He'd backed out for the same reason he always backed out. He wanted all the fuss and publicity and people chasing after him but, it didn't matter which club it was, he never wanted to go *anywhere*. He changed his mind again but I was so disgusted I refused to go with him. He went to see Bamber on his own.'

The following day, 1 November 1974, Dryden was distraught as he read in his morning paper that Clough had signed for Brighton. He would have to wait another year or so before getting an unexpected second bite at the cherry.

Clough came and went as he pleased at Brighton. Preoccupied with his efforts to get back at Derby, his political campaigning, his flirtations with other clubs and even a visit to New York to watch Mohammed Ali, he was never committed to the club like Taylor was. Bamber remembers, 'He had his heart in it for a while but I knew he'd leave as soon as a big club came along. Sometimes he'd go missing from Sunday to Thursday. I didn't know where he was half the time. To be honest I didn't mind too much. Peter was always there and Brighton was on the map.'

To put it another way, Clough's sojourn by the sea was a glorified publicity stunt for the club. The crowd trebled to 16,500 for Clough's and Taylor's first match in charge, a goalless draw against York City. The *Evening Argus* photographer had to fight for space for the first time in his life. The entire British press corps, it seemed, descended on the Goldstone Ground, which is precisely what Bamber wanted. Clough was even interviewed by American television.

Bamber had Clough's measure from the first day: 'I arranged to meet him in my office after training. He sauntered in late wearing a tracksuit top and boots. As became his custom, he put his feet up on the desk, then spread his arms out and sighed, "Mr Chairman, I've shot it. I've been off for three weeks and training's whacked me." I said, "Brian, you're a bloody liar. It's been pouring with rain all morning and your boots are as clean as a whistle!" He smiled back and replied, "You've caught me out already."'

Clough took it out on an eighteen-year-old winger called Tony Towner. As Clough left the chairman's office and headed along the corridor, he saw Towner leaning against the wall. 'When the chairman and I walk through,' he stormed, 'you stand to attention or you'll be out of this club in two seconds!'

The new management team brought in new players by the truckload, but results were not impressive. In one disastrous week, Brighton lost 4–0 to Walton and Hersham in the FA Cup, and 8–2 at home to Bristol Rovers. Clough did not castigate the players. He saved that for when they won! When Ronnie Howe, an amateur, scored a hat-trick against Charlton, Bamber rushed to the dressing room to congratulate him. Hat-tricks were not commonplace at Brighton. The chairman wished he had stayed put. Clough was shouting at the team and telling Howe he would be out of the side unless he pulled his socks up. Bamber says, 'I couldn't believe my ears but later I understood. It was brilliant psychology. Brian liked me going into the dressing room. I loved watching the pair of them at work. The players were in absolute awe of him. Before a match, Brian ranted and raved, then Peter came in and quietened them down. What a double act!'

But things tailed off, in Clough's case at least. Bamber noticed that a change came over him. He became more cavalier, more and more eccentric: 'I thought it was wrong for the manager to slop around in a tracksuit all day. How could he do that and tell the players off for not wearing a tie? His behaviour with the television crews was entirely wrong as well. I permitted Brian to keep his contract with LWT but the poor cameramen were kept hanging about for hours. Even then, they could never be sure that he would turn up. Brian and I got on very well socially, but he was a different animal as soon as there were a group of people in the room. Then he became the showman. He'd have half a pint of beer in public, but as soon as we were on our own again, he couldn't wait to get at the champagne. I had a moan at him only twice. Once when he didn't level with me over the Iran national team offer – I thought it was a stunt, but he never admitted it; the other occasion was on a club tour to Majorca. Brian was sun-worshipping by the pool all day with two blokes waiting on him hand and foot. I found out they were his friends, who'd come out with us. "This is a bit off, isn't it, Brian?" I said, but he didn't seem to care.'

Further cracks were appearing in the Clough–Taylor relationship, largely because they saw very little of each other. Brighton introduced Sunday football as an experiment but Clough responded by boycotting match days. Taylor says, 'I remember sweating it out over a 1–1 draw at Cambridge on my own. Brian said that he didn't agree with Sunday football. That's how it was. I realized that he wasn't the person I thought. He was walking all over Bamber, who couldn't do a thing about it. Brian should have repaid his loyalty. The chairman had taken us on with the FA inquiry hanging over our heads. Brian shouldn't have accepted the job if he didn't want it.'

When Clough was sacked from Leeds less than two months later, Bamber toyed briefly with the idea of bringing him back to Brighton. He decided against because, by then, Clough and Taylor were not on speaking terms.

8
Politician

Yorkshiremen, as John Cleese and company reminded us in one of their immortal sketches, are very good at reaching for their working-class roots when the occasion demands. Whatever tales of deprivation others may conjure up, a Yorkshireman can usually top them. For some reason, his past is always with him.

So it is with Clough. His very name could have been hewn out of the Cleveland hills (a clough is a small wooded valley) and his voice has the cutting edge of the wind off the North Sea. If he had been born ten years earlier, when Teesside was gripped by the most fearful depression, you could have said that his socialism was forged in the fiery furnace. It fact, in the fifties, Middlesbrough was a bustling, thriving centre. Dole queues were for the indolent. For all that, it was a tough working-class culture that surrounded him. You voted Labour and supported the football team. Socialism was the dominant part of that culture and it has been a powerful force in his life. Clough has remained instinctively loyal to it, as he has to most elements that have shaped him: the family, discipline, etc. It matters not that he lives in a country mansion with a Mercedes in the drive and champagne in the fridge. He will argue that those are the fruits of his hard work; that how you think is more important than how you live. Consequently he can think like a pauper and live like a lord, protected by the 'I want everyone to have a Mercedes' philosophy. As long as Clough has anything to do with it, the green, green grass of Quarndon, his home village in Derbyshire, will never turn blue.

Clough's political conscience grew sharper as Taylor's faded. Yet it was Taylor, with his trade-unionist upbringing, who first turned the young Clough's head. Taylor had a passion for oratory. He loved to listen to people who could move the masses (as indeed Clough could). As a teenage goalkeeper at Coventry, Taylor queued at the opera house to hear Aneurin Bevan speak. Hardly the traditional night-out for a footballer! He also introduced Clough to Harold Wilson, the rising star of the Labour Party, when Clough and Taylor were at Middlesbrough. The pair went to hear him at a local working men's club one Sunday afternoon. 'I didn't have to drag Brian along,' says Taylor. 'He was as fascinated as I was.' Nearly twenty years later, Clough, in his own humble way, would help to install Wilson as prime minister at the expense of Ted Heath.

The two general elections of 1974 fell during Clough's fallow periods – the first after his resignation from Derby, and the second after his dismissal from Leeds. With little else to occupy his mind (managing Brighton seemed more like a hobby), he threw himself into the political arena with some gusto and a surprising degree of skill. He nailed his colours to the mast of Phillip Whitehead, the then Labour member for Derby North, who had become a friend during the championship days at the Baseball Ground. With Clough drumming up support around the constituency, Whitehead won the seat in the February election against all odds.

Whitehead says, 'I put a lot of that down to Brian. He had a considerable effect on the vote in an area of the country which was crucial to us. All the computers predicted failure, but we won by 1200 votes. My greatest memory of him was on polling day: a bedraggled figure looming out of the sleet and drizzle with his loudhailer telling everyone, "I'm Brian Clough and I think you should come out and vote for the Labour Party. Get down to the polling station now." He went around the estate drawing people out of their houses like the Pied Piper.'

Neither Whitehead nor the Labour agent, John Beadle, could believe their luck when Clough promised to work for them practically full-time. 'How can you do that when you're manager at Brighton?' Beadle asked. 'No problem,' came the reply. 'I only go on Fridays and I'm back on Saturday night.'

His commitment to the cause did not stop at canvassing. He was not prepared to be a tame figure paraded for propaganda purposes like a Jack Charlton or a Colin Welland. No, his heart was firmly in the local struggle. His interventions were more considered and more passionate.

Pro-Clough fervour was still running high in Derby although he had moved (nominally at least) to the south coast. He had a Messianic following in the town and the Protest Movement was still bubbling, stoked up every now and then by Clough himself. He delivered two highly charged election speeches at the Beaufort and Brakensdale schools, attracting a packed house on each occasion. His theme was 'a slice of cake for all' but, inevitably, football took precedence over politics. The questions switched from 'What about the workers?' to 'When are you coming back to Derby?' Clough told them, 'Let's get Phillip elected first, then we'll see what happens.'

Two days before the 1979 general election, Clough addressed another huge gathering at St Anne's Church hall. Nottingham Forest had just won the European Cup but Clough's heart was still with the people of Derby. With supreme effrontery (call it hypocrisy, if you like), the Forest manager parked his famous Mercedes outside the hall and harangued the audience on the evils of wealth and privilege. Whitehead remembers it well: 'In tirade and rhetoric, his speech was quite extraordinary. He launched a savage attack on Sally Oppenheim, the Conservative candidate, complaining that there was more gold on her fingers than in Fort Knox. All this while his Mercedes sat outside!'

With great dexterity, the speaker reconciled his possessions with his socialism by explaining that *he* earned his money, and paid his taxes. What he deplored were speculators and those who had fallen upon wealth through no ability or effort of their own. In that group he included football directors. 'These are the people holding the country back!' he stormed. The delivery, according to Whitehead, was 'slightly bombastic' but there was no doubting its sincerity. The ovation was deafening.

Whitehead was impressed: 'He had them rocking in the aisles one moment, crying the next. A great rabble-rouser, expressing himself in that populist way of a Joe Ashton or Dennis Skinner. He also displayed great skill when fielding questions, which is a true test of a good politician. He could think on his feet and refused to be drawn into blind alleys. I remember sitting alongside him thinking: This guy's good.'

In that 1979 campaign, the National Front had been more than usually active. One hothead suggested to Clough that they should be out 'smashing the fascists' instead of sitting in a cosy meeting. Whitehead winced inwardly. He feared it was a come-on to which the unsophisticated speaker would reply, 'Yes, let's do it.' Instead, Clough took a deep breath and answered, 'No, don't do that. Ignoring them is the thing that will hurt most.'

That considered response was a measure of how much Clough had mellowed since his early years at Derby. In those heady days he made the mistake of shooting off his mouth at the merest pretext. Gradually, he learned that the media devours you if you are always available for comment. If the content had improved, however, the delivery style had not. John Beadle and the party organizers were worried about the expletives which bounced around St Anne's hall that May evening. Beadle says, 'Every fourth word was "bloody" or something worse. I wished he'd tone it down. No wonder we couldn't get the speech on radio.'

Clough also dug into his pocket to support the cause, while displaying a certain naivety about party affairs. Shortly before Forest's magnificent semi-final victory over Cologne in the European Cup in April 1979, he took a front-page advert in the *Derby Evening Telegraph* declaring, 'Clough supports Phillip Whitehead'. Beadle had to explain the electoral laws, which prohibited anyone other than party agents spending money during the campaign. Clough got around it by making a donation of £100 to cover the cost. A week later, he persuaded Beadle to insert another advert to the same effect, though the agent was sailing close to the limit on his allowance. Again Clough made a donation. 'It was very generous of him,' says Beadle. 'There is no question that politics was an important part of his life in those days.' So important, indeed, that he incurred the wrath of the Forest chairman, Geoffrey McPherson, by planning to miss a league match in order to concentrate on the election campaign. McPherson advised him to stick to football not politics, a remark which Clough turned neatly on its head at St Anne's hall. Referring to his chairman, Clough said, 'He should stick to politics not football because what he knows about football isn't worth knowing.'

Clough had caught his first glimpse of the inside of the House of Commons at a reception held in honour of Derby County's championship success in the summer of 1972. His hosts were Whitehead and Tom Pendrey, the MP for Stalybridge, who lived in Derby and was a keen supporter. Both wanted to acknowledge the enormous psychological boost the club had given to the town after the Rolls-Royce crash in February 1972. Derby was on its knees, with 26,000 disbelieving factory workers thrown onto the scrapheap. The knock-on effects were disastrous too: small shopkeepers went out of business and the Derbyshire Building Society sagged precariously as panic-stricken investors withdrew £2 million inside a week. The Chamber of Commerce paid Clough and Taylor a handsome tribute, saying they had done more for Derby in two months than anyone else had in two years. Clough considered that to be one of the finest compliments he ever received.

He knew it was crucial to provide Derby folk with some upbeat activity to compensate for their demoralization. He was, of course, in a unique position to provide it. Only Clough could have splashed out a staggering £175,000 on Colin Todd while the supporters were staring financial ruin in the face. The timing was deliberate; the effect was galvanic.

Grandiose acts have always appealed to him. He has a knack of sensing the mood and responding in precisely the correct manner: the instincts of a politician. What a tremendous public relations exercise it was for Clough (and, by association, the Labour Party) to be seen handing out free tickets to picketing miners during the 1972 strike. It was not so good for the club. Loyal supporters who couldn't get tickets for the FA Cup tie against Wolves were less than impressed. So were some of the 'tattier' members of the board, as Whitehead describes them. Clough says he has a special affinity with the miners – 'I'm not sure how many of them see the sun when it shines' – but if you had had to choose a winner between philanthropy and political opportunism, you would have needed a photo!

His political allegiances have been notable through the years for the occasional inconsistency. He puts on a show of fierce anti-Conservatism, which borders on the vicious whenever Mrs Thatcher's name is mentioned, yet he saw nothing irregular in contributing to that well-known Tory mouthpiece the *Daily Express*. He once upbraided his mother for displaying Tory literature in her front window at Valley Road and made great play of tearing down election posters near his Derby home, yet he supported the Conservative group leader on West Hartlepool Borough Council during the local elections of 1965. Councillor John Curry just happened to be chairman of Hartlepool United Football Club and Clough needed him as an ally. Curry was surprised that an apparently staunch socialist should canvass on his behalf: 'Brian said he was bound to support me for what I'd done to help him and the club. That was his nature. He wasn't one to let politics or religion stand in the way of ambition.'

When a trade union dispute erupted on his doorstep at Nottingham, Clough could not resist getting involved. Nottingham became the focal point of the 1979 NUJ strike. The journalists' union was locked in a national pay dispute, but could not persuade staff at the *Nottingham Evening Post* to join the walkout. The stumbling block was a dictatorial managing director called Christopher Pole-Carew who threatened his journalists with the sack if they went on strike. They were in turn threatened with expulsion from the union if they did not. The crunch came when ten journalists walked out and were instantly fired. In a show of solidarity, a further eighteen joined them, including members of the sports department, who were not known for their militancy. Few had ever been seen at chapel meetings and the rest of the strikers were amazed at their support. It was said that Clough had been the catalyst, urging the sportswriters to back their union or face his wrath.

As soon as they took industrial action, Clough tried to ban the *Evening Post* from covering Forest matches, but was overruled by his directors. When the sacked journalists published the rival *Nottingham News*, he showered them with favours, allowing them to follow Forest's European Cup campaign at the club's expense and providing them with a world exclusive for the front page of their first issue - the million-pound signing of Trevor Francis. As the fledgling publication battled for advertising revenue and readership, Clough arranged for the *News* to run the first colour photographs of Francis in his Forest kit as a centre-page spread. The edition was a sell-out. According to editorial staff, the Forest manager was 'crucial' to their successful launch. He even visited the hastily acquired offices in Low Pavement to rally the troops. There are few things Clough enjoys more than a battle against injustice.

He relented when he realized that it was doing the club no good to be at loggerheads with the city's main evening newspaper. Although Pole-Carew was as entrenched as ever and the *Evening Post* had been 'blacked' by every union in the land, Clough amazingly agreed to contribute a weekly column for nothing. It went against the grain and several angry unionists wrote to tell him so.

Much ill-informed comment has been made about Clough the frustrated MP. He has, of course, done nothing to discourage it. Why should he indeed? It is good for the ego. One or two luminaries were seduced by his posturing, even Ian Wooldridge, the marvellous *Daily Mail* columnist. He was moved to write in the early seventies:

> At a guess I should say that . . . in between three and five years' time . . . after a long while sunbathing himself to boredom, he'll pop up in public life again in the far less taxing role of a Labour MP.

If Clough was ever serious about going into politics, he did not understand the most elementary requirement: being a member of the Party! He did not join the Labour Party until April 1986, an oversight which astonishes political colleagues like Tom Pendrey and would certainly have astonished the various constituency parties who were supposed to have courted him over the years. Harold Wilson moved heaven and earth to have Lord Chalfont in his cabinet within a day of the peer's joining the Party, but it's doubtful whether he could have done the same for Clough. To be nominated and accepted as a prospective candidate, you are expected to have been a paid-up member for at least twelve months. For years, Clough (and everyone else, it seems) was unaware of his ineligibility. Myth built upon myth, although it is certainly true that factions within the constituency Labour parties of Richmond, Loughborough and Stretford at one time or another deemed him a man worth pursuing. He was always ready to respond but seldom made the first move.

It was during his Middlesbrough playing days that the crew-cut centre-forward with the big mouth was first talked of as a local government candidate in one of the city wards. Nothing came of it. The most serious approach after that came from Richmond constituency Labour Party in North Yorkshire. It wanted a charismatic figure to put up for the 1964 general election. None of the trade unionists fancied the job – they gravitated towards the safe Labour seats and the marginals. Richmond was a hopeless task. It covered a sweep of rich agricultural land from Teesdale to the Lancashire border and included the wealthy market town of Richmond itself. Conservative country if ever there was any.

Richard Hoyle, a local farmer, had stood in 1951 and 1955, when the Tories beat him with 15,000 majorities. He was now president of the general management committee of the Richmond Division. He remembered Clough and his prospective father-in-law, Harry Glasgow, calling into Middlesbrough bowls club for a beer on Saturday nights. Clough had hit the headlines since then and Hoyle had an idea. At their meeting above a public house in Northallerton, the committee fully supported his suggestion to go for Clough. The player had been out of action for six months or so since his knee injury, and had hinted that he might be interested in a political career.

'I thought he'd be ideal,' says Hoyle. 'He was famous, well liked and talked a lot. Richmond was an easy nomination to get because it was such a no-hoper. It would have been a great experience for a beginner. Brian would have rubbed shoulders with the greats like Gaitskell and Wilson. We were all convinced he could make inroads into the floating vote. Because the Liberals weren't standing, we knew there'd be a few thousand who were undecided. That's where Brian could have made a big impression. We were disappointed he turned us down.'

Clough gave the offer due consideration. His footballing future looked bleak; he was almost ready to give anything a try. If it had not been for Alan Brown, his manager at Sunderland, he would have thrown his hat into the ring. He says, 'I wanted to change the world in those days but Alan made me realize that my future was in football not politics. Looking back, that was very shrewd advice.'

Next in line, so the legend goes, was Loughborough - an entirely different proposition from Richmond. In fact, it was not a proposition at all - not officially anyway. The constituency Labour Party was still smarting from defeat in the 1979 election, in which John Cronin lost his seat and the Conservatives took up residence for the first time since 1945. The Party wanted to select its candidate early to give the newly elected member, Stephen Dorrell, a run for his money. But stories that they approached Clough were well wide of the mark. His name was mentioned as a possible celebrity to open the annual Autumn Fayre, the major constituency fund-raiser. Members wanted a big name and hoped they might capitalize on Clough's known political persuasions. In the event, they dismissed the notion without approaching him, realizing that he would be otherwise engaged on a Saturday afternoon in October.

'At no stage did the Party discuss the possibility of his

candidacy,' says Mike Shuker, the secretary. Without its knowledge, a Party member from nearby Measham took it upon himself to speak to Clough. Clough thought he had been offered the candidacy; the busybody member thought Clough had agreed to be nominated and, with a little embroidery on all sides, a thoroughly fictitious report reached the newspapers and television. And an almost identical set of circumstances persuaded Clough to announce that he had been approached by the Stretford constituency Party two years later. He still believes he was. Once more, the inquiry came from an over-zealous individual within the ranks, and never carried any official backing. Clough said he would have enjoyed taking on the sitting MP, Winston Churchill, and warned that, if Churchill got any 'smugger', he would change his mind. Cloud cuckoo land. As Tom Pendrey points out, 'Brian had the mistaken belief that, because an individual person wrote to him asking if he'd like to be considered as the candidate, it constituted a firm offer. It was a little naive of him to think that. There's a hell of a process to go through first.'

The association between Clough and Pendrey goes back to 1967, when Pendrey's wife, Moira, was standing for Derby Borough Council. Alan Hinton and Alan Durban were friends of the Pendrey family and offered to canvas for her on election night. Clough forbade it. An irate Moira Pendrey challenged him: 'Why don't you let these guys put their feet where *your* mouth is?' Clough did not budge. He did not want his players mixed up in politics. A clear case of 'don't do as I do, do as I say'. The same applied some years later with Paul Hart, incidentally. Before he would sign Hart from Leeds, Clough requested that the potential new chairman of the Professional Footballers Association relinquish those duties. For a trade union supporter, it was an odd stance to take. The reason behind it was Clough's dislike for barrack-room lawyers when he was the employer. He had had enough problems with Justin Fashanu and Willie Young, who were both PFA representatives at the club. Hart, to his immense credit, refused to back down although, out of deference to Clough, he withdrew from the running for PFA chairman, that office going instead to Brian Talbot.

Pendrey has always been impressed with Clough's style away from football: 'He's done an awful lot of good behind the scenes that few people know about. At Derby he was marvellous with youngsters, especially the under-privileged. I like the way he stands up to be counted on the major issues too. His Mercedes and his £80,000-a-year contract don't bother me. He generates money for others and enjoyment for thousands.'

It was Pendrey in his capacity as chairman of the All-party Football Committee who invited Clough to be 'MP for a day' in the summer of 1980. There were hilarious scenes as packs of photographers chased him along the road to Westminster, some taking their lives into their hands as they spilled into the traffic. Clough loved every moment of it, though Taylor was less at ease. The charade continued with the biggest press conference the House had ever seen. The apocryphal story was out that Clough had been offered the candidacy at Loughborough and scores of reporters wanted to know what his decision would be.

'I'll never forget it,' Pendrey says. 'Brian sat there surrounded by pressmen and photographers with his shoes off under the table as though he was thoroughly at home in his new environment and had been doing this all his life.'

Clough told the press that he was seriously considering the offer because it was 'a great honour to be asked'. What a shock they would have had to learn that he was not even a member of the Party!

Harold Wilson was one of the 'comfortable politicians' Clough grew to dislike. He thought he'd gone soft. Michael Foot was more his type. Through Pendrey, Clough arranged a meeting with Foot at Derby's Midland Hotel. Every detail had to be right. 'Brian was thrilled to meet him,' recalls Pendrey. 'He was anxious to know Michael's favourite tipple and made sure there was a bottle of best Scotch whisky waiting for him at the hotel. We went to the Baseball Ground in the afternoon because Michael was a big soccer fan. Later Brian thanked me profusely for introducing him to "the greatest political personality" he'd ever met. He admired Michael for his oratory, his beliefs and his fiery nature.'

Foot invited Clough to speak for him at an eve-of-poll meeting at Ebbw Vale in the May 1979 general election. 'He came as a friend and ally,' says Foot. 'He has always had a strong political sense and a keen understanding of socialist principles. Right from the outset I was convinced of his sincerity. His speech at Ebbw Vale was very well received. The rank and file Labour supporter loves him. He is one of them. If people would only listen to him more carefully, they'd deal with hooliganism much better than they do. Brian knows how to spread discipline among the team and its supporters. A word from him and they behave. He has been wasted in a political sense. Sports minister might have been his métier.'

Pendrey takes a different line but believes Clough should be harnessed by a future Labour government should there be one: 'I would personally recommend that Brian be appointed chairman of a new committee to work out a code of conduct for football. We would use him to knock a few heads together and get some much needed action in that area. Nothing was done after the Chester Committee report, but I can guarantee that everyone would have to jump if a Clough Committee report came out. He would be quite dynamic in getting his views across and would break down endless barriers in sport, recreation and leisure. What's more, he would ensure that the Ministry of Sport was elevated to its rightful position instead of being the laughing stock of government. A Labour government would be ill advised not to use this willing and marvellous talent. As a Member of Parliament, I'm afraid he'd have his limitations, although he'd be a good by-election candidate. He'd be terribly frustrated in the House. I can't imagine Brian being summoned on a three-line whip on something he didn't think was important. Most of his ambitions would be thwarted by civil servants and dyed-in-the-wool colleagues not as enlightened as he is. No, he'd be a fish out of water in the Commons, but there is an important political role waiting for him.'

Would Brian Clough have made a good MP? There is no one better qualified to judge that than Phillip Whitehead. He has few misgivings about the man's qualities and the strength of his socialism, but he believes Parliament would not have suited him: 'To be caught on the treadmill of our Parliament, which works longer hours than anywhere in the world and operates insanely by most people's standards, would, quite honestly, have driven Brian mad. He is undoubtedly a political animal with a mesmerizing style who cares about ordinary people. The trouble is he cannot suffer fools. Because he has been so successful himself, he expects others to be equally so. He would find the dolts and toadies one has to put up with in the House quite unbearable. Brian would have been marvellous on the big occasions, but useless on the mundane ones. Sadly, they are the vast majority.'

It's a view endorsed by John Beadle: 'He would never have made an MP. He wasn't organized enough. His speeches are usually couched in football terminology because that's what he is, after all – a football person. He'd have been bored out of his mind on the backbenches.'

Beadle it was who tried to persuade Clough to pay his £8.60 subscription and join the Labour Party. Not once, but many times. The reply was always the same: 'I've supported them all these years, *and* given them money. What else do I have to bloody do?' What stopped him joining? Beadle: 'He won't subscribe to anything unless he can be deeply involved in it. He refuses to be a passenger along for the ride.'

Clough eventually signed on the dotted line before the Derbyshire West by-election of May 1986. Talking to Party members before a press conference to support the Labour candidate, Bill Moore, Clough said, 'I think I ought to join this time, but keep it quiet.'

Brian Howard Clough is now a member of the Duffield branch, which means that he is entitled to attend all Party meetings and have his say. Watch out Duffield! He did a small amount of canvassing for Moore, visiting workings men's clubs in Belper and Matlock and once confounding his chauffeur by ordering him to park the Mercedes outside a street-corner pub in Hurst Farm council estate, Matlock. Unannounced, Clough wandered over to a dumbfounded group of youngsters who were drinking outside and engaged them in political banter for ten minutes before jumping back into the car and racing away for a television appearance. His public role in Moore's campaign, however, was a model of brevity. At the press conference Austin Mitchell introduced Clough as the first speaker and sat back to enjoy what he thought was to be a lively tirade. Clough uttered six words: 'I'm here to support Mr Moore,' then shut up. He was noticeably quiet too during the 1987 general election although lending his moral support when requested. So has the political fire started to dim? 'No,' says Whitehead. 'Clough in his fifties is a much more substantial figure than Clough at thirty-five. I don't agree with people who believe he is winding down. I think he's awaiting a fresh challenge.'

9
Who Dares Leeds

On the face of it, the invitation to manage Leeds United was heaven-sent. Straight from the Third Division into Europe! For once in his life Clough was inheriting a smooth-running machine, not a yardful of pig iron from which he was expected to build a Rolls-Royce. Quite apart from being league champions that summer of 1974, and therefore assured of a place in Europe's premier competition, Leeds were an institution. Over the previous thirteen years, Don Revie had painstakingly reconstructed a club which, while generating more antipathy than most, seemed certain to dominate British football for a long time to come. Shankly's Liverpool was the only comparable force.

Clough should have run a mile. Those trusted antennae let him down badly. His destiny has been to inject life where all trace of it had disappeared, to rebuild after a long period of decay. Very few managers have successfully taken over a club of someone else's making, and Clough's was the most spectacular failure of all. At Leeds there were no working men's clubs to visit to drum up support; no directors to bow down before him; and, ominously, no impressionable young players to bully and cajole into his way of thinking. If he had thought about it long enough, he might have known it was the last job in the world for him.

What he had come to was a club bursting with experienced internationals. Many of them had seen more trophies and visited more foreign shores than he had. What is more, several of the senior players, such as Giles, Hunter, Bremner, Lorimer and Madeley, were only a few years younger than their thirty-nine-year-old manager. Where had he blown in from – Brighton? Who were they?

The rationale behind the appointment has to be questioned.

Manny Cussins and his ageing board displayed at best a lack of judgement, at worst a chronic lack of sensitivity. It was a folly eclipsed only by the panic-stricken decision to sack Clough a little over six weeks later.

A vampire might have taken to a clove of garlic with more relish than the Leeds players and supporters took to Clough. The feeling was mutual. He hated everything Revie stood for and did not care who knew it. In January 1973, a mere eighteen months before moving into Elland Road, Clough had five hundred guests after his blood at a sporting dinner in honour of Peter Lorimer. Having waited patiently for his turn to speak, Clough began, 'You've made me wait for ages - now you lot can wait while I go for a pee!' (Among the audience was the Labour leader, Harold Wilson.) On his return from the gents, Clough resumed, 'Despite the fact that Peter Lorimer falls over when he's not been kicked and protests when he has nothing to protest about . . .' He did not get any further. The rest of his address was drowned by raised voices and scraping chair-legs. Lorimer, having received his award and left early to prepare for a cup tie, missed those few well-chosen words. To this day he has no idea why Clough was invited to be guest speaker in the first place. Revie once said of Clough, 'If all the managers and players acted like him, knocking each other all the time, there very soon wouldn't be any game left.'

It annoyed Clough intensely that Revie's methods had proved so successful. Whatever accusations are levelled at him, Clough has the good of football at heart. He cannot stand to see the game sullied in any way. His players' disciplinary records over the years stand up to the closest scrutiny. He swears like a trooper himself but hates it when football crowds resort to foul language. Leeds, then, embodied everything he disliked in the game. He considered them a dirty side who had perfected every underhand trick - and he was not alone in that view. On his way to Billy Bremner's hearing following the Charity Shield fracas (see page 142), he told Don Shaw, who travelled with him, 'I hate managing them but what can I do? They're filthy and they cheat. They've got it off to a fine art. If the pressure's on, someone goes down in the penalty area to give them time to regroup; then one of them gets boot trouble, which is just an excuse for the trainer to pass on messages from the bench. You wouldn't believe what they're capable of. Either I'll bust them or they'll bust me.'

Shaw was on that trip because the Derby Protest Movement was still angling to have Clough restored to the Baseball Ground. He says, 'We never stopped discussing it right through the Leeds days. Brian was not only receptive, he was dead keen. At the drop of a hat he'd have walked out of Elland Road and gone back to Derby.'

Leeds's aggressive play enraged Clough after they won 3–2 at the Baseball Ground in 1973. He lambasted them in a newspaper column, virtually proposing that Hunter should be locked up. Two weeks later, Leeds went back to Derby for an FA Cup tie and beat them again. There was never any shortage of needle between the two clubs. The pitched battle between Hunter and Francis Lee a couple of years later stemmed from the same mutual dislike. Leeds thought Derby had won the championship by default in 1972. Clough and company were in Majorca fully expecting Leeds to collect two points in their final match at Molineux and complete the double.

Hunter's thoughts are revealing: 'It was easy for Derby. They were sunning themselves while we sweated blood. We were forced to play Wolves on the Monday after the Cup Final. We could only field half a team. Derby were a good side but, if we'd had a fair crack of the whip, we'd have done the double.'

Leeds had a reputation as the perennial bridesmaids of football. For all their dominance between 1965 and 1974, when Revie left, they managed only four domestic trophies: two league titles, one FA Cup and a League Cup. They were First Division runners-up no fewer than five times, beaten FA Cup finalists three times; beaten European Cup finalists twice; European Cup Winners' Cup runners-up once; and Fairs Cup runners-up twice, though they did win that competition three times. All in all, a saga of near-misses and deep frustration. The Derby championship affair was another major irritation. It certainly didn't improve relations beween Clough and Revie.

So what on earth persuaded the Leeds board that Clough was the man to take Revie's chair? This is Manny Cussins's explanation: 'We wanted a manager who was as big as the players. Someone with experience and a proven winner. It was my decision to go for him. I was impressed with the display of loyalty from the team and the fans when he walked out on Derby. It has to be a special person to inspire devotion like that. What Brian had said about Leeds wasn't a problem. If he soft-pedalled, I was certain he'd win everyone round. I liked him a lot. In fact I preferred him to Don Revie.'

Cussins was delighted to get Clough from Brighton, but mortified to lose Taylor. Indeed the deal might have collapsed but for some quick thinking by Clough. The scene was the Courtlands Hotel in Hove, where Cussins and a fellow director, Bob Roberts, had spent a couple of hours negotiating with Clough and Mike Bamber. What Clough did not know was that Taylor had agreed at a private meeting with Bamber beforehand that he would remain at Brighton. No sooner had Clough shaken hands on the move to Leeds than Taylor announced, 'I'm not going.'

Bamber recalls, 'That came as a bombshell. Clough was furious and Cussins was worried sick. Both of them had assumed Taylor was part of the deal. We adjourned for a while and headed up out of the basement meeting room to the hotel lounge. On the stairs, Cussins whispered to me that he hadn't expected any complications and didn't like what he was hearing. Clough sensed his apprehension. He realized that his dream chance could be slipping away. Suddenly he nipped past us into the waiting arms of the press and television. Before anyone else could get a word in, he announced to the whole world, "Gentlemen, I've just been appointed manager of Leeds United." It was an amazing thing to do because nothing had been finalized. Cussins found himself with a *fait accompli*.'

Taylor says the deal would have collapsed if Clough had not spiked Cussins's guns: 'When I said I wasn't going with him, Leeds were ready to call the whole thing off. Only Brian could have got away with a thing like that. Once he'd made the announcement, Cussins could hardly contradict it, could he?'

The press conference itself was interesting. The five-sided meeting had been arranged secretly at Clough's request. Yet no one except Clough was aware that the press had been gathering in the lounge while the negotiations went on below stairs!

The upshot was that Clough went to Elland Road for a salary of around £22,000 – £10,000 more than he was getting on the south coast. Cussins had offered £40,000 to be split between Clough and Taylor and it was taken as read that Clough took the larger share. As it happened, Taylor had been unimpressed both with the nature of the negotiations and the lack of perks: 'Cussins was asking us to pack in on the south coast and move up there at our own expense. That was no good to me. I said, if he wanted us that badly, there had to be more than a flat wage. His answer astonished me: "You're in Europe next season, what more do you want?" What a way to talk to people. That finished me.'

In retrospect, Taylor's decision not to enter the lions' den with Clough was a shrewd one but he insists it had nothing to do with fear. He was in his element on the coast, where the family had moved into a sea-front apartment. By contrast, Clough had kept his base in Derby and shown little inclination to move it – probably an indication of his intention to leave Brighton at the earliest opportunity. Taylor says, 'Brian was desperate to go to Leeds irrespective of the offer. He was certain that I'd follow but I didn't tell him about my private meeting with Mike Bamber nor that I'd virtually promised to stay. I was well aware that Brian was heading for big problems at Leeds, but the two of us together thrived on problems and challenges. I'm sure we could have overcome opposition from directors and players. When there are two of you, you're much stronger. Working alone, neither of us reached the same heights.'

An understatement, if ever there was one. This was the first time Clough had flown solo since he and Taylor had started out in management nine years earlier. He soon became a lonely and disillusioned figure, lost without his 'mate'.

For the moment, however, he was full of himself. He confessed that he would have loved to walk straight into the Leeds job when he walked out of the Baseball Ground. Now he had achieved his ambition, he aimed to follow Revie's achievements by winning the league championship again – 'but even better'. Clough is not known for his diplomacy and, despite his later attempts to camouflage the error, he began life as manager of Leeds in the most tactless fashion imaginable. Instead of taking charge of the players who were about to report back for pre-season training, he returned to Cala Millor in Majorca to resume the family holiday he'd interrupted.

Bamber remembers, 'Brian called in to say goodbye. Cussins sat outside in his Rolls. I wished him a safe drive north with his new chairman. "North?" he replied. "He's taking me to Heathrow. I'm going back to Majorca." I told him he was mad. He had a duty to be at pre-season training and he shouldn't mess about with a club like Leeds. Typical Clough – he wouldn't listen. I think that was one of the biggest mistakes he made, but he was too arrogant to see it.'

Clough's decision to put holiday before club caused dismay in Leeds. Allan Clarke was to become one of his few allies, but even he was disgusted: 'Cloughie was out of order. Pre-season training is a vital part of the season, especially if you've just taken over a new club. As a player, the one man I wanted to see at the training ground was the manager, not the coach. He was the one picking me. Clough should have set an example.'

Clarke's room-mate was Billy Bremner, the club captain. He was renowned for his short fuse and his loyalty to the Revie school of football – a difficult character to figure out. Peter Lorimer says, 'We were never quite sure about Billy. A very good captain but nobody knew what went on in his mind. He'd say one thing and mean another.'

If there was one person with whom Clough could not take liberties it was Bremner. The fact that his contract was up for renewal increased his insecurity, rendering him a potentially dangerous foe. When Clough sent him a telegram declaring that it was 'an honour to manage Leeds' and inviting Bremner and his wife for a few days in Majorca, it fell on deaf ears.

Did Clough really believe Bremner's loyalty could be bought so cheaply? Bremner was heard muttering in the corridors of Elland Road: 'If he's looking for a pal, he can count me out.' Contrary to popular belief, though, Bremner does not seem to have been the chief mutineer.

The new manager compounded his error by turning up two hours late for the club's pre-season get-together. It was an important event on the social calendar. Players, directors, wives and everyone connected with Leeds met in informal surroundings to cement the family atmosphere Revie had striven so hard to achieve. It was Clough's first opportunity to get to know the rest of 'the family'. His unpunctuality spoke a thousand words. His rudeness had been noted in high places, notably at the home of Sam Bolton, the vice-chairman, who was by no means convinced that Clough was the right man for the job.

Bolton was a well-respected if elderly figure in the game. He was an FA councillor and senior vice-president of the Football League. At home, a plain-speaking Yorkshireman who had made his money out of his packaging business. Before he was finished, he would have Clough all trussed up and ready for export. There's little doubt Bolton was looking for ammunition to fire at Clough. He could hardly have had a more encouraging start.

His trump card was the closeness of the players and the backroom staff. What Revie had created would not be lightly torn apart.

Eddie Gray typified Leeds. He had left Glasgow's Castlemilk council estate at fifteen and did the rest of his growing up at Elland Road: 'When I joined Leeds, it was Don's club in every way. Billy Bremner was there, so was big Jack Charlton, Norman Hunter, Paul Madeley, Paul Reaney and Terry Cooper. We'd all joined straight from school and grew up like brothers. When Don invited me down, I remember my mother saying, "Be sure to look after him." He did, as well. Looked after us like a second father. He was strict, but boys of that age needed telling how to behave. People think he was dour and methodical but he encouraged his players to play open football and enjoy a laugh. Even to this day, "the boys" send each other cards at Christmas as though we're still part of the family.'

Hunter says of Revie, 'He knew exactly what was best for his players and made a point of getting to know their families. The night before a Wembley cup final he'd say to the wives, "You've put up with us being away all season - now go and enjoy yourselves" - and pay for them to go to a West End show. It was a great club and a great atmosphere. We were a very close and happy group.' And that from a man not given to sentiment on the playing fields of England!

Revie was a daunting figure - protective towards his flock to the point of paranoia, perhaps, but it is arguable that he achieved a closer bond with his team than almost any club manager before or since, with the possible exception of Matt Busby. Lorimer remembers Revie telling him, 'If you've any problems at all, no matter how small, just knock on my door. You're all my sons.' The players felt at ease with him. Respect without fear. To Revie it was essential that players were relaxed and happy if they were to produce their best. If a member of their families went sick, a bowl of fruit would arrive on the doorstep. At the birth of a child, Revie would either turn up in person or at least make sure the flowers and the greetings card were delivered. His attention to detail was legendary.

There were plenty who believed Revie went too far down that

road – Clough, for one. He did not like mollycoddled footballers – an attitude which again brought him into conflict with Bremner, the club captain. During the 1974 Charity Shield game (Clough's first in charge) the player was sensationally sent off with Kevin Keegan. Bremner and Keegan were both fined £500 and Clough took the further step of insisting that Bremner pay out of his own pocket. 'You can't do that to me,' Bremner remonstrated. 'Don paid all our fines.' Clough replied, 'Don's not here now. You will pay the fine.'

The conversation was overheard by Jimmy Gordon. 'I'll never forget the look on Bremner's face,' he says. 'Brian had no chance after that.'

In fact Clough subsequently went out of his way to befriend Bremner, who, he believed, was a frightened man after Revie's departure. Team-mates noticed how the manager made a point of sitting next to him on the coach from Wembley, trying to bolster his morale after the sending-off, and of including Bremner in his talks during the suspension period in order that he might not feel forgotten. In addition to that, Clough asked the suspended captain to do the assistant manager's job at a reserve game Clough could not attend. Bremner would report back to him on the form of McKenzie and Joe Jordan among others. Alas, Bremner reneged, making believe he had a prior engagement. Clough says, 'I was prepared to show the white flag of truce but he shot me down while I was still fifty yards away . . . I would have liked him angel-faced and all when he was a chick just breaking the shell. Instead I found a tough cockerel.'

Jimmy Gordon had answered Clough's SOS to join him at Elland Road, telling Dave Mackay, 'Brian could be in trouble and I have to help him.' Privately he believed his old boss was on a hiding to nothing: 'He'd said so much against Leeds in the past that players like Bremner and Giles would never forgive him. I agreed with what he said. Leeds under Revie were a dirty team. They'd have kicked their own grandmother. Going there was suicidal but I had to do it.'

Every former Leeds player consulted about this turbulent period refers to Clough's initial team talk. As if he had not done enough damage already, Clough gave the self-destruct button another tweak at that first get-together. The air crackled with electricity as Clough and his team came face to face. Until that moment he had been a distant, shadowy figure prowling around the training ground; observing, speaking to no one, but unnerving everyone in that unique way of his. He had told the players he wanted to get the feel of the place before making any statements. Now he was ready: 'Gentlemen, the first thing you can do for me is throw your medals and your pots and pans in the dustbin because you've never won anything fairly. You've done it by cheating.'

Even accepting Clough's love of mischief, it was a thunderously stupid remark. He was probably right to think that he had to make an impact but he was not talking to a bunch of deadbeats at Hartlepool United.

Lorimer, like the rest, was very upset: 'That hurt. No collection of players had worked harder to create success. The physical emphasis in our game had gone. We'd matured into a very good footballing side. Clough had no right to talk to us like that. Who the hell did he think he was? We'd won more things than he ever had. When he started calling Revie names, there was real anger in the room.'

One by one the manager went through the squad. For some there was encouragement. Pointing to Allan Clarke, Clough said, 'You scored eighteen goals last season. I want nineteen this season.' Clarke was impressed. It was the positive attitude he liked.

The striker was highly amused when Clough turned his attention to Eddie Gray and barked, 'As for you, young man, if you'd been a racehorse you'd have been shot.' An unsubtle reference to Gray's interminable injury problems.

Gray, astonished, replied, 'Didn't your career end in injury?'

'Yes,' said Clough.

'Then you ought to understand how I feel.'

Johnny Giles says, 'Eddie was a superb footballer and a smashing bloke. He didn't need that and he didn't deserve it.'

In Clough's eyes, Giles epitomized Leeds United. The feud between the two men is a deep and enduring one. Clough knew that the Irish international had been Revie's choice to take over at Elland Road. This was his message to Giles: 'God gave you intelligence, skill, agility, the best passing ability in the game and a lot of qualities which have helped to make you a very wealthy young man. What God didn't give you was six studs to wrap around someone else's knee.'

'So what?' said Giles. 'If people kick me, I kick them back.'

Norman Hunter was next in the firing line. Clough is credited in some quarters with inventing the 'Norman bites yer legs' catchphrase. He told the player, 'No one in the game likes you and I know you want to be liked.'

Hunter shrugged his broad shoulders and replied, 'I don't give a damn what people think about me. I'm an established England international, why should I worry?'

So it went on, Clough shifting from one insult to another and singularly failing to make any impact except a negative one. His attempt to shock them out of their complacency misfired. Each of his barbed arrows, aimed with deadly precision, bounced off the target. Giles: 'We were supposed to doff our caps and behave like chastized schoolchildren in front of the headmaster. Who did he think he was kidding? He was talking to grown men!'

In the meantime Clough tried to do what he had done at Derby – take the administration by storm as well. He complained that the ghost of Don Revie lurked around every corner and ordered his desk to be put to the torch. It so upset Revie's secretary that she resigned, which is probably what Clough intended.

Revie's reputation as a taskmaster was exaggerated. Training at Leeds had not been as rigorous as was widely assumed. Usually the team was so busy playing matches that training was kept to a bare minimum. Giles and some of the older pros worked out their own requirements, which often consisted of nothing more taxing than a brief workout, a soap-down and a massage. Clough put the cat among the pigeons by introducing extra training sessions and toughening up the routines. Paul Reaney says, 'Revie had us running up hills forwards, Clough had us doing it backwards.' The new manager was a different animal at the training ground, where he felt a good deal more at ease. So much at ease that he enthusiastically joined in the five-a-side practices and surprised some of the players with his shooting ability. His speciality was squeezing in shots from acute angles. The players noted how much he disliked losing.

At those times an onlooker might have been deceived into thinking that everything in the garden was rosy. But these were the lighter moments, disguising the jealousies and neuroses building up on all sides. The contracts of eight senior players were up for renewal and, with Bremner suspended and Clarke and Mick Jones injured, Clough realized that his first-team squad was paper-thin. Signing new players had never been his forte. He admits that he 'cannot spot a player', but he got away with it because Taylor usually assumed that responsibility. So, when £450,000 went on two reserve players and a ball-juggler who had been staging a one-man strike at Nottingham Forest, a few eyebrows were raised.

Clough had also shortlisted a few famous names for export. He considered that Giles was finished at thirty-three; wondered how long Bremner could keep going; and resolved to sell David Harvey, the goalkeeper who had won the 'Player of the Year' award after an outstanding season. The players got wind of it on the television news, when they learned that Clough was trying to buy Peter Shilton. On top of that, Terry Cooper was set to join Nottingham Forest for £75,000 until the Leeds directors intervened. Hunter figured prominently in the clearout plans. Clough mistakenly deemed Hunter 'over the hill' and nurtured thoughts of replacing him with Colin Todd. Rumour fed upon rumour and the standing joke when the team reported for training was: 'Who's leaving today?' Clough's first acquisition was Duncan McKenzie, signed for £250,000 from Forest. McKenzie had scored 26 goals in his best ever season at the City Ground but was in dispute over wages. Clough paid him £200 a week, trebling his salary, and set out to prove that he could be more than an expensive luxury. The player was later told by Clough that he was one of the worst-paid on the books! McKenzie made his debut at Wembley, where Liverpool won the Charity Shield on penalties. It was a sign of things to come.

As results continued to go against the league champions, Clough turned again to Derby and enlisted the help of his two most faithful disciples. John McGovern was out of favour with Mackay now that Bruce Rioch had arrived at the Baseball Ground, and John O'Hare, having recovered from a long period of injury, was also surplus to requirements. Both might have been forgiven for thinking their best days were behind them. Instead, both were on their way to join the champions of England for a combined fee of £130,000. Leeds supporters were aghast. If McGovern and O'Hare were not good enough to play for Derby, what were they doing at Leeds?

McGovern has only to point to his display of medals to silence his critics, but at the time it seemed a strange deal by Clough. It was difficult to see how the addition of two reserve-team players constituted team building. The real explanation was that Clough wanted familiar faces around him in an alien environment. Now there were three more members of staff (Gordon, McGovern and O'Hare) driving up from Derby each day and another commuting from Nottingham. Clough was displaying the classic behaviour of a lonely, mistrusted man. Indeed, he was such an outcast at his own club that he took his eight-year-old son Nigel training with him during the school holidays. Bringing the kids was unheard-of at Leeds. Revie would have had a fit! While Nigel Clough was doubtless a willing companion, his father wanted him there as a comfort. Clough rarely travels alone. It was an odd state of affairs – normally it is the players who are on edge when a new manager takes over. In this case, it was the manager himself who was nervous.

One warm August night, a little over two weeks into his reign, Clough found it impossible to sleep. From his room at the Dragonara hotel in Leeds, he made a desperate attempt to save himself from the gathering tempest. He could not face the thought of being out on the streets for a second time in less than a year. He dialled a Brighton number.

Peter Taylor's telephone rang at 2.00 a.m. and was answered by his wife, Lill. She was surprised by what she heard at the other end: 'Brian was crying and in a terrible state. He said he'd give his right arm for Peter to join him. I felt really sorry for him. Peter was still asleep and Brian said not to wake him. He just blurted it all out: how the players were ganging up on him and making his life a misery. Between sobs I could hear him say he'd made a terrible mistake going to Leeds. He was convinced there was a conspiracy to get him out.'

Taylor did wake up and spoke to his old partner for fifteen minutes: 'He begged me to go back with him. Said we'd crack it together but he had no chance on his own. I must have been one of the few people who didn't realize what he'd been going through. There was no point kidding him. I didn't consider it for a second. I was committed to Mike Bamber and the Brighton board. It was Utopia down there. Brian wouldn't take no for an answer. He told me to name my own price and asked me to come up the very next day. He was bitterly upset when I turned him down.'

Duncan McKenzie was enjoying himself in the First Division. It didn't seem to matter too much that he could not quite adjust to Leeds' style of play, nor they to his. His bubbly personality soon endeared him to his new colleagues and the big increase in earnings blinded him for a while to what was going on. 'When I came down to earth again,' he says, 'it was obvious there was serious unrest. The players could not understand Clough. He didn't mention the opposition or give team talks, which was unusual in football and undreamed-of at Leeds. They were used to Revie's dossiers. The backroom staff had chapter and verse on every player that ever kicked a ball. Clough told them to forget it. He was all for a couple of pints and a bottle of wine before a game and he encouraged the players to join in. They thought he was crackers.'

McKenzie too was a victim of one of Clough's nocturnal calls. Both were staying at the Dragonara and at about one o'clock in the morning, after the team had flown back from a testimonial game for Ted Bates in Southampton, McKenzie was awoken by the phone:

'It's Cloughie here. I want you down in reception in five minutes.'

McKenzie knew better than to protest. He washed, dressed and stumbled down to the lounge. Clough ordered him to sit.

'Don't let me ever see you get off a plane in that condition again!'

'What do you mean?' asked a bewildered McKenzie.

'You were drunk.'

'But, boss, I don't drink. I only had two tonic waters.'

'Oh,' said Clough. 'Well, never mind. I've ordered a pot of tea.'

The pair sat in a near-deserted lounge sipping tea and chatting. McKenzie says:

'He just wanted someone to talk to. A good manager can't afford to have too many friends among the players, but Clough had fewer than most. He wanted me to be a spy in the camp. He'd noticed me sitting with certain players and wanted to know what we'd been discussing. He said people didn't realize the enormity of what he'd taken on. The whole team was over thirty and he had to prescribe some foul-tasting medicine. That's when he was trying to sell David Harvey and Trevor Cherry to Leicester. I told him most of the conversations were small talk. It was partly true. I couldn't tell him the whole truth.

'In fact the talk was of nothing *but* Clough. They began to think everything he did was wrong. When the manager's kids were off school, players would sometimes be told to go home for four days and report again on Friday. They weren't used to that. The rebellion mounted.

'On the way to Wembley for the Charity Shield, we stopped at a service area on the M1. We were sitting in the foyer when Clough looked through the glass doors, saw it was raining and ordered everyone out for a walk. Bremner was seething. He said, "Walk! I've never been for a walk in my life." We then had the ridiculous spectacle of the league champions of England trudging around in pouring rain on a motorway car park. Even Madeley was mumbling - and you never heard a peep out of him!'

The season opened with a 3–0 defeat at Stoke City. That was unthinkable. Leeds could stop practically any team in the world scoring against them if they wanted to. In the previous season, they had gone a record twenty games without being beaten. Ironically, the run ended at Stoke. Clough was welcomed warmly enough by the fans on his home debut, even though Leeds lost again, 2–1 to QPR. His solitary success in charge of Leeds was a 1–0 home win against Birmingham. A draw at Loftus Road and a 2–1 defeat at Manchester City further loosened Clough's hold on the job and, when they could only manage a 1–1 draw at home to Luton, the crowd booed him off the pitch. So, after six games, Leeds were in the bottom three with this record:

P.	W.	D.	L.	F.	A.	Pts.
6	1	2	2	4	8	4

Poor but not catastrophic, considering there were thirty-six games to go. No one was prepared to wait, especially at Leeds.

Clough was in a dilemma - convinced on the one hand that Revie's team had 'shot it', but forced to admit to himself that Giles, not Bremner, ran the midfield and that Hunter's influence was greater than he had imagined.

Vice-chairman Sam Bolton was growing a little exasperated. This was Leeds, after all, and only the best was good enough. Their poor form of course was illusory. Leeds' fortunes were to improve sharply under Jimmy Armfield. The team Clough had wanted to disband reached the European Cup Final that same season and were unlucky not to win it. Giles played for two more years before player-managing West Brom to promotion from

Division Two; Hunter had three years in the First Division with Bristol City after leaving Leeds; and Gray made a successful comeback.

Hunter is eager to dispel any thoughts of sabotage on the pitch during Clough's reign: 'It's nonsense to suggest we didn't play for Clough. No one held back. We had our reputations to think about and, besides, our professional pride wouldn't allow us to play below our best. I'd never experienced a run like it. We played our butts off and things just didn't go for us. I remember the Manchester City game in particular. We played some super stuff that day and still got beaten.'

McKenzie takes a different view: 'There was no malicious intent to play below their best, but some players refused to accept responsibility for our predicament. If they had acted like mature pros, we'd never have been in that mess.'

Clough had been compelled to abandon his rebuilding plans. For one thing, he wasn't there long enough to sell the players he planned to offload; for another, Leeds ran out of cash after buying McKenzie, McGovern and O'Hare. Surprising for such a wealthy club. He had to make the best of what he had, which, under the circumstances, he had no earthly hope of doing. To put it mildly, moral support was hard to come by. At a team meeting to discuss the QPR defeat McKenzie remembers how the coach, Syd Owen, who had been Revie's right-hand man, heckled Clough from the back of the room: 'Every time Clough said anything, Owen sighed, shook his head and mumbled, "What rubbish!" I heard it plainly enough so Clough must have heard too. Owen was siding with the players and undermining the manager's authority. That heightened the tension.'

McGovern and O'Hare were the centre of attention, but for the wrong reasons. O'Hare: 'They wanted to know what Clough was like at Derby. They thought he knew nothing about the game and couldn't understand how he ever won the league title. Bremner and Giles were the most inquisitive. They couldn't fathom his casual approach to the job. I told them he always did things differently, that's why he was such a good manager. They didn't seem very convinced.'

What a sea-change for McGovern. When he had left Derby, the city was still mourning Clough's sudden departure and praying for his second coming – now, at Leeds, they couldn't get rid of him soon enough! He says:

'From the moment I arrived, players were huddled in little groups discussing the manager's credentials. I sat in the team meetings thinking how ridiculous it was. I said nothing because I was still an outsider. Moving to Leeds was supposed to be the icing on the cake for me, but it finished up sackcloth and ashes. The fans hated me. I had to wear Bremner's shirt while he was suspended and they crucified me for that. Billy was their big idol and to them I represented one thing – Brian Clough. As soon as the results went badly, they got at him through me. I'd never been used to adulation even at Hartlepool but the hostility at Leeds reached Everest proportions. Brian supported me all he could, but eventually had to leave me out of the side. He called me into his office and said, "There's no way I can play you because you don't deserve to take all this. I've got to leave you out. You understand, don't you?" He was trying to protect me.

'When he spoke to us at Derby, players would stop in their tracks and listen. At Leeds they just walked away and ignored him. The respect had gone. I'd never seen Brian treated like that and I was disgusted by it. His record spoke for itself.'

The end came on Thursday, 12 September, fifty-three days after his appointment and forty-four days after taking charge. If anything, Clough's position with the directors had been even flimsier at Leeds than at Derby. Three, Sydney Simon, Bob Roberts and the chairman, Manny Cussins, were pro-Clough; two, Sam Bolton and Percy Woodward, had been anti-Clough from the outset. It was while Cussins's staunchest ally, Roberts, was on holiday in Majorca that Bolton and Woodward seized their opportunity. They phoned the chairman at home and announced they were coming to see him. The message was: 'Get rid of Clough.' Cussin says he resisted but was outvoted: 'I didn't think it was right to sack him but Leeds is a democratic institution. There was nothing I could do.'

Curious then that Cussins did not see fit to contact Bob Roberts, or at least delay any decision until his return. No one else, not even the club secretary, Keith Archer, was privy to what was going on. Meetings between directors were hurriedly and secretly arranged. No minutes were taken. If what the chairman says is right, the famous players' court at which Clough was virtually sentenced to hanging, was nothing more than a charade: a device engineered by Bolton to make it look as though the manager was a victim of player power.

At any rate, the whole squad was summoned to a meeting in the players' lounge before training. Bolton had arranged it. Cussins was alongside him. Clough stood leaning on a table nearby. He had been warned what was to come at the previous night's board meeting and knew in his heart of hearts that it was all over for him.

Bolton addressed the gathering: 'We had a board meeting last night and felt there was unrest in the camp. Can you enlighten us?'

The discussion was slow to get started. According to McGovern, Clough offered an olive branch: 'Can we start all over again and improve things?' But it was not delivered with any enthusiasm. McGovern says he thought Clough would erupt with rage at being called into what amounted to a public trial. Instead he held his peace. 'He handled the situation superbly,' says McGovern. 'He stayed completely calm. He knew things were stacked so heavily against him there was no use saying any more.'

There was a question from the floor about why the board had approached Clough in the first place, given that he and Leeds had been at loggerheads for so long. At this moment McKenzie walked into the room. He thought he was turning up to a normal training session. He was confused and not entirely certain whether he should be there. As he arrived, he heard Manny Cussins saying, 'It wasn't just me who appointed him, boys.'

Before things developed, Giles raised an objection. He didn't think it right to be discussing the manager in his presence. As he turned to ask Clough if he would mind the players talking privately to the directors, Clough was already on his way out, disgusted and sickened by it all. En route to his office he told Jimmy Gordon, 'That's it. There's no way I can continue to manage this club. I'm resigning but don't worry, I've made sure your job's safe.' Jimmy Gordon replied, 'I'm not saying without you.'

Back in the meeting, one or two players had their say. Both Giles and Hunter admitted that it was hard to work with Clough after what he had said to the players. Others queried his methods. Younger players, Joe Jordon, Gordon McQueen, Terry Yorath and Frank Gray, took no part in the discussion. Nor did Paul Reaney, apart from protesting to McGovern alongside him, 'This is all wrong.' McGovern and O'Hare were in an invidious position. Less than a year before they had been part of the mutiny which had fought to reinstate Clough at Derby. Now they were party to his execution. Neither of them spoke or was asked his opinion. McKenzie said nothing either: 'I was horrified but it was no use arguing with people who had the knives out. It would be like having a conversation with a drunk.'

No one spoke in Clough's defence. Not Clarke, not Reaney, not Terry Yorath or Trevor Cherry, not Manny Cussins. Bolton was hearing what he wanted to hear. A 'players' revolt' would suit him perfectly. One or two members of the team said that the vice-chairman seemed to be 'revelling in it'. It must have been music to his ears when the *coup de grâce* was delivered by, of all people, Paul Madeley. He was a model professional who trained hard, played hard and went home. The strong, silent member of the team, respected and liked by everyone but very much his own man. McKenzie, who roomed with him, says he never had a hair out of place, would take a shower at half-time if his knees were dirty, and kept his pyjamas on a coathanger. Madeley sat impassively until Bolton invited his comments. Without changing expression he replied, 'What the lads are trying to say, Mr Bolton, is that he's no good.'

Game, set and match. Bolton and Cussins promised to look into the matter post haste, but of course they already had.

As the players filed out, one of them was lost in his own thoughts. Allan Clarke's reticence had surprised his colleagues. It was well known that he had a soft spot for Clough and vice versa. Besides, Clarkey was usually so outspoken at team meetings. So why the uncharacteristic behaviour? Until given this opportunity to put his side of it, Clarke has studiously avoided mention of the Clough affair and its unpublicized sequel. After a thirteen-year silence, he now tells the story of his secret mission:

'Paul Madeley's remarks left a nasty taste in my mouth. I couldn't believe it of him. During the League Cup match at Huddersfield that night I was in a trance. I kept reliving that terrible meeting. It should not have taken place. I said nothing because I was so angry I might have done something I regretted. When I got home that night I couldn't rest. I had a long chat with my wife and we agreed I should take the matter further. I tried to phone Clough at his hotel just before midnight, but found he was out at Manny Cussins's flat. I left a message saying I wanted to see him at the ground next morning. It was our day off, but I went in specially. I had a perfect right to see my manager but daren't let any of the other lads know what I was doing. They'd have lynched me!

'I told Brian my thoughts about the meeting. I wished to be dissociated from it and promised him all the support he wanted. He thanked me but gave me the impression it was too late. He was seeing Manny again the following day so I told him I'd like to be there as well. Brian asked me if I was sure. I had no hesitation, although I knew I'd be taking a grave risk.

'Manny was astonished to see me, but didn't try to stop me going in. I had to keep a low profile to make sure no one else saw me. It was cloak and dagger stuff. Then I started on the chairman, pleading with him to give Clough more time. I told him it was treachery for directors to listen to players' views behind the manager's back. Didn't he realize they had axes to grind? As soon as directors do that, the manager has no chance. Manny said I should have been a lawyer not a footballer. I said I wanted to be a manager myself one day and, if a board of directors ever treated me the way they'd treated Brian, I'd tell them where they could stick their job.'

Clarke finished with this impassioned plea to Cussins: 'You've employed the best man in the business. He's only been here five minutes and you're trying to get rid of him. Back him instead and let him get on with the job.'

It did no good. Clough and Leeds parted company an hour or so later that Thursday afternoon. Coincidentally, Cussins was still a director when Clarke was appointed manager of Leeds some years later. Like Clough, Clarke believed he could sort out a difficult boardroom - and, like Clough, he failed.

Next door to where Clough and the directors were finalizing details of his compensation, Hunter was meeting his testimonial committee, as he usually did on Thursdays. On the way out, Clough put his head around the door and said, 'Make as much money as you can for him. He's been a good pro for this club.' After all the derogatory things he had said about Hunter, it left committee members speechless. Clough even tried to take Hunter to Nottingham Forest when he became manager but the deal broke down over money.

It has been widely assumed that Hunter was one of the 'gang of four' who had most to do with Clough's departure. He is at pains to dispel that rumour, although cynics would expect nothing less: 'It's rubbish to suggest there was a faction bent on destroying Clough. What motive would we have had? I don't deny that I wasn't one of his greatest fans, but if anyone was doing the ganging up it was the directors. None of us had any secret meetings with the board that I'm aware. They knew they'd dropped a clanger and used the players to get rid of him. Not one of us believed the outcome would be the sack.'

The other three players who have shouldered the blame for Clough's failure are Bremner, Madeley and Giles. Certainly they were antagonistic towards him but there is little evidence to suggest a premeditated and organized coup. Bremner seemed to calm down after his initial outbursts and, according to most of his fellow professionals, was not nearly as hostile as he was portrayed. He was given three opportunities to put his side of the story in this book but declined each time. He had more than enough on his hands trying to manage a football club – Leeds United.

Clough was well aware of Madeley's contribution to the meeting. Shortly after leaving Leeds he invited McKenzie and O'Hare for a drink in Derby. His first words to McKenzie were: 'He's a nice one, your room-mate, isn't he?' But it would be naive to suppose that a manager's fate could have hinged on one man's remark.

Giles is an interesting study. Clough has never concealed his dislike for the man. And once he has made his mind up about something or someone, dynamite won't budge him. His belief that the Irishman sabotaged his reign at Leeds stems from the knowledge that Giles was Revie's choice to take over. Clough appeared to assume from the start that Giles would be resentful of the man who took the job *he* wanted. There is some truth in that but it is worth examining the facts.

Giles never sought nor was offered the Leeds job. It's true he would have been the players' choice as well as Revie's, but he had no thoughts of retiring as a player. He read of Revie's recommendation when returning from World Cup duty that July of 1974. Revie told him the directors were in favour. Giles says events were moving too fast for him. He did not really want the extra responsibilities at thirty-three and was quite happy just to go on playing. Family and friends finally persuaded him that, if it was offered, the managership would be too good to turn down.

There was no word from the board for two reasons. First, they had fallen out with Revie over the England job. Cussins received permission from the FA for Revie to stay on for six weeks until Leeds found a replacement, but Revie cleared his desk and vanished the next day. Second, according to the chairman, they believed Giles would head back to Ireland after the collapse of his insurance business. The club had helped to bail him out. Giles in effect was turned down for a job he did not apply for. Here is his considered opinion of what went wrong under Clough:

'The man cut his own throat. He arrived with entirely the wrong attitude, immediately on the defensive, as if expecting the players to dislike him. His remedy was to be bad-mannered and there's no way we were standing for that. Where was the common courtesy? If we were told to be somewhere at ten o'clock, we were there at ten o'clock – not twenty-five past and let the buggers wait. That was his style. He tried to treat us like kids which was too silly for words. I realized it was an act he was putting on because he was insecure. His way was to knock you down. Once you submitted to his will you were okay. He was as good as gold then. The trouble was, he couldn't crush any of us. Why did he have to?

'He had a go at me after a pre-season friendly against Aston Villa. I laid on a good ball for Allan Clarke to score and Norman Hunter congratulated me. Cloughie butted in: "Never mind the pass, what about the way Clarkey stuck it in?" It was a pathetic attempt to make me look small. Clarke could have scored with his eyes shut. I knew it was a good ball anyway – I didn't need anyone to tell me. We were a team and we didn't make a fuss of any one player. It was entirely the wrong thing for Cloughie to say.

'It was obvious he wasn't the right man for us. I admire what he's done before and since Leeds, but this was the one occasion he didn't go to a run-down club. When he was dealing with internationals and model pros, he proved he had no class and no diplomacy. He had no idea how to talk to intelligent beings.

'It's no good his blaming me for getting him out. I didn't resent him nor did I envy him the job. Managing Leeds was the last thing on my mind. I could have had the job after he left but told the board I wasn't interested at any price. It's hard for people to accept this, but Cloughie did me a big favour by taking it. It gave me a chance to find out about managers and directors. He can't ever accuse me of not playing for him. I gave a hundred and ten per cent and he knows it. He didn't plan to use me, but after I came on as sub in the Villa game, I did so well he couldn't leave me out. I played right up to his last game and, although I didn't agree with his methods, I did my very best for him. If I'd been against him I wouldn't have played at all – I'd have been injured or found some other excuse. The ultimate satisfaction was playing in a winning team. I got no pleasure from seeing the club go downhill.

'The results were bad because morale was wrong. It isn't something you switch on like a tap. Cloughie's first job should have been to get the conditions right for the players. He never made me feel at home. He was only too happy when Spurs talked to me about becoming player-manager. He fixed that up himself so I knew I wasn't wanted.

'One of his major mistakes was throwing in his lot with two men at the expense of the others. He chose Clarke and Bremner, which was a gross misjudgement. Clarke was wide-eyed and impressionable. Cloughie made a terrible fuss of him and brought out all the bad points we'd spent so long getting rid of. When he first came to Leeds, Clarke thought he was the bee's knees. It was a hell of job getting him to knuckle down and realize he was just another player. Under Clough, he started strutting about the place again, believing all the flannel he was getting. The rest of the team were sick to death of it.

'Clough got it all wrong about Bremner too. He thought the way to our hearts was through Billy. Because he was captain, Clough got the idea the other players followed him. He couldn't have been more wrong. We spent much of our time trying to *avoid* Billy. He had the respect of the team as a player, but he had a terrible temper, he was a heavy smoker and he could drink!

'I'd like to make it clear to Clough that I didn't complain to the directors about him. And to suggest he was ousted by a gang of four is ridiculous. When the directors asked us what we thought, most of the team said they weren't happy. How could they be happy? Thanks to Clough the place was in turmoil. It should have been easy to take over a team at the top of the tree. Somehow he blew it.

'He calls me "shithouse" because he won't face the truth. He's got it all wrong.'

What Clough did not get wrong was his compensation. Walking out on Derby had taught him a thing or two about that. If he missed out then, he certainly made amends at Leeds. Although he had not signed his four-year contract, the club honoured it just the same. It cost them around £120,000, including the new Mercedes. Clough pocketed something in the region of £60,000 tax-free, having been guided by a financial expert introduced to him by Peter Taylor. Leeds paid off the taxman.

Clough's parting shot to Jimmy Gordon was: 'That's it. Let's pack our bags and get out. Here's the letter saying the club will pay your tax.' Gordon received £3500, enabling him to pay off his mortgage, and was also allowed to keep the club car. Clough was made for life, as he readily admits: 'Leeds provided me with the financial security to ensure that I could insist on doing the job my way.' Shades of Frank Sinatra! What he meant to say was that from now on he would be a dictator.

Getting the sack might have deflated a lesser man's ego. Not Clough's. Shortly after leaving Leeds he met his old Brighton players at the Midland Hotel in Derby, where they were preparing for a league match at Chesterfield. The team was having dinner with Taylor and Bamber when Clough walked into the restaurant in his familiar tracksuit. Manager and chairman were a little surprised to see him; the players carried on eating. Clough took offence at that, shouting, 'Hey, you lot – just because I've been sacked doesn't mean you can stop respecting me. When I walk in the door, you stand up!' They all leaped to attention.

Bamber comments, 'What an amazing character. If it had been me, I'd have been crawling under a stone.'

10
A Walk on the Water

They used to call Nottingham Forest a 'gentleman's club' because it clung to Corinthian ideals which did not put too high a premium on success. Walter Winterbottom once said it was the club everyone wanted to manage. A democratically elected committee rather than a board of directors tended to believe that winning at all costs was a heathen philosophy. Better to have taken part... and all that. At one time, they would not permit advertising on the ground, believing that it tarnished the game. Quaint, but unrealistic. In many senses it was the last place on earth you might think of looking for Brian Clough. Certain members thought it was the last place on earth to which he should be invited. They had observed the goings-on at Derby and Leeds and were appalled at the prospect each time Clough's name was mentioned. It irked them that Derby's success had eaten away at their fringe-support areas but it did not irk them sufficiently to want Clough for themselves. Brian Appleby, the chairman who eventually gave the unemployed Clough a job, was warned by his predecessor, Jim Willmer, 'We don't want success at that price. Set him on and you'll live to regret it.'

Set him on they did, at a time when Clough was considering the possibility of going into politics, or even teaching: 'My wife suggested I try for a university course and channel my energies into another line. Teaching appealed to me but I had no 'O' levels. It would have meant five or more years' study – if I could get through. I was in a very healthy financial situation but there had to be more to life than counting brass. I had to work and be involved. Football was what I did best.'

Appleby telephoned his stubborn committee colleague with the message: 'This man is coming to Forest. We are one of the most unprogressive clubs in the country. It'll be disaster otherwise.' To be fair to Allan Brown, the sitting tenant, Forest had narrowly missed promotion the season before and were denied an FA Cup semi-final place because of a crowd invasion at St James's Park, Newcastle, when they were leading 3–1 with twenty minutes left. The tie was replayed twice, Forest eventually losing 1–0. Viv Anderson, Martin O'Neill, Tony Woodcock, John Robertson and Ian Bowyer were on the books. Within three seasons they would have kicked the dust of the Second Division off their feet and be sitting astride Europe.

In the meantime, Clough and Appleby squared up to the difficult challenge ahead. The barrister and the back-street kid were poles apart in intellect and ideology. To Clough, the chairman represented the privileged classes he despised. And, to make it worse, he knew he was unlikely to win a boardroom debate against Rumpole of the Bailey! For his part, Appleby had to be careful not to damage his reputation by fraternizing too closely with ordinary football folk. He appointed Stuart Dryden, a magistrate, to be his vice-chairman, telling him, 'I'll support whatever you do but I don't want to know what goes on.' In other words, he did not want to be associated with the sordid (as he saw it) wheelings and dealings of the game. Dryden remembers, 'He saw Clough and Taylor as riff-raff. The best at their jobs, but riff-raff. He and Brian hated each other.'

Appleby choked with rage when on a European excursion Clough offered the theory that the people who ran football clubs were 'a bunch of nobodies'. Dryden was mildly irritated because Clough had made it clear that he was excluded from the generalization, which made the next committee meeting embarrassing for him. But the vice-chairman's displeasure was mild alongside Appleby's: 'The remark was very unfair and it hurt. It was quite ridiculous to say that men who were successful in their own fields were nobodies. I called Clough in and demanded an apology. He was full of remorse and said he'd erupted on the spur of the moment. The trouble was that people expected him to be controversial and he went over the top. I told him to keep a lower profile. Brian Clough is cordially disliked by most directors and he feels it necessary to launch attacks on them. He pretends to enjoy weak directors but I think he prefers people who know what they're doing and have some expertise. Otherwise he shows them contempt.' Another director, Derek

Pavis, was so incensed that he threatened to sue unless a public apology was forthcoming, which it was.

By and large, it was a more reticent Clough the players met when he took over from Allan Brown in January 1975. The resident staff would not have noticed but John McGovern, signed for a fourth and final time, was struck by the change in him: 'After the setbacks at Derby and Leeds, he had lost some of that fantastic energy. I'd known him for so long that I could see immediately that something was missing.' What was missing of course was Peter Taylor, locked in a promotion campaign at Brighton and too busy to give his old mate a second thought. Speculation had been rife that Forest would eventually re-harness the partnership, though, for the time being, both were eager to prove that they could go it alone. The Forest secretary, Ken Smales, swore that everyone had a spring in their step from the moment Clough walked through the door. Appleby says, 'It was a transfusion of life to a dying club.' Clough's first match in charge appeared to confirm that belief – Second Division Forest beat Spurs 1–0 in an FA Cup replay at White Hart Lane. It was a misleading sign. Both that and the following league seasons proved disappointing. Clough, despite his magical qualities, was not pulling up any trees, let alone strolling on the Trent. Slowly, and a trifle hesitantly, he was rummaging out the dead wood and introducing new faces – or *old* faces, to be accurate. Jimmy Gordon came back onstream almost at once. Since leaving Leeds, the ex-miner had lived on the dole for two months before finding work as a storeman at Rolls-Royce in Derby. The pay was modest, but he was reasonably happy. Then he was invited to a Christmas party at Keeling's house. Clough met him and asked if he'd like to get back into football.

Gordon recalls, 'I telephoned the next day and said yes. It was good to be back, but I wondered about the quality of the team when I joined. There were some very ordinary players. Pretty soon they were terrified of Clough. I warned them that he'd be playing hell with them if they didn't give two hundred per cent. I acted as the go-between, trying to calm some of their shattered nerves.'

With McGovern, inevitably, came O'Hare: 'I hoped it would be a matter of time before he came for me. When he did, I wasn't sure it was the right move. I took a fifty per cent drop in wages to

Above: Into the lion's den. Clough is welcomed at Elland Road for his first home match in charge of Leeds Utd

Left: Sir Harold Thompson was 'paranoid' about Clough

Above: The Clough residence at The Common, Quarndon

Right: Clough thought the world of his parents, Joe and Sally

Celebrating a new contract at Forest in June 1976. Also in the picture Ken Smales *(far left)*, Stuart Dryden *(on Clough's left)* and Chairman Brian Appleby Q.C.

Author and subject in Madrid's San Bernabeu stadium before the 1980 European Cup Final

This is what happens when you are banished from the touchline. Abused by Wimbledon fans at Plough Lane, Clough watched most of the match from the police control box

Beware – watching Nottingham Forest can damage your health! Clough, captured by ITV's Midweek Sports Special after the QPR match. He thought the FA 'dipped their bread' by fining him £500 and banning him from the touchline

play in the Second Division and had to sell my house to make ends meet. If I'd foreseen what was to come, I needn't have bothered. Cloughie was a different bloke at Forest. The arrogance had gone along with some of the confidence.'

After a season and a half, Clough was getting nowhere. His second attempt at managing on his own was less acrimonious than, but just as fruitless as, the first. The one crumb of comfort, for Clough at least, was that Taylor had missed promotion at Brighton. Clough monitored Brighton's progress carefully over that eighteen-month period. When the close season came, he made his move.

One midsummer day he telephoned Dryden: 'How do you fancy a drink at Widmerpool Cricket Club?'

'Why there?'

'I'm playing in a testimonial match.'

The pair sat outside the pavilion sipping beer as the shadows lengthened on a balmy evening, Clough in his whites, Dryden in the dark:

'Duncan McKenzie was playing in the match. I thought Brian must be trying to buy him back. Out of the blue he said, "I'm going to Cala Millor tomorrow to fetch Taylor."

'"Taylor? He's manager of Brighton, isn't he?"

'"You're not bloody worried about that, are you?"'

Three days later, Clough called from Majorca: 'I've done what I came for, but we must let things die down for a while.'

Discretion was needed because Taylor had broken faith with Mike Bamber, a man he liked and admired. A man, furthermore, who had consoled him after the disappointment of missing promotion, saying, 'Never mind, Peter. Get yourself a Rolls and a four-year contract. If that's what you call failure, I'll have more of it.' Clough had discovered that Taylor was holidaying at his apartment in Majorca and went after his man without warning.

Taylor says, 'I was surprised to see him. We arranged to meet at a café and Brian talked me into joining him. His timing was brilliant. He had read the situation perfectly. I'd shot it at Brighton, and he had a two-bob team at Nottingham. We both knew we were banging our heads against a brick wall on our own. Together we could do any job. There was no point delaying any longer.'

Back at the Goldstone Ground, Bamber smelled a rat. Taylor

had told him he would be staying in Cala Millor a week longer. Pre-season training was a mere three days away when he first made contact with his chairman.

'I hadn't heard from him all summer, which was unusual,' says Bamber. 'Normally he'd be rushing around looking for players. I knew something was afoot. Next morning he came to see me very embarrassed and said, "I'm sorry, I'm going back with Brian." It was a big shock. I hadn't expected a reunion so quickly. Within half an hour Peter had cleared his desk and gone. I felt very hurt. In fact it upset me so much that I had three days off work. When he drove away I told him, "Your mate must be the best salesman in the world!"'

Appleby, in contrast, was delighted: 'Clough was desperate for him. I told Taylor, "If you can get us into the First Division in three years, I'll be happy." He thanked me for that, saying most people wanted success overnight.'

The pair repaid Forest a thousandfold in the next three seasons, guiding the club to promotion, the league championship, the League Cup and the European Cup. There has been no more dramatic rise to the top, nor could there be. The backbone of the European Cupwinning team were the players who had been scratching around in the lower reaches of the Second Division. Players like Tony Woodcock, who had been on the point of joining Fourth Division Lincoln or Doncaster: 'We became so used to success we thought it must be like that all the time. It became a way of life for Viv Anderson and myself. Some of the older heads like Larry Lloyd told us to savour every moment because it only came once in a lifetime unless you were very lucky.'

Taylor had acted like a battery recharger on Clough, who rediscovered all his old sparkle. Clough sat his partner in the manager's chair and said, 'You're running the show, so sit there. You're at your best when you're telling me to shut up.' He sat on the carpet at Taylor's feet, pretending to lap at the fountain of knowledge. For a while at least Clough handed over the reins. 'Take your time and do what you always do,' he said to Taylor. 'Observe and replace. I shan't say much.' Clough concentrated on what he was best at. Taylor comments, 'He was brilliant at handling directors, turning on the charm and winning people round. His other strength was public speaking. I sat back and felt he was in complete control. He made me laugh and made me cry. I never tired of it.'

Taylor went through the club like a dose of salts. When he finished, nothing was in the same place. His first target was John Middleton, the goalkeeper. He says, 'They thought they had a keeper who would play for England. When I told them he couldn't keep goal, it knocked them for six.' Next to leave was Sammy Chapman: 'He'd shot it. We had to replace him fast.'

Which brings us to an overweight Scotsman who had been languishing at Forest for seven years, promising much and delivering little. Clough warned Taylor, 'Forget him, he's finished. You'll get no response.' Taylor did a double-take when he saw John Robertson. Beneath the spotty face and slap-happy attitude he detected hidden qualities. He tried the short, sharp shock: 'I told him he was a disgrace to the game. Accused him of living out of a frying pan and said he ought to take the words "professional footballer" off his passport.'

Because of his lack of pace, Robertson had only considered himself a left-side midfield player, not a winger. That's how he had played under successive managers and that is how he played under Clough and Taylor until they were on the brink of the First Division. His transition to winger came almost by chance. Clough had planned to build his team around Terry Curran, who was going through a purple patch on the right wing. When Curran was injured, O'Neill was tried on the right wing, but with orders to drop back into midfield when Forest were under attack – a role Curran could not perform. O'Neill's success there freed Robertson from the workhorse job. He proved more effective wide on the left. The management was still dubious, however, and when Curran returned from injury, O'Neill was squeezed out of the pre-season matches leading up to Forest's first season in Division One. Clough and Taylor agonized over whether they could afford to play two wingers in the higher grade of football. Very late in their preparations, O'Neill was given a further run-out on the wing in a friendly against Shepshed Charterhouse. After half an hour, Taylor pulled him off, saying, 'I've seen enough.' O'Neill kept the position; Curran, for all his explosive talent, did not play in the First Division; and Robertson the left-winger was born. He must be the only example in football of a playmaker who did not perform from midfield. Everything, but everything, was channelled through him. Take Robertson out of the Forest side and you would reduce its effectiveness by as much as 50 per cent.

'Brian and Pete saved my career,' says Robertson. 'I was wasting away at Forest. The life was nice and easy until Pete took me apart. After that, Brian helped me an awful lot by watching every aspect of my play and pulling me up on little things. He never missed a trick. Every piece of advice he gave me was spot-on, although I didn't always think so at the time. No great mystique, just good common sense. It helped that I was in awe of him, like we all were, but to say that he ruled by fear is garbage. If he had, we'd have been frightened to walk out onto the pitch. You knew you daren't take liberties but, for three or four years, I couldn't wait for Saturdays. Just to get out there was a joy. I *wanted* to play for him. Sounds soppy but it's true. We were so confident that fear never came into it.'

O'Neill was a slightly different kettle of fish. 'Squire', as they called him, because of his university background and gift of 'the gab', had a hard time under Clough and Taylor. He was aggrieved on two counts – first that the policy of giving the ball to Robertson with monotonous regularity left him starved on the other flank and, second, that he was rarely given credit for his contribution: 'I never felt I was wanted at Forest. I played my heart out for Brian and Pete, but I can only remember receiving praise three times in all those years. I believe that's where their psychology went wrong. If they'd given me more encouragement, they could have got twenty per cent more out of me. In fact I played my best football at Norwich after leaving Forest. They thought I was a smart Alec, and I think it started during a discussion Brian was having with the team before Pete arrived. He was telling us his plans for the new season when I chipped in: "Oh, does that mean we'll still be *here* next season?" Brian gave me a long, lingering look as if to say, "Maybe I've read this lad wrong. He's a bit of a clever dick." Looking back, if there was one time in my career when I wished I'd shut my big mouth, that was it. Things were never quite the same again. All I got was the lash of someone's tongue. I may not have been the greatest player in the world, but I helped to produce one – Viv Anderson. My job was to win the ball off the left-winger or the left midfield player so that Viv's spider legs could take him on the attack. Times I'd be on my back after winning the ball with Viv streaking into the distance. Brian would be bawling from the dugout, "Get up there and support him!" No peace for the wicked.'

The Irishman had a reputation as a barrack-room lawyer, which did not endear him to Clough. If ever there was an issue, O'Neill would be the one voicing the players' feelings: 'Yet, if the truth be known, I was petrified when I went in to see him. Could hardly get a word out. Not only that, I felt all my sinews tighten whenever I saw him coming over the hill to the training ground. I'd wonder: will it be my turn again? Once he got me so tangled up with my new contract that I came out thinking I'd had a £20 a week rise, only to discover on studying the details that I'd negotiated myself a cut!'

In January 1980, on the coach home from a 4–1 victory at Leeds, Taylor called O'Neill over and told him that Coventry wanted to buy him. It would be in his best interests to leave.

There followed one of the most unusual transfer deals that never was. It involved the Coventry striker, Mick Ferguson, with O'Neill the £250,000 makeweight in a £750,000 part-exchange deal. Ferguson and his wife arrived at the City Ground around midday along with manager Gordon Milne and the Coventry secretary. Having exchanged pleasantries, Clough invited Mrs Ferguson to lunch and disappeared for two hours to an Italian restaurant on Trent Bridge. The rest of the party were left kicking their heels. O'Neill made polite conversation with Milne because no one else seemed to acknowledge his presence. When Clough returned, he went into conclave with Taylor. Ferguson was called in to hear Taylor telling him he could use the day's events to extract more money out of Coventry. 'But I don't want to,' said the player. 'I want to come to Nottingham Forest.' Taylor replied, 'No you don't. Get back in there and have a word with your manager.'

O'Neill recalls, 'Pete was virtually pushing Ferguson through the door. The poor chap found himself asking Milne for a pay rise when it was the last thing on his mind. The situation dragged on into the evening, with people coming in one door and going out of another like a Brian Rix farce. At one point I was left alone with Brian and he acted as though nothing was happening. We just sat watching an old movie on his television set, Brian with his feet up on the desk reminiscing about the forties. I thought I must be dreaming. Darkness began to fall and still no one knew what the hell was going on. In the end, I went back to see Milne, told him I was sick of hanging around, and signed the transfer forms. I put my nose around Brian's door and said I was leaving and, by the way, I'd just signed for Coventry. He went mad: "You've done nothing of the sort, young man. You're going nowhere. Make sure you're on that bus in the morning." Ferguson and his party went home and the Coventry striker was left waiting for a phone call which never came. It was an incredible affair and I've still no idea what it was all about.'

Taylor, incidentally, has no clear recall of the details except to say that Ferguson was probably ruled out because of a poor medical report. The fact that such a bizarre episode should not have stuck in his mind perhaps tells us something about the way he and Clough operated. What seems remarkable, even outrageous, to most of us is a matter of course to them. There was no mystery about their job. It just came naturally. It was a three-way process: Taylor motivated Clough, who motivated the players, who won everything in sight, although that is a gross over-simplification. As in all successful partnerships, there was a degree of overlap. Clough was capable of energizing an amoeba and, almost to a man, his players will tell you that *he* was the inspirational one. Because they saw less of it, Taylor's role was harder for them to understand. Except, that is, when he assumed the spotlight, as he did on one or two notable occasions. Then, even Clough was reduced to the rank of spectator.

Such an occasion was Forest's opening league match on their return to Division One in 1977, when they faced the formidable task of overcoming Everton at Goodison Park. The side had been stiffened by the addition of Kenny Burns during the summer, otherwise it was the same team which had scraped promotion. O'Neill remembers the atmosphere before the game: 'With fifteen minutes to go to kick-off, we felt about two feet tall. We'd have settled for crossing the halfway line a couple of times! Those last few minutes were nerve-racking until Pete came into the dressing room and defused the tension with one of the most brilliant stand-up comedy acts I've ever seen. For ten minutes until the bell went for us to take the field, it was an endless stream of jokes and funny stories. If you'd paid for a cabaret you couldn't have got better. Some of us were still laughing when we went out to play.'

Everton ran them off their feet for twenty minutes before

Peter Withe scored from a corner. Thereafter it was one-way traffic, Forest surprising the nation with a comfortable 3–1 win which set the tone for the season. McKenzie was playing for Everton that day: 'We couldn't believe how good they were – and so composed for a team which had just come up.'

Humour was a key factor in the Clough–Taylor success story. It was noticeably absent before Taylor rejoined his partner at Nottingham and it is sadly missing today. The essential Clough is a serious soul. Magnetic, hypnotic even, but not a natural comedian unless fortified by alcohol. In his darker moments his severity can spread to those around him. Walk into the City Ground when the players are not there and you will be lucky to see a smiling face. Jimmy Gordon was recently asked by a director, 'Why don't you come back, Jim? No one sings around here any more.' Taylor comments:

'Fun was a vital part of our relationship. Brian had a sense of humour with me and I had no inhibitions with him. I never curbed myself in his presence, which was beautiful. When he walked into the office in the morning a bit down in the dumps, I was the one who got him laughing. Brian didn't do a lot of that. I used to have him in stitches with any old bit of nonsense. It was my job to do it because no one else could. In the end he was asking for it. He needed me to get him out of his moods. It's important for Brian to have someone like that behind him. Otherwise he doesn't function properly. Goodness knows how he manages today. I shouldn't think he knows where the next laugh's coming from.

'We could have survived together in a telephone booth as long as the common denominator was football, but for the first time in our careers, after a couple of years at Forest, we took separate offices. Life was so hectic that we both needed more space. There just happened to be an empty room next door so I took it. Lill helped me decorate and furnish it and before long it was like an apartment. Brian used to tease me no end about it, but I'll tell you something – he spent more time in there than he did in his own office. He loved sitting on the sofa with a drink in his hand while I spouted about the future. If we had something worrying us, we'd tell the switchboard to divert all calls and sit for a couple of hours talking about everything under the sun. We never approached it with straight faces. There was always a laugh and a joke to create the right atmosphere. Then, out of nowhere, the answer to the problem would arrive. Brian would say, "That's it, we've cracked it." It never failed.'

There were times when Clough could not handle Taylor's boundless enthusiasm and almost child-like optimism, which were apt to overpower. Soon after he moved to the City Ground, Taylor was up to his usual tricks - boasting and forecasting wonderful things. 'Go easy with your bloody predictions - you frighten me to death,' said Clough, who had been warned by Dave Mackay, a former Forest manager, that he would 'never achieve anything there'.

'What do you mean, frighten you to death?' Taylor asked.

'You're putting a noose around your neck telling everyone what we're going to win.'

'That's me.'

'I know, but can't you tone it down a bit? They'll crucify us if we don't succeed.'

'If I had,' says Taylor, 'I don't think either of us would have been so successful. Predicting was part of it. Infecting people with my optimism so that *they* believed they could conquer the world.'

There was no question of toning things down when both were high on adrenalin during those extraordinary after-match sessions in Taylor's office. Friends and relatives were treated to a marvellously uninhibited double-act full of improvised wit and repartee, Clough teasing his partner mercilessly about his fully furnished quarters and the sherry in the cabinet, and Taylor playing up to it. The timing of their routines was perfect: each knew instinctively when to speak and when to shut up, almost as though they had rehearsed the whole thing. The act served them well at many crucial moments. They unwrapped it at West Park Lodge the night before the 1979 League Cup final against Southampton. Forest checked in at 9.30 p.m. expecting to order their breakfasts for morning and retire early to bed. Clough and Taylor had other ideas. Clough told the team he wanted them back down in reception after they had dropped off their bags. A few quizzical looks were exchanged in the lifts. What was he up to now? Surely not a team talk at this time of night?

Larry Lloyd describes what happened: 'They ushered us into this partitioned-off lounge and a waiter came in with a dozen bottles of champagne and jugs of orange juice. Archie Gemmill was in a huff. He was a nine-o'clock-to-bed man and it was already past his bedtime. He asked Clough if he could go to his room. Clough said, "No one leaves until this lot's finished!" John O'Hare said he wasn't a champagne man – he'd prefer bitter. "Bring us twelve pints of bitter," Clough called to the waiter. There was no escape. We got stuck in while the pair of them told tales about the old days at Hartlepools. They had us in stitches. When the sandwiches arrived, most of them disappeared down Taylor's neck in one handful! That started Clough off laughing. By the end of the evening we were helpless. I went to bed at about 1.00 a.m. a bit the worse for wear – we all were. Next day we were 1–0 down to Southampton. It took us forty-five minutes to shake off the hangover, then we slaughtered them.'

Clough and Taylor repeated the dose before the second leg of the European Cup tie at Liverpool in September 1978. The team downed a few drinks at their Scarborough hotel before leaving for Anfield and put paid to a few bottles of Chablis at lunch for good measure. Having slept it off during the late afternoon, they produced one of their outstanding performances, a 1–1 draw which sent them into the next round and on their way to the trophy. No other management in the history of football would have dreamed of preparing a team in that fashion. As Lloyd says, 'When we won the title at Liverpool, Shankly toasted us in water at the celebration dinner. Yet there was Cloughie shovelling it down us! I tried it once when I was managing Wigan and it worked. Only Clough could have thought of it.' The same strategy was employed on at least two more important occasions. Immediately before the Hamburg final, Clough and Taylor took the players to Cala Millor for a week. Apart from the fitness zealots like McGovern, who ran three miles each morning, no one exercised anything more than his right arm! Anderson says, 'No one who saw us stumbling around the streets of Majorca in the early hours would ever have dreamed we were about to play the most important match in our lives!'

Clough continued the tradition after Taylor had departed. Celtic thought they had set themselves up for the knock-out blow in 1984 when they drew 0–0 at Forest in the UEFA Cup with the home leg to come. (Clough had taken one look at the icy ground and told his troops, 'A goalless draw will do us tonight.') The Scottish papers wrote Forest off for the return leg, but Clough, no doubt remembering the Cologne and East Berlin campaigns, was ultra-relaxed. When they arrived at Glasgow airport, he instructed the coach driver to drop them off at the Celtic manager, David Hay's favourite pub, where the players drank their fill in a long and carefree lunchtime session. On his way out, Clough said casually to the barman, 'Put it on David's account.' Before the poor chap could protest, the party had moved off to their hotel. Preparation for the game consisted of another drinking bout in the evening and half an hour's training on the morning of the match. Celtic were not mentioned once – not until Forest had beaten them 2–1 and defied all predictions once more.

Those little touches of genius – for that is what they were – set Clough and Taylor apart from the rest. Where they led, others followed meekly after. Taylor tells the story of how Bobby Robson, then the manager of Ipswich, telephoned to pick their brains about the value of mid-season breaks on the continent. Forest had been doing it for years. Taylor: 'I don't know why Bobby bothered to phone – the answer was as plain as the nose on his face. Bobby and the others were too trapped by convention. They didn't experiment like we did. We never had any trouble out-thinking him or anyone else. Now everyone goes for breaks in the sun.'

Getting the best out of players who had apparently come to a dead end in their careers was a particular forte of Clough and Taylor. Apart from the most obvious example of Robertson, the rehabilitation of Larry Lloyd was a major triumph. Coventry had paid just under a quarter of a million to Liverpool for the England international centre-half at the end of 1976. They were getting poor return on their investment. In Lloyd's own words he was 'giving it the big-time Charlie' at a small club, an attitude which made him unpopular with his team-mates. Add to that a back operation and it was easy to see why he played only forty games in two seasons. In short, he was a player to avoid, which is precisely why Taylor went for him. If he was certain there was talent underneath, Taylor did not mind polishing his way through several thicknesses of trouble to reach it. He could bully like a good 'un and Clough could terrify the life out of anyone. It was a useful combination when it came to the likes of Lloyd: 'I was only any good where there was a strong manager. Not many could handle a big, proud, arrogant bugger like me, but Clough did. Till I went to Forest, I thought Bill Shankly was strong! Clough *made* me change my ways. When he said, "Hey, big 'ed, cut it out," I did as I was told.'

Lloyd nearly came to blows with Taylor and Clough early in Forest's championship season. The team ended their unbeaten run at Arsenal – one of only three defeats that unforgettable season – and Taylor accused Lloyd of 'bottling it' over Arsenal's third goal, scored by Frank Stapleton. Lloyd leapt to his feet, fists clenched: 'Say that again and I'll bury you!' Clough and Taylor stood their ground and Lloyd cooled down. 'Both were shitting themselves,' he says. Clough did not much care for Lloyd, yet he recognized the immense value to the side of a big centre-half who could intimidate the opposition and allow his team mates to play. When Lloyd broke his foot, David Needham took his place, but was back on the sidelines as soon as Lloyd recovered. Clough said to Needham, 'David, you're a nice lad, a gentleman. I even *like* you and that's a bonus. I *hate* that bastard, but I always put his name ahead of yours on the teamsheet. What's the matter with you?'

Clough, by the grace of God, weathered his most serious storm with Lloyd in Athens during the first European campaign. Lloyd was the only player who reported without his club blazer. He was wearing jeans and a sweatshirt. He tells the story:

'I was astonished to see everyone in uniform. I checked with the captain, John McGovern, and he confirmed that there'd been no instruction about club blazers. The only other person casually dressed was Clough. He was in his tracksuit bottoms and that bloody green top he always wears. He went missing for ten minutes and came back in uniform. He asked me if I was getting changed, but I said I wasn't because I'd packed my blazer.

'He asked me three times, but I refused to find my case and unpack. Back at the ground on Friday morning he walked into the dressing room and flung an envelope at me. We used to call it "the red tree" because those envelopes always had the Forest emblem in the corner. Clough said not to open it then, but I did. Inside was a fine – "red trees" are always fines – a hundred pounds for breach of club discipline. I said I wasn't paying.

'Clough said, "You'll pay it."

'"Why? I haven't been in breach. We weren't told to wear blazers. I was on time. I'm not paying."'

It was the start of a long argument which continued hammer

and tong in front of the others for several minutes. Clough put his foot down: 'Every word you say now will cost you an extra £50.'

'Make it £500 'cos I've plenty to say.'

'Done.'

'Okay, but you'll never get the money.'

'Shut up, big 'ed, and, by the way, I've just dropped you for tomorrow.'

'I'll get the union on to you.'

'Get out of here. I don't want to see you again.'

With that, Lloyd left and Needham was picked for the game at Ipswich, which Forest won 1–0. Lloyd stormed into the offices on Monday to hand in his transfer request, only to find that Clough had gone to Spain for a week. In that week, tempers cooled and Lloyd withdrew his request. He paid the £100 fine and the matter was forgotten.

Thereafter, Lloyd had to keep an eye out for Clough. Jimmy Gordon would warn him at the training ground, 'Hey, better be on your best behaviour this morning. He's on the warpath, especially for you, big man.' Gordon was first into Clough's office in the mornings, partly to tell him the plans for the day, partly to assess his mood. If it was bad, he would forewarn the team. He says, 'When he had one of those moods on him, he always picked on the biggest man, not the little rabbits.'

Promotion to Division One had brought its problems for the committee. Taylor wanted three players: Burns, Gemmill and Peter Shilton. He didn't care in which order. On top of that, Clough was insisting on a new stand. Both of them loved playing to a grandstand full of people. They had achieved their ambition at Derby. Now the Forest directors were being asked to find £2.6 million to build one. Clough told Dryden, 'If I don't get it, I'll go somewhere else.' It was as simple as that.

Acquiring Burns and Gemmill was easy enough, although the directors were a little worried about Burns, the Scotsman with the fiery reputation. Once more the rather unusual choice had been Taylor's. His fascination with 'naughty boys' led him to trail the Birmingham City player at Perry Barr dog-track to spy on his alleged gambling problem. Taylor reported back that he was only a small-time merchant. He could handle that. Once under Taylor's wing, Burns became a different character. 'He was a lamb underneath,' says Taylor. 'People had completely the wrong impression of him. His wife had him under her thumb. There was never a problem.' Even so, Appleby was less than overjoyed to have a pub-brawler in the camp. When Clough and Taylor were offered the Derby job, he told them, 'Don't leave me with Burns or I'll slash my wrists!'

Gemmill was signed from Derby in exchange for Middleton and £20,000 while Clough was at a civic dinner. No sooner had the waiter brought the soup than Clough was leaping up and down answering the phone trying to secure the deal. He eventually returned to the table rubbing his hands and saying, 'Good, we've got him.' By the time he sat down to eat, the other diners were on their puddings. Clough called to the waiter, 'Hey young man, this soup's cold!'

Stuart Dryden was caught cold over the Shilton signing. Clough was driving him along the M1 to see a reserve match between Liverpool and Forest one night when the manager said, 'I've arranged for you to see the chairman of Stoke City. We're going to sign Peter Shilton.'

'What about the chairman of Nottingham Forest – don't you think he ought to know about this?' Dryden responded, but neither knew the whereabouts of Appleby so the mission continued.

Dryden had been empowered by the chairman to do as he saw fit. Nevertheless, agreeing a world-record £275,000 for a goalkeeper was rather a large decision. In those days goal scorers attracted the big fees; no one had gone overboard on a goal stopper. It was a gilt-edged investment though. Before selling Shilton to Stoke City, his home club Leicester calculated that he saved them ten points a season. If that wasn't worth a quarter of a million, what was?

'There was a hostile reception from the committee when I told then what we'd done,' says Dryden. 'Within six weeks I didn't hear a murmur of protest.'

Within six months Clough was kissing Appleby on the cheek! Forest had won the First Division championship by seven points from Liverpool. The final 0–0 draw against Birmingham meant that they had gone a record twenty-three home games without defeat. Their goals-against column showed that Shilton (and Middleton) had conceded only 24 all season.

'It was a very emotional moment when we went onto the pitch to collect the trophy,' says Appleby, 'Brian threw his arms around me and kissed me. That was the first outburst of emotion in a purely business relationship. I was very moved by it. It was the only recognition that he and I had any closeness whatever. Throughout my three years I never interfered with him. You don't with a man of that calibre. Even at my stage of life, I felt a shiver of anticipation whenever he walked into the room, and I'm not easily impressed. The place would crackle with excitement. Very few people have the ability to do that.

'My most vivid memory of him was on the coach coming back from a magnificent 4–0 win at Old Trafford in December 1977. He was singing "You've either got or you haven't got style" and it was infectious. He loved football played in that adventurous, buccaneering spirit. Archie Gemmill had shed ten years that day. Somehow Clough had breathed new life into him. It was the same with Burns, whose chairman at Birmingham, David Wiseman, had said, "Don't buy him, he's trouble"; and it was the same with Larry Lloyd, Frank Clark and John Robertson. Suddenly these people had become great players. That wasn't coincidence. That's the genius of Clough. He rekindled their pride in themselves and their thirst for the game.'

That same evening, Taylor said to his chairman, 'I hope you've enjoyed the football you've seen this season because you won't see us play like that again.' He had reasoned, rightly, that meanness and method were the keys to unlock Europe. The buccaneering spirit that Appleby spoke of gave way to stifling defence and the counter-attack. Forest were admired enormously for presuming to sit on top of Europe. For a provincial city with no football tradition, it was little short of a miracle. But the flair was missing. Yes, they were the best team in the continent for two seasons, but they did not fire the imagination like Real Madrid or Benfica or Manchester United had done. Where were the Di Stefanos and Puskases, the Eusebios, the George Bests? Forest's man of the match in Madrid in the 1980 European Cup Final was Kenny Burns, an out-and-out stopper who had reduced Kevin Keegan to anonymity. Did it have to be like that?

Taylor comments, 'Winning became the only thought. We were obsessed with defence. Looking back, I think we overdid it. We didn't score as many goals as we should have but all our triumphs were based on solid defence so there was no point changing horses. Brian and I discussed this for hours. He tended towards the more open style of play – he would, being a centre-forward. It was me, the goalkeeper, who kept reminding him of Harry Storer's words: "Build from the back." People called us "boring", but I think that was unjustified. We would never tolerate the long ball. It was all about possession and a team that doesn't give the ball away can't be boring. We liked defenders who pushed it around at the back instead of whacking balls up to the attackers. When we sprang forward, all hell was let loose. Everyone had to be involved then, fullbacks, central defenders, the lot. Once the side broke up a bit we tried to introduce more flair. That was the point of buying Francis.'

In the run-up to the 1979 European Cup final the Swedish champions, Malmo, worried them more than Hamburg did a year later, simply because they were so ordinary. 'I went to see them and couldn't believe my eyes,' says Taylor. 'I came back and told Brian, "They're such a bad side I'm worried. We daren't let the lads know. Our motivation's got to be spot-on for this one or we've had it." It turned out to be a real struggle. I'll never know why. We should have won 6–0. Brian and I went through hell on the bench. We were glad when it was over.'

The trump card had been Trevor Francis, playing his first European match and scoring the winning goal. It was a much cockier Francis who strutted around the dressing room in East Berlin the following season after Forest had gone into a three-goal lead at half-time. Dinamo Berlin had won the first leg 1–0 at Nottingham, providing ammunition for the doubters who believed that Forest were about to surrender their European crown. Two goals from Francis and a Robertson penalty on a freezing-cold night in Berlin had the team bubbling during the interval. It was Clough's turn to give the pep talk but, appreciating that talk was the last thing they needed, he opted for quite a different tack. 'Sit down and don't say a word,' he instructed them. For ten minutes you could hear a pin drop, the enforced silence broken only by Francis giggling under his breath. On another day, Clough would expel his players from the dressing room to spend half-time shivering on the centre circle. For each different set of circumstances there was an answer, and usually the right one.

Taylor was the man for gut feelings. He wandered out into the cold German air before that match to see the Berlin players warming up. He says he knew instantly that Forest were through: 'They looked like zombies – heads on their chins, terrible. I went back into the dressing room and told the team, "This is easy. They're beaten before they kick a ball."'

Similarly, before the Hamburg final, Taylor told reporters, 'We're all right here. I took one look at our players this morning and I knew they were in the mood. We'll win.' He had spent most of the coach trip telling the team that Keegan was over the hill. Clough smiled quietly. He didn't think Forest had a chance.

Sitting on the bench with Clough and Taylor for part of that evening was John O'Hare. It is a tribute to him, but more so perhaps to the management, that, at thirty-four, he could come on as substitute in a European Cup final and hold his own in midfield when he might have struggled to get into a Second Division side. The system was so efficient, the players so hyped-up, that Clough and Taylor could have played the groundsman and got away with it! That is not to compare O'Hare with a groundsman. It was his farewell appearance: 'Sitting in the dugout with Clough was an enlightening experience. His was the most acute football brain I've come across. He assessed situations when the untrained eye wouldn't even *see* a situation. I learned more about the game in ninety minutes than I would from a lifetime of reading books.' It is a fallacy, however, that Clough and O'Hare were bosom pals, despite the number of years they spent in each other's company and the readiness with which Clough turned to him when he was recruiting players. O'Hare says:

'When it came to personal matters, I got on better with Peter Taylor. I always went to him in preference to Brian with a problem. Once at Derby when I was having a tough time, Peter told me to go and find the nicest holiday I could for my wife and myself and send the bill to the club. We had a lovely time in Majorca but, when I handed in the bill, Brian went crackers and demanded to know where I'd been for the money. At Forest, likewise, Peter told me to consult a private specialist when we had a domestic illness and assured me the club would pay the bill. They did, but we kept it quiet from Brian. He could be warm at times, but Peter was warmer. Brian was a complex man. You could not get close to him, neither were you sure which was the real Clough. Towards the end of my time there, his behaviour was getting out of hand.

'Before we played Ajax in the European semi-final, we were leaving the hotel for a walk when we saw half a dozen teenage supporters waiting outside for autographs. They were minding their own business but Brian suddenly barged into them, shoving them violently out of the way. They were terrified – didn't know what had hit them. Why he did it no one knew. He could easily have caused a brawl. He was so rude to waiters and hotel staff it made us squirm. I didn't feel when I left that he was all that committed. We hardly saw him. He'd walk down to the training ground, spend ten minutes there and disappear again. In a sense, the club was being run by Jimmy Gordon. It got to the stage where everyone tried to avoid Brian. The players were frightened of him and so was the staff. It must have been awful working next to his office all day. He still had this pulling power, though. Players went to Forest because of his reputation. Once you were there, he made you feel that you owed him a debt. *He* won things for you, not you for him. That was his secret.'

There was an odd sequel to the 1980 European Cup final when Clough insisted that the team should stick together and return to their mountain retreat twenty-five miles outside Madrid rather than meet up with their wives. In view of what they had just achieved, it was a remarkable decision. For once in his life Robertson took the bull by the horns: 'I couldn't believe he was serious. All the way on the coach back to the hotel I kept complaining that it was unfair not to allow us to see the wives. He argued that we came as a team therefore we should go back as one. I said it was ridiculous. I was determined not to give in and kept up the banter until we pulled up outside the hotel. As we were getting off the coach, he said, "One more word from you, Robbo, and I'll knock your teeth out!" That was the end of the argument.'

Eight of the team broke the curfew, taking taxi rides to the hotel where their wives were staying and spending the night there. O'Neill was one of them: 'We timed it so that we arrived back at the team hotel at eight o'clock next morning. We walked into the foyer moments before Peter Taylor came down. He was always the early bird. "Hello, lads, you're early for breakfast," he said. I don't know whether he suspected or not. Pete was the sort who would have let it go. We knew we were safe because, once Clough started celebrating, there was no danger of seeing him at eight o'clock in the morning!'

Robertson had also been part of the conspiracy, although his courage failed him on another continental occasion when

Woodcock, Anderson and Birtles decided to break a curfew and slip into town for a few drinks. Anderson says, 'Robbo came as far as the foyer but no further. We tried to persaude him but he wouldn't step outside. He just clung onto the door, saying, "I daren't, I daren't."' Who says Clough does not rule by fear?

Nothing could be so strange, though, as the case of the dented cup. Clough spent a sleepless night thinking about it before phoning Dryden at eight o'clock one morning – unusually early for him. He wanted to see the chairman urgently. Dryden listened as the grizzly tale unfolded. In a moment of weakness, Clough had lent the club's seven-month-old Mercedes to a policeman friend in Derby. The said constable had driven a few of his colleagues to a police 'do' at the Ripley headquarters. Not only that – Clough had allowed them to take the European Cup as well. So far not too bad. The call to Dryden was to say that the officers had had a few drinks and the Mercedes had gone off the road, through a hedge and into a ditch: it was a write-off. And, to compound matters, the trophy, which had been in the boot, was battered and dented. 'It was a tricky one,' says Dryden, 'but we covered up well. We got the car replaced after inventing a mechanical fault and sneaked the European Cup to a silversmith's in town to have the dents knocked out. No one was any the wiser.'

Forest's failure to retain the league title was a major source of irritation to Clough, not only for the obvious reason. He was committed to paying huge bonuses for something the team had not achieved, although he only had himself to blame. In one of his more expansive moods he asked the players during the close season how many points it would take to win the championship a second time. Forest had done it with 64 in 1978, but the consensus was that 60 ought to be enough in a normal season. 'Think you can do it?' asked Clough. The players nodded and he offered them a generous incentive. For the first 53 points, they would receive the usual £25 per point bonus, but for each point beyond that it went up to £1000 per man. In the event, Forest collected the 60 points they had predicted, but Liverpool did better. Clough had to be content with the runner-up position and a £100,000 hole in the profits, with each man pocketing a £7000 windfall. Clough stormed, 'I'm paying you all this bloody money and you didn't win a thing.'

Money was frequently a bone of contention among the

players, who found Clough a hard taskmaster. On a tour to Israel, McGovern, as captain, was sent in to confront the management over the little question of spending money. Under the PFA guidelines players were entitled to £7 a day out-of-the-country allowance. Taylor answered the door.

'The lads need some spending money, Pete.'

'Spending money? No, they don't. You're all having a marvellous time seeing the world. What a great experience.'

'But it doesn't buy a round of drinks.'

Taylor relented, offering them £2 a day. Anderson was relieved and delighted when the brown envelopes came around, each containg £25 for the duration: 'I had the shock of my life when I opened mine and found £50 instead. I had Jimmy Gordon's envelope by mistake. Can you imagine a manager who thinks the coach is worth twice as much as the players?'

They should have been grateful for small mercies. On a later trip to Malaysia, Willie Young, as captain and PFA representative, had to do the bargaining. It cost him the captaincy! Young recalls, 'The allowance should have gone up to £9 a day but we were getting nothing. The boys were spending their own money. They sent me to ask Clough what was going on. He said, "Get out! We'll have no barrack-room lawyers at this club." I told him that, if we were raising money to get the club out of trouble, why didn't he just say so and I'd report that to the boys. Clough replied, "It won't worry you, son, because you're not going on the trip and you've just lost the captaincy." In the end I *did* go on the trip because it was too late to change the tickets.'

Clough had his most serious run-in with Young (not an easy customer) over a removal allowance when he signed from Arsenal. Young, who is a keen horseman, bought a riding school near Newark. Clough argued that the allowance was supposed to be for buying a house, not a business, and refused to pay. It came to a head nine months later at a Torquay hotel where the team was staying for a couple of days. Young explains:

'He'd been having a go at me after a friendly match we'd just played, and then started baiting me in the restaurant. He was at one end and me at the other. He tried to put me down so that everyone could hear. I told him I wasn't putting up with that kind of treatment. If he wanted me to play along with his way of doing things, he should pay me what I was entitled to. Later I walked into the bar and, to my horror, Clough was sitting there.

In that sarcastic way of his, he said, "Come and join us, son."

'I said, "I wouldn't drink with you if you paid me!"

'Clough: "It doesn't matter, son, because you're going home first thing in the morning."

'Young: "Tomorrow's a day off and I'm not going anywhere."

'The argument went on and on, then Clough went to bed and Ronnie Fenton started having a go at me. I told him the only way I was going on that bus was if he picked me up, threw me on and locked the doors. I said I'd kill him if he laid a finger on me. Fenton backed off. Mike Keeling came to fetch Clough the next day and *he* went home instead. I never did get my money.'

Clough's parsimony finally drove Anderson away from his home-town club. The manager spent weeks on end trying to prevent him going to Arsenal. The player comments, 'It was a wrench but what swayed me was Clough's attitude over European bonuses. We went without until we reached the UEFA semi-final when he promised to look after us. But even after full houses against Celtic and Anderlecht we didn't get a bean. That was the end for me. I wouldn't have minded so much if *he'd* taken a pay cut!'

Money seemed to pervade everything at Forest in those days. Management and players may have allowed it to distort their vision and consequently to sabotage their progress. Dryden says that before each European game he spent half an hour walking around the pitch discussing Clough and Taylor's share of the receipts: 'It wasn't common practice to reward managers that way but we were happy to do it at Forest. Peter was very open about his earnings – it was uppermost in his mind most of the time. Brian was equally fond of money but perhaps less obvious about it.' Taylor had thought it right in the early days for Clough to take the lion's share of what was due to them but, during this period at Forest, the pair of them decided that Taylor should lose his 'assistant manager' tag once and for all. From now on, they would be on identical contracts.

Directors from other clubs would scratch their heads and wonder how a little club like Nottingham Forest had managed to climb so high, build a modern stand and smash the transfer record by paying a million for Trevor Francis. 'Who's the sugar daddy?' Taylor was asked. There was none, of course. In their first year in Europe, Forest made three quarters of a million pounds and the stand, by providing extra seating at increased cost to the supporter, was generating its own revenue, even though the club would be committed to interest charges to the NatWest Bank for a few years ahead. Money came from the sale of players, too. Woodcock cost nothing and went for a small fortune, Birtles the same. Who needed a sugar daddy? The case of Francis is interesting, because the first man to cost a million did *not* actually cost a million at all. Clough and Jim Smith, the Birmingham City manager, had reached the figure of £950,000, which Smith interpreted as seven figures. He was anxious not to incur the wrath of the Birmingham fans and thought that a million pounds for their star player would soften the blow. He told his directors the deal had been done at that figure, only to find Clough stubbornly sticking to £950,000. 'Not a penny more,' said the Forest manager. Through an intermediary, Smith made frantic contact with Taylor and they agreed to split the difference. It was £975,000, with Forest giving Birmingham permission to 'call it a million'. So a myth was born, although arguing over the missing £25,000 seems fairly academic. Forest recouped their outlay with a little profit when they sold Francis to Manchester City for a *real* million pounds!

Forest's finances were a masterpiece of economic engineering which proved that you can survive at the very top without gates of 50,000. In the post-Hamburg era, however, money was on everyone's lips. According to McGovern, 'It was like a cancer spreading through the club. Instead of looking forward to the next match, people were more interested in what their cut would be. The feel of the place was never the same again. If you were sensible you handled your money well, but some frittered it away. It led to petty jealousies and arguments, the like of which I'd never noticed before. When that was allowed to happen, discipline had gone for a burton. What had been a very tight ship was springing leaks. The management must accept a lot of the blame. I've given them plenty of accolades in the past but, this time, they deserved the strongest criticism. They lost their way completely. Success vanished overnight. We went from European champions to no-hopers inside eighteen months. That was criminal.'

It came to the point where most of the team was in dispute over contracts and European bonsues. At one meeting Clough threw the contracts on the table and stormed out with his arms in the air saying, 'As far as I'm concerned, the whole lot of you can bugger off!'

Even Jimmy Gordon was not immune. Clough called the trainer into his office one day and told him, 'I've got a benefit arranged for you but half the money goes to Forest.'

Gordon says he was too stunned to speak: 'I discussed it with my wife that night and she was of the same opinion as me – that it was grossly unfair. Next morning I confronted the boss about it. I told him he was good at spending everyone's money except his own. It was the only time we had cross words in all my years at Derby or Forest. After the game (Forest *v.* Derby) the ticket-office manager gave me £4000 and said £3000 had gone towards the club. It was better than nothing, but I thought it was unforgivable of Brian considering the service I'd put in.'

To cap it all, Forest plunged back into the million-pound market they had opened up themselves, but this time with the gay abandon of a child in a sweetshop. Justin Fashanu was a hopeless misfit. It was only after paying £1 million for him that Clough and Taylor realized he could not play their style of football. 'It was bad judgement on my part,' says Taylor. 'I thought he could improve with age but I'd read him wrong. Justin didn't *want* to play football.' Ian Wallace was a good player, but even he would have to laugh at the seven-figure sum Forest invested in him. Peter Ward's transfer provoked a disagreement between Clough and Taylor, Clough believing he could be bought for less than the £500,000 or so Taylor had agreed to pay Brighton. In between, Asa Hartford had come and gone in a flash, with Taylor announcing to a bewildered press, 'We made a mistake.' He says now, 'You can call it bad management or good management, getting rid of Asa so quickly. I prefer to call it good management.'

Whatever it was, the combination of uncharacteristically imprudent forays into the transfer market and poor results convinced Clough that Taylor was losing his edge. He had begun to question his partner's judgement for the first time, although he did not admit it in the presence of others. As one director said, 'You could criticize them both, but criticize one in front of the other and the balloon went up.'

More accurately, the Forest balloon had burst – not with a loud bang, rather with a barely perceptible whine. McGovern's case illustrates the point. Clough asked him to stay on as a squad player who might play fifteen or twenty games a season; Taylor in contrast thought McGovern was finished and wanted him out.

Depending on which of them was in the office on any particular day, McGovern was in and out of the team like a yo-yo. There seemed to be two sets of players – Clough's men and Taylor's men.

McGovern comments, 'Taylor put me on the list, Clough said no, then Taylor put me on it anyway. The captain was on the transfer list and the manager didn't know. It was ludicrous. I certainly couldn't handle it. I wasn't used to indecision. Once there's a division between the guys running the show, it seeps through to the players like a dog sensing that you're afraid of him. Some days we didn't see Clough, other days we didn't see Taylor. They were drifting apart. I came home once and said to my girlfriend, "I don't want to go into training any more." For me, a fitness fanatic, that was unthinkable. I went and played squash to keep fit. The spark was missing from matches too. If I'd known then what I know now, I'd have said something. Players were getting away with murder in team meetings – any excuse to miss the next match. The magnetism and the buzz had gone.'

What hurt him most of all was that the club had erected a platform and, instead of building on it, fell off. Leeds, a comparable club in many ways, had gone on to build a dynasty from less impressive footings, as had Liverpool too. Forest's life at the top had come and gone inexcusably quickly: 'For two seasons we knocked Liverpool out of the League Cup and European Cup and the whole of Europe was frightened of us. We had the chance to keep Liverpool down and dominate British football. We proved we weren't a flash in the pan. You can't be lucky and win leagues and go forty-two league games without losing a match as we did. But we blew it because greed consumed too many people. Brian's shown that he may have rekindled the fire since but I'm bitterly disappointed that he slipped in between. There was no reason why a successful formula should have failed.'

Clough clearly gets his 'buzz' from building success from nothing. Like a number of gifted men in their chosen spheres, however, he also seems to derive a vicarious pleasure from self-destruction once a certain level has been achieved. It is as though once his masterpiece is on the canvas in front of him, he gets bored with it and wants to start again from scratch.

11
Your Country Doesn't Want You

The cruellest irony of Clough's career as a player and manager is that he was rejected by England in both roles. Cruel because he had a thoroughly legitimate claim in one and an overwhelming claim in the other; and ironic because they were two things he yearned for.

He was delighted with his interview for the England manager's job in 1977, reporting back to Taylor, 'It went absolutely brilliantly. If it's straight, we've got it.' The 'if it's straight' is rich in significance. Clough rightly suspected a conspiracy to frustrate him. On the admission of Peter Swales, a member of the FA selection committee chaired by the crusty professor Sir Harold Thompson, 'We were ninety per cent against him before he walked in. It would have been a miracle if he'd got it.'

Not only that. 'Tommy [Sir Harold] was paranoid about Clough,' says Swales. 'He didn't want to grant him an interview in the first place and promised to "sort him out" once he got him into the interview room.'

Sir Harold never got a chance. Clough outmanoeuvred him beautifully. He disarmed his hostile reception committee that bright December morning by breezing in full of confidence:

'Good morning, gentlemen,' he began. 'It's a bit early for this, isn't it?' Before anyone could reply, Clough addressed each of them in turn: 'Good morning, Sir Harold, nice to see you looking so well; good morning, Sir Matt . . .' and so on.

Swales describes his performance: 'He was magnificent. I'd been used to seeing him wearing shorts and carrying a squash racket, but he was dressed in a very smart suit and behaved impeccably. He gave by far the best interview of all the candidates – confident, full of common sense and, above all, patriotic. He came as near as dammit to winning us all round and getting the job. If Ron Greenwood hadn't been around, he'd have clinched it.'

On the sensitive issue of national team management compared to club management, Clough had a typically forthright attitude: 'Football's football. There are eleven men on the field whether it's England or Nottingham Pork Butchers, and they all want managing.' He cracked a few stern countenances with that one before bringing the interview to a close himself and departing with the words: 'You're not such a bad bunch after all.'

But the committee went for Greenwood, the establishment man, and passed up a glorious opportunity to alter the course of English football. It turned its back on the most obvious and best qualified candidate, condemning us to a decade of disappointment. Can anyone imagine Clough surrounding himself with a committee of managers like Greenwood did in Italy during the 1982 European Nations championship? At one point during training in Turin there were more managers on the pitch than players: Bill Taylor, Geoff Hurst, Bobby Robson, Don Howe, Dave Sexton and Terry Venables – not to mention Greenwood himself. They seemed to spend most of their time huddled in discussion. In his autobiography, Greenwood reveals how he asked his back-up squad to write down their choice of team for the World Cup qualifying match against Italy. The only one who declined was Clough, who had been appointed youth-team manager. He believed that Greenwood should have been capable of selecting his own team.

Would Clough have persisted with two goalkeepers, Shilton and Clemence, because he could not decide which was the better player? And can anyone imagine Clough, as Greenwood did, canvassing the team's opinion on formation and tactics? There is no *certainty* that Clough would have achieved more than Greenwood or his successor, Bobby Robson, but his credentials left both in the shade. Clough, for all his faults, was a winner. He had won the league title with one unfashionable club and was about to guide another, Nottingham Forest, to the pinnacle of Europe.

Greenwood was well respected for turning out attractive footballing sides at West Ham, but he had never won a championship, despite the presence of Bobby Moore, Martin

Peters and Geoff Hurst. By the time the Hammers won the FA Cup in 1975 and the European Cup Winners' Cup the following season, Greenwood had relinquished control of team affairs and moved upstairs to be general manager. To all intents and purposes, the man entrusted with the job of taking England into the European Nations championships, and subsequently the World Cup Finals in Spain in 1982, had *retired*.

He had been out of the mainstream for more than three years and was given to melancholy walks along Brighton beach. In his book he says he was depressed and 'disenchanted with football'. Sir Harold disturbed his introversion. England had been left in the lurch by Revie's speedy exodus and the president of the FA sent an SOS to Greenwood:

> We need a firm, stable hand immediately. Everyone's being roasted including myself and the rest of the international committee. We don't like it. See what you can do.

In fairness to Greenwood, who is one of the game's gentlemen, he did a reasonable job during his three-match probation period. England drew a friendly against Switzerland at Wembley and beat Luxembourg and Italy 2–0 in the World Cup qualifying matches. More goals against the impoverished Luxembourg team might have squeezed England into the finals in Argentina, but the damage had already been done under Revie.

Greenwood had rediscovered his enthusiasm for the game. The FA were unanimous that he should continue the work he'd started. They were an elderly body of establishment figures disinclined to go catching tigers by the tail. Interviewing the other candidates – Clough, Lawrie McMenemy, Bobby Robson and Allen Wade – was a formality, not to say a waste of time. The sitting tenant was always going to be favourite, even at the age of fifty-four. Indeed, but for Sir Matt Busby's intervention, Clough would not even have been invited for the interview. Sir Matt appreciated the public relations value of being seen to interview the people's choice.

Clough was discarded because they were terrified of him. There would have been more chance of getting Ken Livingstone into the House of Lords. The FA saw themselves as upholders of Her Majesty's government's reputation overseas and could not possibly risk an outburst by Clough in any delicate international scenario. Why, the bounder might just as likely tell some official from the German Democratic Republic that their country was run by nobodies – then the cell doors would clank behind the whole team, old boy.

Dick Wragg, a public school colleague of Sir Harold, claims to be a good friend of Clough, but even he could not lend his support: 'It wasn't just a football job. It was a question of international diplomacy. We needed someone to restore the good name of the FA. Clough wasn't that man. He never was nor ever will be a diplomat. He was too abrasive for his own good.'

That much is possibly true, but had not Wragg, the vice-chairman of the selection committee, and the rest of his colleagues got their priorities around their necks? Was it not more important to restore the good name of English *football*? The finest ambassador would have been the man who produced the most successful side. What use is a diplomat who achieves nothing? For years before Clough arrived at the City Ground, Forest had a series of charming, non-controversial managers who got nowhere. Victorious opponents laughed all the way home. Is it any wonder that England became a second-rate soccer nation when this, in Wragg's words, was the prevailing philosophy: 'Winning is not the be-all and end-all. We had to have dignity as well. We had to feel that we could travel across Europe and look people in the eye again. Ron Greenwood did exactly the job that was asked of him. It hurts me that we haven't won anything since 1966, but how many countries win things? We haven't had enough world-class players. I look back and ask myself if there's anything I or the FA could have done and the answer is no. You cannot blame us.'

It might be a little easier to swallow if England had failed heroically. In Italy in 1980 they were negative, timid, hidebound by theory, and awash with indecision. Defeat against Norway and Switzerland in 1981 threatened to eliminate the team from a second successive World Cup finals, although Keegan and Brooking inspired a famous victory in Budapest to save England's skins. Once in Spain, it was the same old story: apart from victory over France in the first match, abject failure. Mexico 1986 failed to provide much relief, victories over Paraguay and Poland flattering to deceive, although it took Maradona's hand to eliminate the side.

One of the first to congratulate Greenwood on his temporary appointment was Clough. He telephoned with this message: 'If there's anything I can do to help, even carrying the kit, you only have to say.' That gave Greenwood an idea. He suggested to the FA that Clough would be a better man to have inside the camp than out. It would keep him quiet and douse public indignation. 'I decided to take him at his word,' says Greenwood, 'and asked him to run the youth team. I went to Nottingham to discuss it with him and he seemed delighted. He asked that Peter Taylor be allowed to work with him. I had great hopes of them. It was not a soft option.'

Despite his reasoning, it must have been obvious to a blind man that Clough had been fobbed off. Taylor explains how the offer placed them in a quandary: 'The job didn't excite us but to have refused there and then would have looked bad. It might have ruined any future chances. Ron was genuine enough about it, but what an insult by the FA! While a man with few trophies behind him was running the national side, the most successful partnership in English soccer was asked to look after the kids. It was a joke. Brian had it written into his contract that he could leave Forest at any time to take the England job. If they'd had the courage to give it to him, we would have set out our stall to win something, not to massage the egos of FA councillors who knew nothing about the game. Success would have kept them quiet.'

Clough and Taylor seem to have tackled the youth job in the spirit with which it was offered. They viewed it as a diversion. Taylor's account of that period is revealing: 'When we heard there was an international youth tournament in the Canary Islands, we suddenly fancied the job. Four days in Las Palmas sounded too good to miss. We had a day off after the final and I managed to wake Brian at about 8.30 in the morning. That wasn't easy. He's such a heavy sleeper. I'd ordered a taxi and told him we were going to get a November suntan. We missed breakfast and fell asleep on a deserted beach. When we woke up we were surrounded by nudists. We thought we were still dreaming! Brian persuaded me to stay all day. That was the highlight of managing the youth team.'

The feeling was mutual. Several councillors had already complained that Clough and Taylor were not taking the job seriously. The pair were conspicuous by their absence most of the time. A fortnight after their appointment they stayed long enough to give the youth squad a team talk but had to leave before the match because Forest were playing the same evening.

Things came to a head on the Canary Island trip. Clough and Taylor set great store by their unique double-act before matches and during the half-time interval. That is when they geed players up, made them believe they were invincible. The last thing they wanted was interference. Imagine their dismay when they found Professor Frank O'Gorman, the doctor, and John Bayliss, a long-standing FA administrator, already in the dressing room slicing the half-time lemons.

Both men were dismissed with a flea in their ears. 'We don't allow outsiders in here,' said Clough. 'This is when a lot of our important work is done and we must have privacy. Please get out.'

O'Gorman never spoke to Clough or Taylor again, and Bayliss was seething with anger: 'I'd been arranging youth-team trips for twenty years and never been spoken to like that.' He complained bitterly to Greenwood. The youth team's part-time coach, Ken Burton, went a step further. He was furious that Clough and Taylor, who were only figureheads in his view, had taken the credit for England's success in the tournament. (They beat Russia 1–0 in the final with a goal by Mark Falco.) Burton resigned, saying to Greenwood, 'I can't put up with that, I'm sorry.'

Greenwood concedes that it was not a satisfactory state of affairs, but he had not helped matters by naming four men to do one man's job. Apart from Clough, Taylor and Burton, he had also appointed John Cartwright as England's first full-time youth coach. 'Jobs for the boys,' says Taylor. 'We could have managed with a single coach, but two coaches, plus a doctor and an administrator, was ridiculous. It was a nice, cosy set-up for the old brigade. They didn't want anything to change.'

After a year in office, Clough and Taylor told Greenwood they could no longer continue because of their commitments to Nottingham Forest. They jumped moments before they were pushed, and Lancaster Gate was a much calmer place once they had departed. Greenwood had miscalculated, but it was a sincere mistake: 'It was a great pity I didn't get the chance to work with Cloughie. I honestly believed he would have been a good influence on the youngsters. I would have taken him to Italy with me for the European Nations championship, and who's to say he wouldn't have taken over from me at a later date?'

The question remains: should Clough have been given the job

in the first place? There is not one member of the interview panel who will say so, but that is hardly surprising. As is his wont, Clough had personally insulted Peter Swales, Bert Millichip and Sir Harold Thompson at one time or another. Their judgements, like anyone else's, were bound to be subjective. Ted Croker, the FA secretary, who also sat in on the interviews, stands by his view that Clough is 'the most successful manager there's ever been', but maintains that he was the wrong man for the England position because of his temperamental nature and inability to get on with people. He has a point, although he does himself a disservice by suggesting that the committee had no preconceived notions. Sir Matt Busby, uniquely on that committee, had experience of management, but still felt unable to give Clough his vote. He was doubtless swayed by events at Derby and the stories he had heard from Sam Longson. The fact that Clough had been sacked should not have weighed against him – the same thing happened to Robson at Fulham – but the circumstances of his dismissal from Leeds would have failed to impress the panel. An England manager has to handle the best players in the country: established internationals belonging to other clubs. Clough at Leeds raised serious doubts about his ability to control footballers of that calibre.

Jimmy Gordon is relieved for Clough's sake that the opportunity was denied him: 'It wouldn't have worked. You can't talk to players from other clubs the way he talks to his own. That would have been a recipe for trouble. In any case, Cloughie couldn't be bothered with scouting around looking at players. Find him a team and he'd knock it into shape, but don't ask him to look for one.'

Howard Wilkinson, recruited during the Greenwood era to help Venables and Sexton with the Under-21 side, believes Clough should have been offered the job, but does not underestimate the task which would have confronted him: 'The England set-up is not like a league club's. The Football Association is a large, bureaucratic institution and it is sometimes impossible to cut your way through as quickly as you might like. It is a rabbit warren of different sections, each seeing its job as important as the next. It would have been tough but I'm convinced Brian could have come to terms with it and gone on to great things.'

In some ways, Clough's approach is similar to Sir Alf

Ramsey's, although they are chalk and cheese when it comes to personality. Both believed in simple tactics and making early decisions. Neither suffered fools gladly. Sir Alf surveyed what was available to him in 1963, took the decision to do away with wingers and stuck to it. Clough would no doubt have planned his campaign in similar fashion and a few unexpected names might well have appeared on his team sheet. As the only man who has won the World Cup for England, Sir Alf has more right than anyone to venture an opinion: 'The FA is wrong to talk about diplomacy and international relations coming before results. That's been Dick Wragg's creed for years at Sheffield United and what have they ever achieved? I'm certain Clough would have done it right. He would have concentrated on team matters, like I did. The other things could take care of themselves. He might have lost patience and walked out on the first day. Who knows? But there is no reason, if he'd have stuck at it, why he shouldn't have been just as good for England as he was for Nottingham Forest.'

Had there been a public referendum, there is no doubt that Clough would have been an outright winner. More significantly, perhaps, in a poll undertaken by the author for the purposes of this book early in 1987, seventy-nine per cent of England's leading club managers believed he should have been appointed manager of the national side. This is how the results broke down:

Should Brian Clough have been England manager at some stage? Yes: 34. No: 1. Abstentions: 8.

That accounted for every club manager in Divisions One and Two. The only person to vote against was Dave Smith of Plymouth Argyle. He thought Clough 'thoroughly inappropriate' because he was not a person to toe the line and was too fond of criticizing others. 'Many of us *think* the things Clough says, but most of us have the sense to keep those thoughts to ourselves,' says Smith. The abstainers included Billy Bremner of Leeds, Graham Taylor of Watford (now Aston Villa), and Alan Ball of Portsmouth. None even wanted to discuss the matter. Of the others, George Graham of Arsenal, Kenny Dalglish of Liverpool and Alex Ferguson of Manchester United all felt, as Scotsmen, that they were not sufficiently equipped or interested to pass judgement.

The overwhelming 'yes' was headed by John Bond the manager of Birmingham City, who said it was 'quite ridiculous' that Clough had never been offered the job: 'He's the best manager in the country by a million miles.'

Another powerful broadside came from Lawrie McMenemy, who was interviewed for the job along with Clough: 'Clough is a hard man to get to know. He would have upset a few people but he can handle players, press and public better than anyone and that is three quarters of the job. The endless stream of FA councillors would have been his biggest bugbear. Nevertheless, for England to have had that talent available and not to have harnessed it is a great loss to the game. Cloughie would have dropped dead for his country.'

Steve Coppell, the winger whose name Greenwood always penned first on his teamsheet, and who now manages Crystal Palace, thinks Clough's moment could still come: 'If the job was judged on qualifications, Clough should have walked it. However, he's becoming more acceptable to the establishment as the years have gone by and I believe that the older he gets the more chance he stands.'

Clough and Howard Kendall have had their differences in recent years, but it did not prevent the former Everton manager saying this: 'If he hadn't been so outspoken, he'd have got it. He'd proved himself the best in the business. I'd have given him the job if I'd been on the selection committee.'

Coventry's John Sillett would not have hesitated in offering Clough the job: 'He would have put some pride back into the England shirt. That's what we've needed since Sir Alf.' And Bryan Hamilton, the Irishman in charge at Leicester City, was equally unequivocal: 'His attitude could have won the World Cup for England. He would have worked out his plan of attack and done it.' David Pleat thought hard before giving his reply: 'Brian is powerful enough not to have to be a diplomat. He would have made himself dictator. I would have loved to have seen it. He is the most amazing man I've met.'

What of the person who knew him best (professionally at least) and would have shared the responsibility of leading England? At the time, Peter Taylor took a more detached view of things, warning Clough before his interview that it was not the job for them. It will surprise many to learn that the pair hardly discussed the possibility of managing their country. According to Taylor, 'If it was Brian's burning desire to manage England, he kept his cards close to his chest. We never talked about it. We were too busy winning things for Forest.'

Clough might not have discussed it with Taylor, but he certainly consulted Phillip Whitehead: 'He asked me whether he should apply. Being a very proud man he was worried that the FA would shortlist him then humiliate him. His instincts were dead right. I told him he had to go through with it. He was a changed man and, if I could see it, so would they. Even then he was very hesitant about applying.'

If Taylor's view sounds like sour grapes, it should not be forgotten that they would have been several thousand pounds the poorer for setting up shop at Lancaster Gate. Greenwood was paid only £25,000 a year, a figure Clough and Taylor would have doubled at Forest with European bonuses. In addition to that, Clough enjoyed a second career as a newspaper columnist, with carte blanche to attack whom and what he liked. He would have forfeited that privilege as England manager. Given that both were money-conscious, it is not beyond the bounds of reason that they would have declined the offer had it been made, materialism being a more workable god than patriotism.

Taylor reflects, 'Running the England set-up would have been a doddle but we were at our best when we had daily contact with players. There's no way either of us could have sat around contemplating our navels for weeks on end. We had to be in there where it was tense, living on our nerves every day of the week. It's rubbish to say that Brian had a chip on his shoulder about England. When it came along he was interested, but he wasted no time thinking about it beforehand or regretting it afterwards. The prestige side of it appealed to him. There's one thing he'd have loved more than accepting the job – turning it down. He's a great one for that. As it turned out, missing the England job was the best thing that ever happened to us. It enabled us to go on and win European Cups.'

But could that really have compared with the satisfaction of winning the World Cup?

12
Death of a Friendship

Pale and drawn, Peter Taylor walked into Clough's office in May 1982 after a 1–0 home defeat by Manchester United. He locked the door, slumped in the chair and said, 'I've shot it. I'm resigning.'

So ended the most famous and successful partnership in the history of football. A seventeen-year association which began under the leaking rafters of Hartlepool and climaxed under the floodlights of the St Bernabeu stadium in Madrid was severed in the time it takes to utter five words.

Clough tried to dissuade his mate: 'You're wrong. Think about it overnight.' But he had failed to recognize that they were no longer 'mates'. They had not been for a long time.

Taylor arrived home after midnight. His wife and daughter were pacing the floor in their dressing gowns wondering what could have happened. He had been noticeably tired and miserable of late and they were worried. Both broke down when he strode into the living room and announced his decision. 'Don't cry,' he told them. 'I feel marvellous. It's a ton weight off my back.'

When Taylor negotiated his pay-off with the Forest chairman, Geoffrey McPherson, Clough astonished them by interjecting: 'I want to do a deal for the pair of us, Mr Chairman, 'cos, if Pete's going, so am I.'

There was a stunned silence as McPherson tried to gather his wits. 'Give me a break, Brian. If two of you resign, what am I supposed to do for a manager?'

The meeting was adjourned but on the way out a furious Taylor took Clough aside: 'What stroke are you pulling?' he demanded to know. 'They can't afford to pay us both off.'

Was it one of Clough's time-honoured ruses to boost his contract once he saw the board backed into a corner or could he genuinely not face the prospect of running Forest on his own?

'Difficult to know,' says Taylor. 'He's such a good actor you wonder when he's sincere.'

At any rate, Clough did not pursue the matter.

His own version of events is somewhat different: 'When Taylor told me he'd shot it, I agreed with him. I negotiated a £31,000 pay-off for him when the club didn't want to give him threepence. They didn't think he did enough work. They didn't particularly like him!'

'Nonsense,' says Taylor. 'I negotiated my own deal. It was £25,000, not £31,000 – the maximum because of my £70,000 contract. I paid for the car myself. I can only imagine Brian wants to claim the credit because he can't bear people to think that he was abandoned. He has to make believe he arranged it all.'

The fracture of such a long-enduring partnership mystified those closest to both parties. It mystifies them still.

Taylor tries to explain what went wrong:

'In my last year at Forest I lost respect for Brian and realized that I had grown to dislike him. Our differences didn't seem to matter when we were winning things. During a lean spell, which is when the truth often comes out, I had time to take stock. I had all the money I needed, a happy family, and all the honours the game could bring. Why did I need to stay with a man I didn't get on with? What really bothered me was that the club was suffering as well as my family. Brian and I weren't happy together. The chemistry which won us so many titles wasn't working any more. Worst of all, we had lost the ability to laugh. The players could feel the tension in our relationship and the results proved that something was wrong. Our secretary, Ken Smales, read the signs. If it hadn't been for him and Paul White persuading me to stay, I'd have left before I did.

'I woke up each morning dreading the thought of work. I was irritable and tired. When that happens, you can't just carry on. Was it me who changed or Brian? I'm not sure. I just know there were sides to his character I could no longer come to terms with. His need for hangers-on was unbearable. I never objected to his friends – some of them were nice people – but in recent years they were in the way. Anything up to six or eight of them would turn up at the hotel when we were having our pre-match talk. That was a time I considered precious, when the players and I psyched ourselves up for the game. His cronies filled the office and the corridors, driving a wedge between Brian and me. Sometimes I couldn't even get to talk to him. He seemed completely unable to cope without people running around after him: driving his car, doing his errands, fetching his drinks and practically tying his shoelaces, while he sat back and ordered them about. He was hopeless at being on his own.

'His craving for publicity irritated me. Brian was never happier than when he was making the banner headlines. In the early days he loved being with people like Michael Parkinson and Geoffrey Boycott, who were bigger personalities than him. It didn't bother me at the time but lately he'd become a media creation – a cardboard cutout of the real Brian Clough. Many of the so-called brilliant one-liners were carefully rehearsed and geared to have the maximum effect. He was a great manipulator of the press. He and they fed off each other like leeches. I watched reporters being treated like dirt – hanging around for hours, then being spoken to like children. At first I believed they deserved such treatment if they were prepared to put up with it, but after a while I began to wonder what motivated a person to behave so abominably towards others.

'Brian needed constantly to be number one. Few of his friends had a normal relationship with him. Many of the associations were based on what each side could get out of it. He wouldn't tolerate anyone who answered back or posed a threat to his dominance. I couldn't stand for that.

'He will be the richest man in Derby cemetery when he goes. It's no secret that I like money and the things it can buy, and I don't deny that we have sailed pretty close to the wind sometimes. It was me, not Brian, who handled all the contractual negotiations. He used to say, "You'll never get away with that," but I always did because I knew what our value was. With Brian it has got out of proportion. He deserves to be highly paid but I've a feeling that materialism has taken him over, and that his one thought from waking up in the morning to going to bed is: how can I earn more money? I didn't want to be a millionaire. I don't think Brian will be happy until he's a millionaire several times over.'

There was such a torrent of public acrimony from Clough after the split that it is hard to believe Clough and Taylor were ever close friends. Readers may detect an undercurrent of jealousy in Taylor's testimony – not professional jealousy but the emotional jealousy of someone who sees a close companion courted by intruders and eventually wooed away from him. Before Taylor jilted Clough, you might say, Clough, spiritually anyway, had jilted Taylor.

Following one further attempt to change Taylor's mind before the first match of the 1982–83 season, Clough broke off all contact. If he was wounded by his partner's departure, he was aghast when Taylor emerged from his apparent retirement eighteen months later to manage Derby. Had it been Rochdale or Darlington, Clough would not have taken it so personally – but Derby? That was the place he had believed he could go back to if all else failed. In Clough's mind, Derby was his bolt-hole. Taylor was suddenly a menace now. Clough knew that a resurrected Derby County would steal his own thunder. Goodness knows, it was hard to get crowds into the City Ground at the best of times!

Clough: 'He says he's shot it then he pops up a year or so later at Derby? That was bloody crackers! If he wanted to get into football, I'd have thought the most obvious thing was to come back to Forest. We gave him the chance.'

Taylor had not really enjoyed his retirement. It was as taxing in many ways as managing Nottingham Forest. Without football, life was too quiet. When Stuart Webb and the Derby chairman, Mike Watterson, approached him about going back, he jumped at the chance – even though Derby were an ailing Second Division club with colossal financial problems accumulating in the background.

The sequence of events which followed is shrouded in confusion but it appears that Clough heard what was afoot and intervened. Webb received a call from Keeling, who gave him a telephone number where the Forest manager could be contacted. Webb fancied the idea of a Clough–Taylor return but told Keeling that Taylor had already been offered the job and accepted. If Clough wanted to be involved, he would have to talk to Taylor himself. Webb comments, 'It would have been ideal if they'd have come together, but I wasn't sure what Brian's game was. He loved leading people up the garden path. I sensed another of his tricks.'

Clough and Taylor arranged a rendezvous at their favourite meeting place, the paddling pool on the Trent embankment. The meeting was as cool as the November air. According to Clough, he told Taylor: 'I wouldn't go back six years ago, I'm not going back now!' He said Taylor was not going to take the job unless Clough went with him.

Taylor talked money, big money, and Clough at least gave the impression that he would consider. As they climbed back into their respective cars, Taylor said to Clough, 'If your answer's no, we haven't met, okay?'

Taylor maintains that Clough promised not to breathe a word of their meeting.

Yet Taylor and the rest of the nation read about Clough's decision in a national newspaper – which would not have picked up the story for peanuts. Taylor says, 'I offered him the earth and he stabbed me in the back. Why? If he had no intention of going to Derby, why create the fuss in the first place and why bother to meet me? I suppose I should have known that he had to stick his nose in everything whether it affected him or not.'

It was generally assumed that Taylor's book *With Clough by Taylor*,[1] written and published while they were at Forest together, triggered off the animosity between them. It does seem strange that he undertook the task without Clough's knowledge, and Taylor confesses that it was perhaps a mistake to have been so surreptitious about it. Clough boycotted the book launch and cursed Taylor on the quiet. His public displeasure has to be seen in context, though. For years *he* had been supplementing his income with newspaper articles and columns. Taylor says he was never consulted about those nor should he have been. But he objected to Clough's earning extra pocket money on the strength of what they had achieved together: 'He was telling the country how we did this, and why we did that. *We!* But when it came to money, I hardly got a sniff. His conscience did him once. We drove out into Derbyshire to thrash it out. He said he could accept my point of view and wrote out three cheques for £250 there and then. One for me and one each for my son and daughter. In future he promised to cut me in but that's where it ended. I have no conscience about the book I wrote. I made one per cent of what he made from his articles.'

If the book was a smokescreen, the John Robertson case was not. It came after the relationship had begun to ice over and

1 *With Clough by Taylor*, Sidgwick and Jackson, 1980.

plunged it into the deep freeze. There were some bizarre dealings between the two men leading up to the Robertson affair.

Clough would have us believe he was a friendly neighbour: 'When Taylor went back to Derby against my advice he was battling away there and no one was more delighted than us at Forest who liked him and had worked with him for ages. I finished up in his house two or three times trying to get Anderson and Proctor then Plummer and Gray to sign for Derby on loan.'

Taylor says he tried to buy or borrow several players from Forest but found them disappearing in the direction of Chesterfield or Barnsley – anywhere but Derby. Then, as Clough says, he turned up at Taylor's country bungalow with Viv Anderson and Mark Proctor in his car.

It is perhaps appropriate to let Anderson tell the story:

'I was at home nursing an injury one afternoon when Clough rang and asked me to go to the ground. When I got there he said, "Come on, we'll go and help Pete out. You can go to Derby on loan." I told him I didn't want to. He put the same proposition to Mark and got the same reply. He left us for a few minutes and we decided that, whatever happened, neither of us was going to Derby. Then Clough more or less bundled us into the car and drove out to Widmerpool in the depths of winter. We sat in Pete's house arguing about it, Mark and I saying we weren't leaving Forest, and Pete saying he couldn't afford our wages anyway. It was embarrassing for all of us but Clough wouldn't take no for an answer. In the end he said, "Right, you're not coming home with me. You can find your own way back." With that he stormed off into the next room. We couldn't call a cab without him knowing so we decided to make a break for it. While the two of them were talking next door, we escaped over the garden and through a fence. It was pitch black and we hadn't got a clue where we were.

'We carried on over the fields till we came to a village. We ended up in the pub waiting for a cab and having a late beer. It was unreal. My wife was worried sick when I got home at about midnight. I worked it out that I'd walked five miles with an injured leg.'

In Taylor's view, 'It was a joke. He wasn't doing me any favours. He was just trying to unload two problem players. He had no time for Viv and didn't get on too well with Mark. What a way for a manager to treat his players.'

Clough's fury when Robertson was plucked from under his nose was understandable. For a man who prides himself on knowing people's thoughts even before they think them, it was unusual for him to be caught napping. Or rather hiking. His antennae must have been out of range on the Pennines, where he had set off on a four-day charity walk during the close season. While he was away, Taylor pounced. He maintains that Clough's absence was a coincidence, but he will protest till he is blue in the face. Robertson was another of Taylor's obsessions, so much so that it distorted his judgement: Derby palpably did not need a strolling genius up-front to get them out of the Second Division any more than Robertson needed Derby.

The player had been feeling insecure at Forest after a cartilage injury in the season in which his contract ran out. Clough had said to him in passing, 'A bad time for that to happen, Robbo!' – which the player took to imply that he might be offered a reduced contract next time. He recovered towards the end of the season, 1983, helping Forest to qualify for the UEFA Cup, but his fears were confirmed when Clough said he might not be able to offer Robertson as much on a renewed contract. That said, the manager made for the hills. Robertson was a free agent.

Technically, Taylor played it by the book when he signed him. He says, 'I broke a few rules signing players for Brian when we were together, but everything was above board with Robbo. It's ridiculous to say I should have asked his permission. If I had, I'd never have smelled Robertson.' Our intrepid adventurer learned of the *fait accompli* when he telephoned home after his hike.

'That finished me with Taylor,' says Clough. 'I'd been breaking my neck trying to get Robbo to sign because I was trying to survive with a very inferior side to the ones we'd had. Thanks to Taylor, we'd wasted £3 million on bad players, then he does that to me. The worst manager in the Football League or the one who hated me most would have paid me the courtesy of letting me know first. I'd earned that much, surely. I'd have felt less hurt and less disgusted and less likely to vomit if it had been any other manager than Taylor. This is the man who shared my table for God knows how many years. Shared everything. There was no relationship left after that. He could paddle his own canoe!'

Taylor had been guilty of nothing more serious than gross lack of courtesy, but then Clough had an 'A' level in that himself.

Robertson owed him more than 'goodbye' and he knows it: 'The worst thing I did was not telling him I was leaving. I asked Pete whether I ought to but he said the less Clough knew about it the better. I wish I'd done the decent thing instead of leaving him to read about it. I don't think he'd have let me go.'

By way of retaliation, Clough clobbered Derby where it hurt most – in the bank account. One of Taylor's closest friends, David Pleat, then of Luton Town, testified at a tribunal to fix the transfer fee that he had made a bid of £200,000 for Robertson. The tribunal accordingly upped the player's fee to £135,000, much more than Derby had anticipated. It meant that Taylor had no money left to reinforce his defence. The upshot would be Derby's relegation, rather than promotion, and Taylor's sacking. *Touché*.

Robertson says he was surprised to hear of Luton's interest and an apparent written offer from Southampton: 'They were both news to me.' Clough snubbed Taylor and Robertson on the way into the hearing. As the Forest and Derby contingents moved towards each other along the narrow corridors of Paddington's Great Western hotel, Clough performed a theatrical 'U' turn and showed Taylor the full width of his back. Taylor: 'It was an awful moment. I've never done that to anyone in my life.'

That was the beginning of the end of Robertson's career. Clough banned him from the City Ground and Taylor was not impressed with the return he was getting from his investment. Derby stretched themselves to the limit to make him happy, but he was a fish out of water as the Third Division beckoned. Clough finally broke the cold war, inviting Robertson to watch a game at Forest before buying him back from Derby. It was a peculiar move, which did not pay off. After a handful of games in the First Division Robertson was put out to grass, Clough this time complaining about his attitude. He said early in 1987, 'If Robbo had shown the same commitment to playing football as he does to drinking lager, he'd still be playing instead of running a pub.' Taylor believes Clough took Robertson back aiming to prove he could succeed where Taylor had failed.

Over the next few months, Clough tore his old partner to shreds in the newspaper columns, saying among other things that, if they met on the A52 between Nottingham and Derby, he would run Taylor over. Taylor's family heard of the comments while they were weekending in Scarborough. It devastated them. 'No one will know how my wife and daughter suffered over those remarks,' says Taylor. 'It hurt more than anything in all my years with Brian. He did it out of pure spite without a thought for the agonies I was going through trying to manage Derby. He knew I was down and out. Why put the knife in like that? It's a terrible thing to say, but I will never forgive him for the misery he caused. Stories about my holding out an olive branch are just newspaper tittle-tattle. It's over.'

The public's impression of a close camaraderie turning sour overnight is incorrect. According to Taylor, resentment and mistrust had been piling up during and since the successful days at Derby. Trouble began with an alleged secret £5000 pay rise to Clough in 1971: 'Brian told me nothing about it, nor did Sam Longson. I saw the contract by accident on Stuart Webb's desk. I took Sam out into the middle of the pitch before a league match and asked him to explain. All he could say was: "How did you find out?" I told him that was a disgusting question. How could he reward Brian and not me when I'd suffered a heart attack running the club while he was away doing his television shows? Brian apologized and helped to make sure I got a rise as well. He promised to make it up in other ways but the damage was done. I'd thought I could trust him with my life but already I was having doubts.'

Taylor's heart murmur confined him to barracks for six weeks. Clough had arranged his admission to Derbyshire Royal Infirmary on a Saturday morning when half the staff were on leave, but thereafter his interest waned. During those weeks at home, Clough visited his partner only once. Even allowing for the fact that he has a detached attitude to others' illnesses (something several of his friends have remarked upon), it is not the way you would expect a friend to behave. Sitting around at home, Taylor nursed serious doubts about the strength of their comradeship. It was as though, outside a football context, they were strangers. Since the early years on Teesside, they had barely socialized at all.

When the two men came to Derby, Clough and the children would sometimes take a Sunday afternoon drive to Findern for tea with the Taylors. Barbara did not join them. Clough would arrive with a bar of chocolate for the children and, while all three boys played football in the back garden, Clough and Taylor would invariably discuss football. It was the desire to make a go of it rather than a love of each other's company which drew them together at that stage. Their relationship had changed slightly. Taylor was his own worst enemy in this respect. An expansive and a very funny man in private groups, he felt awkward on public occasions. Clough is right in essence when he says, 'Socialize – how could we? Taylor hid all his life!'

Taylor would do anything to avoid engagements and dinners; he froze if a petrol-pump attendant recognized him, and was reduced to disguising himself in a trilby and dark glasses for a day at the races. Ultimately, even those trips dried up because of Taylor's fear of being pestered. He was little better at Forest. Stuart Dryden, the former chairman, says he only once managed to get Taylor to have dinner with him and that he would never pop into the pub for a drink: 'He'd get as far as the door then make some excuse.'

Clough often accused him of not living life to the full: 'You behave like a top manager, you spend like a top manager, when are you going to relax and *live* like one?'

Their best times were on trips to Wembley or to Europe, when their respective families could fill a railway compartment, a coach or half an aeroplane. Otherwise, socializing was limited to their Majorcan 'branch office', Cala Millor. Taylor came across it in 1972 when he wanted to reward the Derby championship team with an end-of-season holiday. The north-eastern coast of Majorca was undiscovered in those days. It is now a playground for the East Midlands, promoted largely by Stuart Webb, who was quick to realize its potential and established his travel agency on the strength of it.

Clough's fear of flying held him back for years. He had his first bad experience on the England trip to Russia in 1958 and a worse one when returning from a break with his mother and father in Jersey. Taylor was there too: 'We came back on a jet and Brian was in a terrible state, white knuckles, hands gripping the seat, staring straight ahead. The plane lurched to avoid a thundercloud and I thought he'd faint. His mum asked if he was all right. He snapped at her like an alligator. It's the only time I ever heard him say a cross word to her.'

Whisky and a valium tablet enabled Clough to come to terms with air travel, but it was 1978 before he too discovered Majorca. He and Taylor bought apartments and first introduced the concept of mid-season breaks which they had written into their contracts. The two families holidayed together but apart.

Clough loved bearing his torso to the sun for hours on end or sitting at his favourite roadside bar. The kids played in the sand and Barbara lounged by the pool in her dark glasses, enigmatically reading a novel. The Taylors would meet them for a drink or a meal, and Peter would laugh at the newest indiscretions of Nigel Clough, a fearless and mischievous lad right up his street: 'I love naughty kids – nice tearaways like Nigel. If he wasn't breaking tumblers or swallowing things he shouldn't, he was up to some other mischief. I'll never forget the day he shinned from one balcony to the next on the seventh floor of a hotel with a sheer drop underneath him. That takes some pluck. Simon ran off to tell his mum and she was hysterical. His parents and uncles and aunts used to stop him doing things, stifle his spirit. They still do. I don't accept that. You've got to give kids like that their head. Kids who are a handful often turn out to be the opposite, as Nigel has. They want help, want to be cuddled, not smacked and turned away. I was as soft as putty with him. He wasn't Brian's favourite because he couldn't handle him. He was still learning how to bring up kids. Nigel and I had a call sign when we spoke on the phone. If he picked up the receiver, I'd do my cockerel impression: "Cock-a-doodle-do!" I didn't have to say any more. Nigel would laugh and shout to Brian, "Dad, it's Pete on the phone." What a cracking lad. I've missed him since we drifted apart.'

Clough and Taylor came into conflict again when Derby made their much publicized attempt to prize them away from Forest. The argument arose not so much over the fact that Taylor wanted to go to Derby and Clough did not, but over the negotiations Taylor claims Clough subsequently had with certain members of the club. Hardy, the Derby chairman, had made a final offer of £50,000 for Clough to divide whichever way he saw fit between himself and his partner. Clough kept that to himself and made no further contact with Hardy. Through the grapevine, however, Taylor got to hear of some behind-the-scenes activity.

He was in a seething rage when he confronted Clough in his office. This, he says, is how the conversation went:

'I want the truth from you like I've never had it before.'

'You always get the truth.'

'Have you or haven't you been negotiating to go back to Derby on your own?'

Clough was apparently non-committal and Taylor fumed: 'I know what's been going on and you'll pay for this.'

Taylor drove home for lunch, followed – although he did not know it – by Clough: 'I was amazed when he knocked on the door. He never came to the house. I said, "Christ almighty, this has got to be important for you to come here!"

'Clough replied, "I swear to you it is. Get me a large scotch, Lill."

'Then he poured his heart out. He was choking. He knew I'd rumbled what was going on. He said he had been thinking of taking the £50,000 job for himself, but got cold feet because he didn't fancy it on his own. It shook him that I had found out. He'd come to see me because he was terrified I'd walk out and leave him.'

One further incident helped to extinguish any embers of friendship that remained. It concerned an alleged ex-gratia payment to Clough and Taylor after they had taken Forest to play in a testimonial match for Paddy Mulligan in Dublin. The *Sunday Times* published an exposé but were forced to print a public apology when Clough threatened to sue. The apology exonerated Clough but made no mention of Taylor. 'I couldn't believe it,' he says. 'One minute Brian and I had been discussing what action to take against the paper, the next he had demanded an apology for himself alone. It left Brian smelling of roses and me in the dock.'

It was expediency which kept Clough and Taylor together, not love and friendship. We should be surprised not by the fact that they parted, but that it was so long coming.

They met head-on when Derby and Forest were drawn to play each other in the FA Cup in 1983, a momentous occasion in every sense. Forest were going through a lean period but Willie Young had struck a fine spell of form at centre-half. It was to Young that Clough turned before the tie: 'Just do one more thing for me, Willie. Keep it up for this match and I won't ask another thing of you.'

Forest lost 2–0 at the Baseball Ground and Clough sought out his centre-half in the dressing room: 'He accused me of taking a bribe from Pete to throw the game. It had completely blown his mind. I'd never seen him under so much pressure. He ordered me to get in the bath and "fuck off" early like I always did. I said, "I never do that. I always sit and think when we get beaten because I'm sick."

'"You're not sick," he said. "Get in the bath then fuck off and see your mate Taylor."

'I was furious at being spoken to like that so, to spite him, I *did* go and see Taylor.

'It just happened that, as I was talking to Pete, Clough came walking by. His face was purple. I shook hands with Pete, then got on the coach. Clough ran to the back where I was sitting and wagged his finger at me: "Did you shake hands with that shithouse Taylor? I don't believe it." He ran to the front of the bus repeating those words then ran to the back again: "Did you really shake hands with him?"

'I said, "Of course I shook hands with him. You told me to go and see him."

'Clough shouted back, "I didn't bloody mean it!" Then he got off the bus and ran round the back pointing up at me through the window. He was like a man possessed. With all the fans staring at him, he bellowed, "That's the last thing you ever do at this club."'

Since then, Clough and Taylor have spoken to each other on the telephone once about a private matter. There was no mention of getting back together. Both have been offered money to effect a public reconciliation – Clough as much as £10,000. If it comes, it will be the most expensive handshake ever and sponsored friendship will have arrived.

13
A Singular Man

Only an ingenu or a sentimental softy would have shed tears for Brian Clough as the one trophy which eluded him all those years, continued to elude him through the eighties. The FA Cup was probably dashed from his lips when ninety-five Liverpool supporters died so horribly at Hillsborough. Fate seemed to have ordained that Liverpool would take that trophy, as indeed they did, sweeping Nottingham Forest aside in the delayed semi-final and triumphing over Everton at Wembley.

Clough was more miffed than hurt, his dislike for Liverpool is surpassed only by his dislike for their manager, Kenny Dalglish. To be tripped up by circumstance with the goal in sight is not such a heartache when you are as wealthy and fireproof as Clough. He had already accumulated riches beyond his wildest imaginings and secured a position of impregnable power within football – a position unshaken even by his meting out instant justice during a mild pitch invasion at the City Ground! Who is to say he did not deserve the money and the status? He ignited two somnolent soccer citadels, provided opportunities for many and hope for thousands while changing the face of his 'industry' and enriching our lives as only larger-than-life personalities can. It has to be said that Clough also alienated a few of us with his discourtesy and appalled many more with his disreputable antics on the touch line.

Yes, the Littlewoods Cup (and the Simod) in 1989 were the first trophies he won on his own but that mattered more to him than it does to us. He will be judged largely on what he and Peter Taylor achieved together. Two men without an 'O' level between them who taught us that if you believe in yourself, everything is possible.

When Taylor walked out of his world, Clough went to work with a vengeance. The first task was to build a fortress around himself and post trusty sentinels at all the entrances and exits. With the help of Nottingham Forest's unique constitution, this he did. The chairmanship at Forest is, in theory anyway, an office shared by rotation and therefore devoid of any real power. There is no room for an Elton John or a Robert Maxwell – no one to call the financial shots, because the man in the chair is but a single shareholder like the rest of the board. Clough has argued that directors should inject money into the club but, if that were the case, the manager would be allowed far less latitude than he has now. Alone among managers, Clough uses his influence to alter the composition of the board to suit his own purpose. That is why you will not hear a dissenting voice.

He edged out the two men who presumed to stand up to him. Most of the others specialize in rolling onto their backs and having their tummies tickled. The chairman Maurice Roworth is a case in point. He admits: 'We don't dictate to Brian Clough – he just tells us what he's doing.' That is to say that Clough is as close to complete autonomy as you can get. If he wanted the world on a silver platter he need only click his fingers or, to be absolutely certain, threaten to resign. The idea of losing him is repugnant to the board and there is the rub. Should Clough retire – and that appears as likely as Mrs Thatcher surrendering the keys of No. 10 – Forest have little to fall back on. Clough has steadfastly stalled over moves to groom a successor, preferring to take everything upon his shoulder's, thereby placing the club's future in some doubt.

There is nothing he enjoys more than teasing his board with speculation about potential heirs. If he is not praising his no. 2, Ron Fenton, to the skies, he is pressing the claims of his old full-back and comrade, Frank Clark. Such is the confusion in the ranks that Fenton and Archie Gemmill, who piloted Forest reserves to honours, are at loggerheads over their prospects. Fenton sees Gemmill as a major threat to his hopes of taking over and feelings ran so high during a post-season holiday in Majorca in May 1989 that punches were thrown from an undisclosed quarter and Graham Lyas, the club physiotherapist sported a black eye in the Spanish sunshine.

Clough's close friend Stuart Dryden, himself a former Forest chairman can see the dangers: 'The amount of power Brian's been allowed to assume is ridiculous. I shudder to think what they will do when he leaves. Trouble is they're all terrified of him. Sometimes the chairman's reduced to serving drinks to the players and Brian should put a stop to it.'

The reason he doesn't is that it is rather convenient to be surrounded by acquiescence. A friendly chairman is no threat. To be fair to Roworth, he has had to tread a tightrope. Should he rock the boat for the sake of the odd principle here and there, or should he turn the other cheek in the belief that an omnipotent Clough is better than no Clough at all?

Whatever view one takes, Roworth's meek performance over Clough's attack on the Forest fans who were celebrating the 5–2 victory over Queens Park Rangers in the Littlewoods Cup, did the chairman a disservice. It was mysterious that he could defend and even support such antics. Roworth would surely have given his own credibility a fillip by chastising Clough for his outburst even if he could not actually bring himself to punish the manager. Instead, the chairman tried to persuade the football world that Clough clobbered his own supporters in the interests of security and other high-minded ideals.

Mr Roworth, why didn't you remove the blinkers from your eyes – see what thousands of television viewers saw to their displeasure? 'We will stand by Brian,' said the chairman, 'there is still overwhelming support for him. We have received 628 letters backing the manager and only 51 against . . . We will be mounting a strenuous defence. I don't like trial by television.'

He was criticized by the Football Association for changing his tune at the hearing. Graham Kelly, the FA chief executive explained: 'His admission that Brian Clough's actions were misguided and wrong would have been better on the day after the incident . . . not three weeks later on the day of the hearing.'

For all that, the FA Commission retreated when Clough apologized during the forty minute session at the City Ground. Some parties were demanding his removal from office or at least a permanent ban from the touchline but the FA fined him £5000 (roughly the price of a swift newspaper exclusive) and banished him from the touchline for three months. Clough, who carried a torch for discipline and self control, knew that leniency had been stretched to faintly absurd limits. Such is the aura of the man and the fear he generates in others that the very fans he whacked were for a time offering to pay his fine. They certainly apologized for bringing their faces into conflict with Clough's fist! A staggering state of affairs and a situation from which one cannot imagine any other manager extricating himself.

The two chief victims, Sean O'Hara and James McGowan became television celebrities overnight and were offered small fortunes to prosecute Clough. Neither did nor was tempted to – again a dubious tribute to the manager's godlike appeal. Attempting to sue him would have been almost blasphemous. And yet O'Hara acknowledges the irony of it all. 'I told the police that if the boot had been on the other foot and I had hit Brian – I would have been locked up. Even so, I didn't want to embarrass Brian or cause him any trouble because I love him. The police kept insisting that I should go ahead with the prosecution because they had video evidence and said they'd support me all the way. They kept reminding me that I could make some money out of it. Even though I'm unemployed I wasn't interested.'

Both victims were offered cash inducements by tabloid newspapers to go ahead with the prosecution. O'Hara put the phone down on the *News of the World* claiming that a reporter was promising him and his family free trips around the world and a luxury lifestyle. He says Clough hurt him by punching him in the face – an incident witnessed by thousands of television viewers on *Midweek Sports Special* – and that he had a tingling in his ear for some time afterwards but still considered he was in the wrong and Clough in the right. 'I shouldn't have come onto the pitch. It was my fault it happened and it won't happen again.' O'Hara and McGowan were both fêted by Roworth and Clough at the Forest ground shortly after the attack. The chairman poured them glasses of wine and persuaded them both to remove their earrings because 'Brian hates those things'. Clough then appeared before his victims.

Says O'Hara: 'I thought I was dreaming, I'd never met Brian before and here he was treating me like a guest. He apologized for what had happened and ended up making us kiss him. My girlfriend was mad at me afterwards. She said I'd kissed away thousands of pounds I could have earned if I'd pursued the matter.'

The police concluded there was insufficient evidence to bring a prosecution – which makes their earlier remarks to O'Hara a little curious. The enquiry was led by Chief Superintendent Michael Holford who had been Divisional Commander of the

Meadows for three and a half years. That division includes the City Ground and for eight months of the year one of Mr Holford's priorities had been crowd and traffic control at the stadium. He had built up a professional relationship with Clough over 14 years and it must have been very strange for him to investigate a football manager and professional friend who set great store by a police presence. The crown prosecutors in Nottingham recommended that no action be taken and the Director of Public Prosecutions followed that advice. A former Forest director who watched the incident from no more than 20 yards back said: 'Brian was going through a bad spell that night. Normally he's away down the tunnel as soon as a game ends. I thought something was funny when he lingered but I was astonished when he lost control. I can't explain it and neither can Brian – but then there's no logical explanation for many of the things he does and says.'

Chief Superintendent Holford agrees that Clough was misguided to react the way he did and can only explain it this way: 'He saw different signals from those observed by the television cameras and was fearful of a pitch invasion. The QPR fans were pretty hostile that night. In 33 years as a police officer I've never witnessed scenes like it afterwards. Press and television went berserk. So many wanted Brian's head it was distasteful.

'People have said that if it had been a steward and not Clough who attacked the fans I'd have behaved differently but that is patently untrue. Anyone who knows me knows that I wouldn't be influenced by the identity of the person concerned.'

O'Hara and McGowan waited in the wings at the Commission's hearing – but were there for the defence, not the prosecution. Forest fed them on cheese and ham cobs but didn't require their testimony. Afterwards Clough thanked them profusely for their support and promised them tickets for the Littlewoods Cup Final should Forest make it. They did, of course, beating Luton 3–1. O'Hara was in the crowd at Wembley but had paid for his own ticket. 'I'm surprised Brian forgot his promise but it didn't bother me too much. The day cost me £20 but we won and that was the most important thing.' A sizeable sum nevertheless for a 20-year-old who has never had a job and was trying to support himself, his girlfriend and a young baby on £52 a fortnight.

In the meantime, humble pie is the regular boardroom diet. Clough cannot resist the temptation to humiliate when he perceives a sign of weakness in others – even though that very weakness is the source of his greatest strength. Dryden says, 'Brian has complete contempt for directors when he thinks they are only in football for the kudos. After the Littlewoods Cup tie against Crystal Palace, the chairman invited him to the directors' room to meet the Palace board and warm himself with a bowl of soup. Do you know what he did? – Turned up with half a dozen apprentices and ordered them to "get stuck in before these buggers have it all". It was uncalled-for and extremely rude.' No one uttered an admonishing word.

The last person to put up resistance was embarrassed into resigning when Clough exposed a so-called betting ring on the directors' coach. It happened during a trip to Old Trafford in 1985, when the said director, Frank Allcock, laid £10 against Forest beating Manchester United. Allcock says it was not as simple as that: 'I was invited by another director to lay £50. He had noticed that the *Sporting Life* was quoting 7–1 against Forest and thought it was a good price. I said no. Another passenger on the bus persuaded me to have £10 "for a bit of fun". The director whose idea it had been took a £20 bet on United from Derek Pavis, a friend of mine who was travelling with us.' Pavis had been the other thorn in Clough's side. He was by now an ex-director, beaten by five votes after Clough rallied the shareholders against him. So there was a situation in which Allcock and Pavis were both betting against their own club. Both lost their money too. Nigel Clough scored a late winner for Forest.

The men involved might have anticipated reverberations – and they certainly got them, particularly Allcock, who had been a member for thirty years and a director for four. The chairman reported the incident to Clough, apparently describing the two protagonists as 'traitors'. Clough immediately latched onto it, hinting that it would be good fodder for his column in the club programme. Despite Roworth's promise to Allcock to 'kill it', the article came to light not only in the programme but also in the *Daily Mirror*. Allcock complains, 'My family was humiliated over a trifle. It can't be right for a manager to attack directors in the programme and the national press. The story made it look as though I was going up and down the bus laying 7–1 odds, which certainly wasn't true.' Allcock, predictably, resigned, blaming Clough for his public execution and Roworth for conniving at it.

Oddly enough, Clough and Allcock had been holidaying together in Spain only two months previously. 'He treated me like a father,' says Allcock. 'We played cards every morning before lunch and, when we got back, he told the chairman, "I've had a fantastic trip and enjoyed every minute of Mr Allcock's company." How could he change so quickly?'

Two further incidents illustrate Clough's grip on the club.

Forest had been beaten at home by Southampton in the third round of the 1985 FA Cup when Allcock, walking disconsolately along the passageway, happened to say to Alan Hill, Clough's assistant and a former Forest goalkeeper, 'The way we're going, we'll have *you* back in goal.' Clough, who dislikes criticism to the point of paranoia, got to hear of the conversation. Meanwhile, four out of five directors stayed behind after the game discussing football, as was their custom. One of the topics of conversation was the recent board meeting to consider Viv Anderson's transfer request. The board had told Clough he could go up to £200 a week more to keep the player.

Allcock takes up the story:

'There was a knock at the door and Clough came in. I'd never known him do that after a match. He said, "I've just come to see what you lot are up to," and sat down next to me.

'I said, "We're talking about Anderson." That set him off.

' "You buggers never give me £200 a week increase but you don't mind me giving it to a player!"

' "We don't discuss your contract. That's between the chairman and the vice-chairman."

' "If you don't give me a hundred per cent loyalty on this board, you can all get out. You've got a good thing going here, watching free football . . ."

'I said, "Free football? We've been watching football since we came out of the forces. I've been to every international ground in Europe. Have any of your cronies been to a World Cup in Mexico and paid their own fare, because I have! I didn't come onto this board to get free tickets. We pay £200 a year for our seats."

'Clough ranted and raved, using some dreadful language, then walked out. A few moments later he came back in and shouted, "If you don't give me a hundred per cent loyalty, fuck off!" '

The second event occurred during a period of financial cutbacks at the club in the mid-eighties. Clough's car had registered

75,000 miles and was ready for renewal. The board agreed that he should be given another car but, with a million-pound overdraft, they could not afford a new one. Pavis was asked to look into the possibility of a sponsored car. He was delighted to report that a local garage had agreed to provide Clough with a top-of-the-range Ford Granada, and an undertaking to change it every year. It would not cost the club a penny. 'You wouldn't drive around in a Granada, would you?' asked Fred Reacher. 'A Granada's no good. Brian says he would like to stick to his Mercedes.' A Mercedes it had to be, with the overdrawn board agreeing to pay lease charges of £581 a month!

One of the manager's many business outlets was a West Bridgford newsagents called Central News, which just happened to have belonged to Frank Allcock. 'Let me know when you're ready to retire,' Clough would say to his director. 'I want that shop for my bairn.' He was always scouting for investments for his sons. 'Don't buy them presents,' he said,' 'set them up in business.' Clough had done his homework. It was a good little business and there were no paper deliveries to worry about. In due course he and Dryden bought the shop and installed the manager's elder son, Simon, to run it. Not unnaturally, the club's magazine and chocolates order for away trips was switched to Clough's new premises. Dryden would arrive at the ground with a large box of sweets and magazines each time the first team, the reserves or the 'A' team were travelling. Allcock queried the apparently sudden fascination for chocolate: 'I used to spend a lot of time looking through invoices. I saw the bill from Central News was running at about £30 a trip. On top of that, Clough would order sixteen 1 lb boxes of chocolates for the wives when the team was away on tour. I'm not suggesting there was anything untoward – I'm certain there wasn't – but I raised it at a board meeting because if we had to consume that amount of chocolate, I wondered why we couldn't have it on account and pay wholesale. Clough wasn't even giving us a discount! He didn't attend that particular meeting, but he turned up at the next one. He walked in late, like he always did, came straight over to me and placed a Mars bar, a Kit-Kat and a copy of the *Sun* on the table. "I thought you'd like a bit of chocolate, Frank," he said. Could you beat that? I had to laugh, but the chairman should have brought him to order. He said nothing. That's what happened if you criticized him – he tried to make you look ridiculous and was allowed to get away with it.'

It is not uncommon for people who have lived in the spotlight under intense pressure for twenty years to turn to alcohol a little too often than is good for them. Clough has been no exception. While he was taking Forest to the semi-finals of the UEFA Cup and the runners-up position in the league in the 1984–85 season, he was noticeably under strain. Some of his close friends were concerned that he seemed to seek solace in whisky a little more than was healthy. It could explain some of the extremes of behaviour which have bewildered those who do not know him and occasionally caused distress to some who do. Against that there is no doubt that he could hold his liquor better than most. Taylor: 'We both liked a drop of champagne. I've taken the glass out of his hand before now and he's done the same to me. It was never a problem to us and I didn't see it affect the running of the club. In the later years at Forest I'd have missed it because I'd be in the office at the crack of dawn and gone by early afternoon. Brian would arrive nearer lunchtime and be there until the evening.'

After a league match at Liverpool in the early eighties Clough admitted to John Robertson that he was finding it difficult to give up the demon drink and devised a scheme to stop himself: 'He came to the back of the coach and said, "Can you help me, Robbo? I can't beat it unless someone helps me. Do you think you can stop smoking if I stop drinking?" We had a bet, although I didn't really *want* to stop smoking. In fact I never really stopped and I don't think he did, but we carried on the pretence. A few weeks later, we were staying at a hotel in London and I went up to my room straight after dinner for a fag. I heard a knock on the door. It was Ronnie Fenton, the trainer, bringing my boots up. I was sure he was checking, so I kept the cigarette behind my back. He left and I carried on. Two minutes later there was another knock. I put the fag in the toilet and answered the door. It was Clough. He went straight into the bathroom and saw what I'd been doing. "We'll call it off for tonight," he said. That really meant that he wanted a drink.'

Over Christmas 1981, Clough suffered a mystery illness thought at the time to be a mild heart attack. He had been entertaining his brother Barry and sister-in-law Judy at home on the morning of 27 December and had seemed perfectly fit. After lunch, he put on his wellington boots to shift snowdrifts from the back door. Within a few minutes he came back inside sweating profusely and complaining of pains in his chest. His wife insisted that he went into hospital for a check-up and he walked into the Derbyshire Royal Infirmary by himself. He was to spend the weekend under observation and the next three weeks off work, although tests in the coronary-care unit failed to diagnose anything serious. He later consulted a Harley Street specialist who came to a similar conclusion.

Later during the afternoon on which Clough was taken ill, David Coleman announced on BBC *Grandstand* that Clough had been taken to hospital with a suspected heart attack. It set the telephones ringing from one end of the country to the other as his family anxiously tried to find out what was wrong. Judy fielded many of the calls: 'I told them Brian wasn't good, but not to worry because he wasn't that bad either.' In the early hours of the morning two days later, she received the strangest call of all: 'The phone rang at 2.00 a.m. and I heard this funny voice whispering at the other end. Then I realized it was Brian, ringing from the infirmary. He wanted a bottle of champagne! I said, "You're supposed to be on the heart machine." But he said, "It doesn't matter, I've seen the sister right. Get our Barry to bring a bottle round now." We got one out of the fridge and Barry took it straight round to him. They sat drinking until four o'clock in the morning!'

In 1986 Jimmy Gordon, now shunned by Clough after his remarks first appeared in this book, received a call from one of the manager's confidants: 'You'll have to have a word with Brian – he's drinking too much.' Gordon says, 'It wouldn't have done any good. The boss wouldn't listen to me. That's the trouble. He won't take anyone's advice. He thinks he's indestructible. I know he likes a drink to help with the pressures of the job, but it's never interfered with his work that I know, and I've never seen him drunk.'

Also that summer, Nottingham City councillor Howard Noble was dozing off in his private hospital bed when he heard a vaguely familiar voice outside his room. 'I want to see Mr Noble,' it said. As Noble opened his eyes, Clough walked in. The manager had called at the city's Convent Hospital to see Alan Hill, who was recovering from a leg operation. Hill had no drink in his room so Clough had a word with the nurse, who informed him there was no bar on the premises before remembering that Councillor Noble, just up the corridor, kept a drop of scotch in his cupboard. 'You could have knocked me down with a feather,' says Noble. 'I was a keen Forest fan but I didn't expect a visit from the manager. I'd never met him before. He said he'd heard I was in the hospital and called to see if I was getting on okay. He said he'd just come from a board meeting. I told him to sit down and asked if he'd like a drink. He said, "I bloody would!" After four or five scotches he left. I found out later what the visit was about.'

Clough once said, 'I've tasted most things but if there's owt better than family life, let me know.' It is a sentiment which no doubt springs from the warmth of his childhood days on Teesside. He has always considered himself a family man, although football goes home with him at night, takes him away from home for long periods and occupies three-quarters of his weekend for at least nine months of the year. 'Do you know why I'm reluctant to go along with Sunday football?' he asked a few years ago. 'Because it breaks into precious, precious Sundays with my wife and children and I resent that.' Alternate Sunday afternoons, in fact, are spent on the touchline at Meadow Lane, Alvaston, just south of Derby, watching Simon play for FC Hunters, the Derbyshire local league side, of which Clough is team manager. To many of us it would seem like a busman's holiday, but Clough finds it therapeutic to shout himself hoarse on Sundays as well as on Saturdays. With his stick and his dog, he has become an accepted part of the Sunday league scene since he and Barbara founded the club in 1982. Mrs Clough's attitude, and that of his teenage daughter, Elizabeth, seems to have been: 'If you can't beat 'em, join 'em.' At one time, Barbara was the club secretary, a role she has since relinquished in favour of the fireside. FC Hunters' most celebrated old boy is, of course, Nigel Clough, who went straight from Sunday league to Nottingham Forest and even now runs the line for Hunters. Simon is a good/average player without sharing his brother's burning ambition.

All three Clough children went to Woodlands Comprehensive at Allestree where, according to one of Simon's contemporaries, they were teased mercilessly about their father, especially at the time Derby were trying to re-engage him in 1977. You would have to live in the East Midlands to understand the rivalry between Forest and Derby County. The fact that Clough lives in one town and works in the other has occasionally made life difficult. He once said, 'Schoolmates and, would you believe, teachers have battered my kids from pillar to post on occasions. They've had to run the gauntlet of nastiness, envy and jealousy, and that's hurt me perhaps more than it's hurt them. But because they've emerged from it so well adjusted, I'm prouder than ever of them.' He could, if he wanted, have put them all into private school, but he has placed his socialist ideals first, believing that Simon, Nigel and Elizabeth (Libby) would benefit from the state system. He criticized Mike Keeling long and loud for sending his children to boarding school. 'I love my kids and I want them around me,' he would say. Both boys stayed on for their 'A' levels – Clough was not going to make the same mistake with their lives as he had done with his own – but neither showed any exceptional academic talent, much to his chagrin. Stuart Dryden says, 'Deep down I think he's disappointed that they didn't achieve more at school. He'd have loved them to go to Oxford or Cambridge and make a resounding success of the thing he failed at.'

Jimmy Gordon remembers Clough's overwhelming desire to give his children everything: 'We used to babysit for them when the boss was at Derby and he often used to take us up to the bedroom to see them. He was so proud of them. "Come and see my bairns," he'd say. I'll picture him till I die sitting on the edge of Nigel's bed stroking his brow and saying, "Isn't he a bonny lad?" Then he'd whisper to him, 'I'll put you right where you should be, son. You'll have the things I never had." That was the only time I really saw the warmth of the man. He has good in his heart. It's a pity he doesn't let it show more often.'

Gordon and his wife Olive were having a meal at Clough's house when Nigel was nursing an injury. 'The boss pointed at him across the table and said, "You'll be in tomorrow and you'll be training." His brother Simon interrupted: "Correction – he'll be in tomorrow but he *won't* be training. He'll go and do as the physio tells him!" The boss climbed down. That's the first time I ever heard any of the kids answer back. Years ago Simon would never have dreamed of it. He has more confidence now. Nigel's too quiet. Too quiet for a centre-forward.'

As for the other side of the family, Clough has admitted before, 'I don't understand women and their hair-does. I've never had dealings with teenage girls. I was somewhere in the middle of our family of eight, and my sisters were either a lot older or a lot younger.' Olive Gordon has seen him turn on the charm with women around: 'It's "Oh, come here, darling, you smell lovely, darling", but the wives see through it now. He can be so sugary it's not true. Barbara must be very patient. We've been at the house when the atmosphere's red hot but somehow she manages to stay cool. She can be very stern, but *he's* the boss. I'll never forget how he kept the Lord Mayor waiting at a reception he was supposed to attend. The speeches couldn't start and Barbara was getting frantic. She kept telephoning home, saying, "Where *is* he?" She eventually found him sitting in the house. "Let the bugger wait," he told her. I don't know why he goes out of his way to cause trouble. Whenever we were asked out to dinner, I used to say to Jimmy, "Anything but this." It wasn't an evening you could look forward too. He could be charming or make you feel terrible. You never knew.'

For all Clough's idiosyncracies the family, including two men in their twenties remained under the same roof until Simon married in 1988. He did so against his father's wishes and chose to marry while Clough was away and unable to attend the wedding. It came at a time when family relationships were already under strain – newspapers reported that his daughter Elizabeth had been cast out of the household because of her liaison with a married man.

It is not so much that Clough was suffering an attack of moral indignation, more likely that he was struggling to come to terms with a reality faced by all parents – that the chicks are ready to fly the nest. Revealingly, he once said of his children: 'They're my life and if they're still at home at 40 I'll be the happiest father alive.' Few know his innermost feelings better than Bill Clough, his brother, who believes Brian is uneasy about being left alone: 'He's faced with an enormous void in his life if and when the kids leave. The boys went everywhere with him from an early age but they have their own lives to lead and I am not sure Brian's ready for that. He likes to think he can still play cards with them like he used to, but the family games have all gone now. That big house can seem very empty when he's on his own. But he can't hold onto the past. He has to let go some time. He's been a very good brother to me and I just hope he can cope when the break comes.

'The last thing we want is to see him brooding, especially on dark winter days, when he can get very depressed. I've told him he must come fellwalking with me in the lakes, but I don't know whether he'll get round to it. He always says, "Get the sun on your back, Bill – it's better than rain!" '

There is not a parent alive who has not had run-ins with teenage children, but Dryden thinks Clough's situation is exacerbated by his attempts to keep the family together for as long as he can: 'He asked me whether I had trouble with my teenage daughters because Simon hadn't spoken to him for a week. I told him of course I did, but that the tension was avoided because my girls had moved away from home at an early age. I didn't think it a good thing for his three all to be at home. With the best will in the world, I believe Brian stifled them and they were certainly in awe of him. They lived in a lovely, comfortable house so it wouldn't be easy to say goodbye to that, but I always said the lads would be better off if they could get away more. To my mind it's unfair, for instance, that Nigel should have to play under his father. It's like being the headmaster's son. It's not good for Nigel or the rest of the team. He'd benefit from joining another club, but Brian doesn't see it. He thinks Nigel's a reincarnation of himself.'

Clough says that Nigel is 'just another player' when he is out on the pitch: 'He's not my son, he's a player with a number nine on his back and he's in the side because he's better than the number nine we've got playing for the reserves. As soon as I can replace him, I will.' That is typical Clough but the answer does not really address itself to the main question: what effect is it having on Nigel and his team-mates? Although he lacks nothing on the field of combat, there is a distinct feeling that Nigel is exaggeratedly shy in civvy street. He has avoided most television interviews. His father says it is by his own choice, but one is bound to suspect the influence of Clough senior. It could be that he has advised his son that the longer he delays the eagerly awaited exclusive the more it will earn him. Or it could be that Clough is apprehensive about media penetration into a side of his life that has always been private. There is a third alternative: that Nigel is so inhibited by his father that he barely dares to answer anyone's questions. When he scored his maiden league goal against Watford at the City Ground in April 1985, he was escorted out by his brother and driven away from waiting reporters, who merely wanted to record his reaction to a happy event. And interviewed on ITV after his two goals helped Forest to beat Luton in the Littlewoods final, Nigel skilfully deflected all references to the old man.

Travelling on the Forest team coach as a youngster helped Nigel to familiarize himself with the players and the routines before signing for his father. At Brighton Clough used to throw him into the bath after training sessions and tell the physio, 'Give him a good scrubbing!' Colin Walsh, who saw his progress from supporter to centre-forward, says that, far from receiving preferential treatment, the youngster was given an especially hard time by Clough, who was anxious to avoid charges of nepotism.

'The manager was always onto him, bullying, telling him he couldn't play or that someone was after his place in the side,' says Walsh. 'We all went through it but Nigel more than most. He coped brilliantly. You have to grit your teeth and hang on. It's like an initiation test. If you can survive, he leaves you alone and moves on to the next one. Nigel survived well and has gone on to become a terrific player.' But did Clough junior feel free to criticize his father in front of the others, and they in front of him, which is surely the acid test? 'Yes,' says Walsh. 'He was always one of us and there is an unwritten code among team-mates that certain things don't get back to the boss. Not only did we moan about Clough in front of Nigel, but *he* did his fair share of moaning about his dad to us. There were no worries on that front.'

At the time of writing Nigel, now a full England international is poised to make his own way in the world. In many ways he's the closest of the three Clough children to his father but he is engaged to his girlfriend and has begun arousing interest among European clubs. The combination of the two suggests that a parting of the ways either domestically or professionally or both is imminent. How Nigel and his father will cope apart will be very interesting because the truth of the matter, despite what Mr Dryden says, is that Nigel only produces his best when he's playing for Forest. His England Under–23 goal scoring record is meagre and for all his undoubted vision and ability to smite a ball with typically Clough-like power, his England debut against Chile was disappointing. He may well come to the conclusion, either now or later, that his father breathed into him a fire that no one else could. He would not be the only one to whom that applied.

If he is a daunting father, Clough can be equally formidable as an uncle. Tea at Aunty Barbara's and Uncle Brian's could be an unnerving experience and was viewed with considerable apprehension at Judy and Barry's house. It was difficult to persuade the children to go with them and, once there, they were in awe of their famous relation. Judy Clough: 'My daughter was screwed up with fear. When she was ten or eleven, she used to sit on the edge of the settee crying and begging to go home. We told her not to be so silly, but Brian was overpowering with kids. It was: "Are you going to study, young lady?" and "What are you going to do when you leave school?" He couldn't be relaxed and happy-go-lucky like the other uncles, although he was generous with them in other ways and genuinely cared about their welfare. If the kids stepped out of line, Brian would be down on them like a ton of bricks. It got to the stage where neither of our two dared to open their mouths.'

Clough's relationship with Barry has passed through the entire spectrum of emotions and now lies in ruins. True to his belief that charity begins at home, Clough engaged his younger brother as an electrician at the Baseball Ground in the sixties but made a point of treating him like the rest of the workers when others were around. He would pass him in the corridor and say, 'Electrician, I want to see you in my office!' As soon as they were tucked away in private, Clough dropped the façade and opened a bottle of scotch. Barry needed all Clough's brotherly love when he had a terrifying accident while trying to hoist a flag on the roof of the old stand. Part of the roof gave way and Barry was in hospital for months with a broken pelvis and leg, as well as back and hip injuries. As soon as he was walking again, Clough gave him his old job back and eventually went into business with him at a Duffield newsagents just north of Derby. He had a thing about newsagents, also helping to set up another brother, Gerald, at Bramcote post office and stores near Nottingham, where it was not uncommon to see Brian selling newspapers on Sunday mornings.

Barry and Brian fell out over a financial matter which led to fisticuffs in the back yard with regulars from the public house next door looking on in some dismay. According to Judy:

'Brian was in a terrible state, banging on the back door and threatening to knock it down if we didn't let him in. Barry told him he'd call the police if he didn't go away. He shouted, "You wouldn't dare!" but I did.

'The sergeant came from Belper and ordered him to leave. Brian replied, "Do you know who I am? What's your number, sergeant?"

'Brian finally did leave but not before he and Barry had come to blows. The two of them were at it hammer and tongs, bashing around among the dustbins. It was very frightening.'

It was a far cry from the old days, when Clough paid off a £200 debt and also bought them their first holiday out of England – a fortnight in Jersey. 'He was very kind to us in those days,' says Judy. 'I have lots of warm thoughts about him but I always had the feeling that, when he did anything for us, it was like a reward for protecting him and an insurance that he could continue to rely on our cooperation. He went to great pains to build a protective circle around himself of people who wouldn't talk out of turn. If he had kept it to the family, it would have been easier. As soon as the wall spread to include so-called friends, that's when it became weaker. I believe Brian's apprehensive about the kids getting married because that would mean strangers coming into the circle.'

When success came to Derby, Clough 'bought' his mother and father and all his brothers and sisters a colour television set each. In the late sixties, it was a status symbol to have colour, especially where Barry and Judy lived. 'We were thrilled to bits because no one else in our street had a colour telly,' says Judy. 'I ran out to the telephone kiosk to thank Brian. He said, "I hope you like it. Let the kids watch *Magic Roundabout* and the football, because the grass is green." A year later we had the shock of our lives when the bill came from Radio Rentals for the next twelve months' hire! We couldn't afford it but we had to find the money because the kids would have been heartbroken if we'd sent the set back. That's typical of Brian.'

As Judy points out, Clough spread his protective net wider than the immediate family. Mike Keeling was an early member of the Clough appreciation society which would surround Clough everywhere he went. Keeling had become Clough's 'pet' on the Derby board, informing him of all the inside moves. The association continued when the pair undertook a number of business ventures together. Keeling was later joined by Colin Lawrence, a local newsagent, and David Gregory, who both accompanied Clough on several European trips. Gregory was a former Derby parks' gardener recruited to tend Clough's impressive acreage at Quarndon.

Intellectually, Clough's friends may not be on the same wavelength as him, but they are reliable, willing to serve and to hold their peace. These are the people Taylor says he found blocking the corridors at the City Ground. Since Gregory was taken ill with arthritis, incidentally, their positions are reversed, with Clough now looking after *his* garden.

According to Dryden, 'Brian doesn't have many close friends. I think I'm one. We have a good working relationship. Once you become a friend, his loyalty is unshakable.' Dryden is in a better position than most to judge. Like Keeling at Derby, Clough had cultivated him as the 'friendly' director on the Forest board. In return for his unswerving support, Dryden was buttressed by Clough in his own hour of need. The Ruddington postmaster was convicted of fraud in 1980 and, in his own words, 'lost just about everything – the Forest chairmanship, my freedom and very nearly my sanity.' Clough sat in court throughout the seven-day hearing and drove Dryden's deeply distressed wife, Mary, home after her husband had been sentenced to six months in Lincoln prison. As Dryden was a magistrate, it was especially humiliating. He was on personal terms with the prison governor and had had a hand in sending down some of the shorter-stay offenders. He was given the dubious benefit of a cell in the hospital wing so that he would be apart from the recognized ruffians.

After appeal, Dryden was moved to Sudbury open prison in Derbyshire, where Clough tried to visit him outside normal hours and was turned away. 'Nevertheless,' says the former chairman, 'Brian was a pillar of strength when my world collapsed. I don't know quite what I'd have done without his support. He stood by me then and has stood by me ever since.'

Dryden has a nickname for Clough. He calls him the 'Quare Fellow': 'He's like two different people. Jekyll and Hyde. You're never certain which one's going to come through the door. He can be kind and gentle or insufferably rude. I don't think *he* knows why he treats people so badly sometimes. Occasionally I've wondered about his attitude to suffering and death. There's a curious detachment from that sort of thing. I've known a good friend who was ill for years and never had a visit from Brian, and I've seen him show no apparent sympathy when a player breaks his leg. It's as though he'd rather not know. The sad death of his brother Des must have upset him deeply but he let out the news almost casually in the course of a conversation about something entirely different . . . Against that he'll go out of his way to raise money to buy wheelchairs for the disabled. He's a quare fellow all right.'

Clough's Jekyll and Hyde qualities are well illustrated by two episodes of such disparity that it is difficult to believe they involved the same person. We shall abandon chronology for a moment to record a series of confrontations which landed him in Nottingham County Court in January 1985, smack in the middle of his tenth anniversary celebrations at Forest. Case number 8211524, John Joseph Pye versus Brian Clough, was heard before an empty pressbox by judge Thomas Heald. At the end of it the Forest manager signed a statement which apologized 'unreservedly . . . for any distress and embarrassment which may have been occasioned to the plaintiff.'

The plaintiff was a local auctioneer who claimed he was manhandled and verbally abused by Clough several times in March and April 1981. Why did it take four years for Pye to take out a private summons? Partly because Nottingham solicitors were reluctant to handle the case (he was eventually forced out of town where he secured the services of Robinsons at Heanor in Derbyshire); and partly because of Pye's determination not to be rushed. Clough could hardly have chosen a more resolute adversary. The plaintiff was a forceful character, not fond of mincing words and well known in local circles for his theatrical performances on the rostrum. He had been a Forest supporter since a boy and a member until 1987. His wife owned one of the largest debt-recovery businesses in the northern half of England, so money was no object.

According to the court papers on which this account is based, the gist of his complaint was that Clough had ejected him from the City Ground during a reserve match on the evening of 31 March 1981. Pye told the court he had been looking for a telephone during the half-time interval and strayed into the foyer where Clough was talking to some apprentices. The manager, having demanded to know who Pye was and what he was doing in the inner sanctum, was dissatisfied with the answers and allegedly 'frogmarched' him to the exit ordering him to 'scram'. Judge Heald listened for close on two hours as Pye described how his attempts to extract an apology only inflamed matters. A meeting with Clough and the Forest chairman, Geoffrey McPherson, ended in more argument. Pye said the manager was 'wagging his finger and tapping me on the nose, threatening to sue me for every penny I had and said he'd have my wife and children out on the streets.'

Clough was not called to the witness stand but under cross-examination Pye was said by the defendant's solicitor, Anthony Goldstraub, to be trying to bring his client, 'a top football manager', into disrepute with false accusations. The plaintiff who has remained a staunch admirer of Clough's managerial talents, replied, 'I would like to point out that I rate Mr Clough one of the top three managers in Great Britain. Before he came to Nottingham Forest we had so few trophies they'd have all fitted on a Victorian mantelpiece.'

The animosity between them finally erupted, Pye said, when Clough spotted him leaving the ground a couple of weeks after the initial row. According to pleadings read out in court, Pye claimed that Clough was so furious that Pye had written to McPherson, that he took hold of him and threw him to the floor four times before dragging him to the visiting directors' and managers' lounge where, in full view of the guests, he tried to force an 'enormous' whisky down the plaintiff. Pye said he was virtually teetotal.

It was an unusual case. The auctioneer had apparently been suing for damages but surprised everyone by settling for an apology. He says that is all he ever wanted. Not only that – Pye agreed to contribute £750 towards the defence costs. 'I thought the payment totally unnecessary,' he says, 'but I was prepared to let it go because I got what I went for. It was the principle that mattered.' His principle cost him more than £3000. After the hearing, Neil Barnes, his solicitor wrote to him: 'Both I and Nicholas Woodward (counsel) had advised you throughout that you would lose the claim and that there was a substantial risk of you meeting your own and Brian Clough's costs . . . To obtain a signed apology from Brian Clough can only be regarded as a success.' The apology also promised to look favourably upon Pye's re-application for membership of Nottingham Forest but he is still waiting to join.

In consideration of the Defendants further offer
to apologise unreservedly to the Plaintiff for any
distress and embarrassment which may have been occasioned
to the Plaintiff in consequence of the Defendants behaviour
towards the Plaintiff on and after 31 March 1981,
and also in consideration of the Defendants offer
to use his best endeavours to influence the favourable
outcome of an application by the Plaintiff for
membership of the club and not by word or
deed to obstruct such application; the Plaintiff
offers to withdraw his claims herein and to
pay £750 towards the Defendants costs;
whereupon the Plaintiff and Defendant accept
their said respective offers and it is agreed that
the plaintiffs claim should be withdrawn on
such terms.

[illegible]

Brian Clough

[illegible]
as Counsel
for Defendant

3.1.85.

A mere six months before those unpleasant scenes, Clough played a significant part in saving the life of a potential suicide who threatened to jump into the River Trent. Two police officers had been called to Trent Bridge in September 1980 where a twenty-seven-year-old man was sitting on the edge of a parapet beyond the iron railings, saying he was alcoholic and epileptic and wanted to end his life. Clough was driving past when he noticed a crowd of people. He pulled up and immediately went into action. Police Constable Lee Summers takes up the story: 'It was a nasty situation. We couldn't pull the chap away without spearing him on the railings. Cloughie took over and relaxed him by talking about football for a good five minutes. He talked about the crowds who were flocking to Forest in those days and asked if the chap was a supporter.

'It did the trick. The fellow calmed down enough for us to reach him and bring him clear of danger. Only Cloughie could have distracted him like that.'

The manager protested at the time that he had done very little, but was nevertheless presented with a 'Citizen of the Month' award, given jointly by Nottinghamshire police and the *Nottingham Evening Post* newspaper. The then chief constable, Charles McLachlan said, 'I think your contribution was twofold – to the man himself and to the police officers. I am very grateful.'

Clough has an uncanny knack of knowing what is going on around him. It borders on omniscience, even telepathy. Once, when he was busily engaged with the England youth squad in the Canary Islands, Dryden received a phone call from him. It was to ask how the postmaster had taken the shock of impending prosecution: 'The news had only just broken and I hadn't told anyone outside the family circle. I haven't a clue how Brian found out about it over there.' For all his support of and friendship with his old chairman, Clough was conspicuously absent at the wedding of Dryden's daughter, where he was to have been one of the principal guests. He sent his own daughter, Elizabeth, in his stead. Dryden says, 'As well as I know him, I was amazed that he didn't even phone to apologize. My wife was slightly relieved, to be honest, because she couldn't handle him in a situation like that. He partially made up for it by sending my daughter a marvellous present.'

Delegating people to fulfil his engagements is a common Clough ploy. When Des Walker won Nottingham Forest's Player of the Year award, the manager sent his wife to do the honours! He will go out of his way to send tapes to coma patients or encourage unemployed youth, then leave some charity organizer embarrassed and stranded by failing to show up. Like his habit of turning up late for appointments he has arranged himself, it might be a studied technique designed to punish those who are impudent enough to expect him to be there in the first place – or it could be simply that he cannot be bothered. He rarely forgets.

Clough's eccentricity is innate. When he arrives for television interviews in his working clothes, he barely causes a raised eyebrow now. He once strolled among Wimbledon's strawberry and Pimms set in his tracksuit during the All-England Championships, telling John McGovern, his blushing companion, that he was proud to be wearing 'the tools of my trade'. Staff at the Kedleston hotel have become accustomed, if not exactly inured, to seeing him arrive for Sunday lunch in his wellington boots and rugby shirt, Clough having failed to see the distinction between dressing for a spot of gardening and dressing for lunch. No one is immune from his eccentricity, indeed his friends seem to suffer more than most. 'One day he invited me to lunch at "the best place in town",' says Dryden. 'A friend of mine very kindly fixed us up at the Victoria club in Nottingham, although neither Brian nor I were members. My friend agreed to sign us in as his guests, and we waited nearly an hour for Brian to arrive. He eventually came walking up the steps in his green and white hooped shirt, shorts and tennis shoes. We didn't know where to put our faces. Behind him were four taxi-loads of pressmen, all trying to sign him as a columnist now that his contract with the *Sunday Mirror* was up. What had been planned as a quiet meal for two turned into an invasion. I didn't even have time to stay for lunch.'

Dryden recently experienced at first hand Clough's legendary powers of walking on water. They had arranged to meet for a lunchtime drink at a quiet pub in the Derbyshire countryside. Dryden was there first, of course. 'It was pouring with rain – a real filthy day, when to my utter amazement, Brian walked in in his stockinged feet! I told him it was madness, that he'd catch his death of cold, but he wasn't bothered. He sat there in dripping wet socks, as though it was perfectly rational behaviour.'

The Forest players were required to perform many strange routines at the training ground, from scouring the hedgerows for mushrooms to seeing how many of them would fit into a five-a-side net. Those rash enough to get into the tiny structure first ran the serious risk of death by asphyxia. What the exercise achieved, other than making grown men look faintly ridiculous, is hard to imagine. Jim McInally, the former Forest full-back, was particularly unremitting in his criticism of Clough's methods and earned a few bob from the *Sun* for his disclosures. Shortly after McInally's transfer to Coventry, Clough spotted a log floating down the Trent during a training session and lined his team up on the bank to salute it. As the flotsam glided past, Clough announced to his bemused troops, 'There goes Jim McInally – let that be a warning to you!'

On European trips, the players could be even less certain of what was in store. At a pretty town called Graz in Austria, during Forest's UEFA Cup campaign in 1984, Clough took the players for a pre-match walk along the river and broke off to slam his fist into a treetrunk. 'We thought he'd finally flipped,' says Colin Walsh. While the team waited for the men in white coats to take their manager away, Clough explained that it was a 'punch tree' and expressed his amazement that none of them knew what he was talking about. Paul Hart says he expected to get a drink out of it! Walsh recalls, 'He stood there belting the living daylights out of this tree and inviting us to join him. It had soft bark which didn't hurt your fists. The manager was right. He obviously knew something about trees.'

Clough treated European trips like mini-holidays and he made sure he and the players enjoyed the break. Once, in Amsterdam, he took them everywhere from the state circus to a Dutch bordello, although the latter caused something of a stir when wives and girlfriends got to hear about it. Clough had thought it would be an education to see the famous red-light district. Not only did they see it – some of the squad sampled the hospitality of a high-class brothel, though it has to be stressed that they stopped short of any impropriety. One of the less diplomatic girlfriends let the cat out of the bag in the wives' room back at Forest, where there was talk of sending a deputation to have it out with Clough. The ladies' fire was quenched after lengthy explanations from the menfolk, but there were a few henpecked husbands as a result of that little escapade.

Apart from a bemused interpreter, the author was the only English-speaking witness to an extraordinary show of pique by Clough in the East German town of Frankfurt-Oder. Forest had won the UEFA Cup game in September 1983 and Clough was clearly eager to hotfoot it out of a cold and miserable town back to East Midlands airport that night. The rules of European competition, however, stipulate that both managers must present themselves at the post-match press conference – something Clough avoids like the plague in domestic football. He was in no mood for niceties when he arrived at the press centre to be confronted by a roomful of East Germans. The English party were seated in the coach, equally eager to get to the airport.

Clough launched a blistering attack on some of his directors who were also relaxing on the coach bathing in the afterglow of victory. He said, 'It's those buggers who should be here talking to you, not me. My job was finished when the whistle went.' After delivering a few more barbs, he left. Watching polite smiles give way to disbelief as the interpreter translated his words was one of the more memorable moments of the European campaign that year.

In the ceaseless quest for revenue, Clough has hawked the Forest team all round the world – to Canada, Australia, South America, Malaysia and the Middle East. They played a few games, earned a few thousand for the club and, more often than not, arrived home jet-lagged and fed-up.

One such safari, to Dubai, literally did not get off the ground because of the manager's bad humour. The source of his irritation initially was a 1–0 defeat at the hands of Arsenal the previous day. His mood was not improved when he was pestered for his autograph in the airport lounge while trying to conduct a team talk. He snapped at the unfortunate autograph hunter, a fellow passenger, 'Get lost you little shit!' That was bad enough, but his cup of woe overflowed when he boarded the plane. As it was en route to Bombay, the flight was chockful of Indians jabbering excitedly and disregarding their children, who delighted in running up and down the aisle making, it seemed, as much noise as they could. Clough was appalled at the din and the pungent clouds of garlic and spices which wafted through the plane. He called to Ian Bowyer, the skipper, 'All we're getting for this trip is a few measly thousand. When we get there you can have the lot because we're too good to put up with this.'

With everyone prepared for take-off, the plane ground to a halt on the runway – there had been an unforeseen hitch, which served only to heighten the excitement among two hundred Indians and plunge some of the women into paroxysms of anguish. Clough decided he had had enough. He summoned the stewardess and told her, 'We're getting off.'

'You can't!' came the incredulous reply.

Clough: 'No problem, dear, I'm going home for my Sunday lunch.'

The stewardess tried to explain that it was impossible to disembark, especially on the runway, and that he would be unable to get back through customs. Clough was past the point of taking no for an answer. He ordered the team off the plane and instructed airline officials to 'sort it out'. The Forest squad must have cut a strange sight standing in the middle of the runway surrounded by airport policemen screaming into their walkie-talkies. Somehow he negotiated the party back into the terminal building, where British Airways agreed to bus them to Nottingham.

Football consumes Clough to the extent that outside interests are reduced to almost nothing. Squash was a fleeting passion, but leisurely pursuits like golf have never appealed. Getting away from it all consists either of sunbathing in Cala Millor, concocting some gastronomic delight in the kitchen (he is good at that), or pottering about in his lovely garden. His knowledge of herbaceous borders would not fill a book but there is nothing he enjoys more than digging or planting trees. His brother Bill says, 'He has a thing about trees. Can't stop looking at them. I've been abroad with him when he's been in raptures over an avenue of pine trees. "Look at them, Bill," he'd enthuse, "aren't they beautiful?" '

Clough used to say that his ideal day when the children were younger included an afternoon walk to the local park and a stroll around the flowerbeds. 'That's where I lose football. People don't appreciate beauty these days. They look at everything but they don't really see. Who really looks at trees and sees their shapes and colours? They're magic. That's what it's all about.'

He has a passion for conifers, once inveigling Einer Aas, Forest's Norwegian defender, into smuggling out a sapling from Norway in his trouser leg! The said tree now sits proudly in his alpine border. Once at Schipol airport, Amsterdam, Clough exported a different type of forest – one he had personally collected from a Dutch garden centre. The players had to sit on the plane with a baby conifer semi-concealed between their legs and carry the tender greenery back to Nottingham for him. The Dutch authorities, knowing his antics by now, had waived the normal customs regulations and allowed him through.

In 1985 he astonished those who know him by developing a fondness for Del Boy, the golden retriever, a fairly recent addition as the family pet. Judy Clough: 'For as long as I've known him, he's hated dogs. In fact, he was frightened of them. He couldn't bear to be in the same room as our spaniel. He'd say, "Get that filthy thing away from me! Dirty smelly, germ-ridden pest!" ' For years, Clough watched at a distance as Taylor made a fuss of Bess, his black labrador prescribed for him by the doctor as an antidote to stress. 'He was never very keen on her,' says Taylor, 'but he had to put up with her. I took her everywhere with me. She was the most photographed dog in football. Brian hated it when she jumped up at him. To be honest, I think he was frightened. For him to have a dog of his own was unbelievable. My family always said that what I did yesterday Brian will copy tomorrow.'

Del Boy was bought from a kennel near the Forest ground as a Christmas present for Elizabeth Clough. She had been pestering her father for a dog ever since Hans van Breukelen, Forest's Dutch goalkeeper in 1983, had brought his giant schnauser out of quarantine. The plan went slightly awry when Clough himself grew attached to Del Boy, whom he soon adopted as his own. The dog was said to respond only to his commands and accompanied him on his walks across the fields near his home. Clough regularly took it to the training ground and once introduced it at a board meeting as a gesture of defiance. Del Boy was one friend he could guarantee would never give away a secret!

Clough is a lonely man who constantly needs reassuring about his worth and importance. 'If people don't recognize him,' says Taylor, 'he creates a fuss and makes sure they do.' Dryden says Clough is *afraid* of not being recognized, which may account for the fact that, when in Cala Millor, he frequents the same pavement cafe. The resort has as much privacy as Derby market place and is bursting with holidaymakers who are bound to stop and point wherever he goes. 'With his money he could go to Barbados,' says Taylor, 'but he must have familiar surroundings. He's a creature of habit. He sits at the same cafe so that everyone can see him. I don't understand why he is so insecure and alone when he has so much going for him. There is something deeply mysterious about Brian. He lives in a world of his own. Barbara and I have been closest to him, but neither of us knows where his soul is.'

It is Judy Clough who perhaps best encapsulates the dilemma facing Clough in his fifties: 'He's made a lot of people laugh and a lot of people cry on his way to the top of the mountain. Now he's up there, he's got no one to share the view with him.'

Index